EVERYDAY BUSINESS LAW

Everyday Business Law

Greville Janner
QCMP

Gower

© Greville Janner, 1988

All rights reserved. No part of this publication may be reproduced, stored in a retrieval system, or transmitted in any form or by any means, electronic, mechanical, photocopying, recording, or otherwise without the prior permission of Gower Publishing Limited.

First published in 1962 as *The Businessman's Lawyer*
Published in 1988 in hardback as *Janner's Business Law*

This edition published 1989 by
Wildwood House Limited,
Gower Publishing Group,
Gower House,
Croft Road,
Aldershot,
Hants GU11 3HR,
England

Gower Publishing Company,
Old Post Road,
Brookfield,
Vermont 05036,
USA.

The author and Gower Publishing Company Limited have used their best efforts in collecting and preparing material for inclusion in *Everyday Business Law*. They do not assume, and hereby disclaim, any liability to any party for any loss or damage caused by errors or omissions in *Everyday Business Law* whether such errors or omissions result from negligence, accident or any other cause.

British Library Cataloguing in Publication Data

Janner, Greville
  Everyday business law.
  1. Law—Great Britain   2. Business Law
  —Great Britain
  I. Title   II. Janner, Greville. Business
man's lawyer
  344.106'62   KD665.B8

Library of Congress Cataloguing in Publication Data

Janner, Greville.
  Everyday business law.
  Original title: The business man's lawyer.
  Includes index.
  1. Business law—Great Britain   I. Title.
II. Title: Business law.
KD1629.J353   1988   346.42'07   87-14365

ISBN-07045-06416

**Printed and bound in Great Britain at
The Camelot Press Ltd, Southampton**

Other books by Greville Janner include:

Janner's Employment Letters*
Janner's Employment Forms and Procedures*
Janner's Complete Speechmaker
Janner's Complete Letterwriter
Janner on Presentation
Janner on Meetings

For details on all these *books* and on *in-company training* on *business law* and *presentational skills*, contact Paul Secher LL.B, J.S. Associates, 25 Victoria Street, London SW1H 0EX. Telephone: 01-222 2102

---

* Looseleaf services – published by Business & Legal Publications Ltd

Contents

Preface xi

PART ONE COMPANIES AND PARTNERSHIPS
1 Business Begins 3
2 Problems of Partnerships 7
3 The Director's Personal Liabilities 11
4 A Director's 'Fiduciary Relationship' 13
5 A Director's Title 14
6 Must You Supervise Your Colleague? 16
7 Take-overs, Mergers – and Self-protection 18
8 Battles in the Boardroom 23
9 Oppressed Minorities 25
10 Winding up the Company 27
11 Removing a Director 29
12 The Protection of Depositors and Investors 31
13 Company Meetings 34
14 Changing Your Line of Business 36
15 Checklist for Closing Down 39
16 Confidential Information 41
17 Banking 46
18 When Your Name's the Same 48
19 Laws of Copyright 50
20 Registration of Trade Marks 53
21 Data Protection 55
22 Travel Costs and the Tax Inspector 57
23 At Your Lease's End 60
24 The End of a Business 64
25 Retirement – Voluntary and Otherwise 68

PART TWO EMPLOYMENT LAW
26 Your Contracts of Employment – a Checklist 75
27 Varying Your Contract 78
28 Attachment of Earnings 81

29	An Employee's Inventions	83
30	Is Moonlighting Legal?	84
31	Restraint Clauses – and Unfair Competition	86
32	Who Gets a Share in the Bonus?	88
33	Sick Pay	90
34	The Stealing of Staff	92
35	Go – in Good Health!	94
36	References – and the Cost of Free Advice	96
37	Redundancy Payments	100
38	Part Time Problems	106

PART THREE INDUSTRIAL RELATIONS, EMPLOYMENT PROTECTION AND UNFAIR DISMISSAL

	Introduction	111
39	Dismissal	113
40	Information and Collective Bargaining	116
41	Guarantee Payments	120
42	Equal Pay, Sex Discrimination and Maternity Rights	121
43	Equal Pay – Cammell Laird and after	126
44	Time Off – Including Time Off for Trade Union and Public Duties	131
45	Employees' Rights in an Insolvency	134
46	Redundancy Rights	135

PART FOUR HEALTH, SAFETY AND POLLUTION

47	Duties to Employees	141
48	Your Duty to Non-Employees	146
49	Visitors – and Trespassers	148
50	Duties to Customers and Clients	150
51	Your Personal Liabilities	152
52	Passing the Buck	153
53	Inducing Employees to Obey the Safety Rules	156
54	Procedures for Coping with the Health and Safety at Work Act	158
55	Written Statements of Policy, Organization and Arrangements	163
56	The Control of Pollution	166

PART FIVE CONTRACTS AND CONTRACTORS

57	Have You Made a Contract? – a Checklist	175
58	Buyers' Rights – a Checklist	178
59	Trade-ins and Trade Descriptions	181
60	Hiring and Leasing	184
61	Your Servants – Your Agents?	187

62	When You Are Mistaken	189
63	Collecting the Money You Are Owed – a Checklist	191
64	Fending Off Your Creditors – a Checklist	194
65	Time	197
66	Import/Export – and Foreign Accounts	200
67	Common Market Law	205
68	Some Principles on Interest	207
69	The Cost of Contractors	209
70	What Can Repairers Charge?	212
71	Rights of the Unpaid	213
72	Unsolicited and Uncollected Goods	218
73	Commission When the Deal Goes Off	221
74	Product Liability – the New Scene	224

PART SIX NEGLIGENCE, NUISANCE AND OTHER 'TORTS'

75	Negligence – Gratuitous and Otherwise	237
76	Vicarious Liability	238
77	Neighbours and Nuisances	241
78	Coming to a Nuisance	243
79	The Value of Life and Limb	244
80	Accidents and Injuries	246
81	An Occupier's Liability	248
82	Guard Dogs	251
83	A Question of Contributory Negligence	253
84	Trespass – and Assault	256
85	Remoteness of Damage	258
86	No Loss, No Damage	260

PART SEVEN CRIMES

87	The Theft Acts	265
88	A Criminal Mistake	267
89	Handling Stolen Goods	269
90	The Trade Descriptions Act – and the Employer's Liability	271
91	Bribery and Corruption	273
92	Race Relations	276
93	Prosecution Laws	278
94	The Rehabilitation of Offenders	281

PART EIGHT COURTS, CASES AND LAWYERS

95	To Sue or Not to Sue?	287
96	Representing Yourself	289
97	When You Need Your Lawyer – a Checklist	291

98	Problems of Legal Aid	295
99	Arbitrations	296
100	When You Owe the World a Living	299
101	Legal Aspects of Billing	301
102	The 'Harassment' of Debtors	303
103	Time Passes	304

In conclusion 307

Index 309

Preface

This book is designed to help you to keep to the minimum your contact with the law. I hope that you will find it easy both for reading and for reference.

When I was first called to the Bar, my wise old Head of Chambers told me: 'My boy, a good lawyer is not one who knows the law. The good lawyer is one who knows where to find his law – and who knows his judges.'

The businessman who is his own lawyer has a fool for a client. This book will direct you to lawyers when you need them – for instance, to avoid trouble with the criminal court or to construct restraint clauses. It also points out many of the traps in time for lawyers to steer you around them.

Civil law – companies and contracts, torts and trespasses, leases and licences and all the paraphernalia of the High Court, the County Court and their Scottish equivalents, the solicitor's office and the barrister's chambers – is rightly regarded by business people with a shudder. Litigation is irritating, expensive and inexplicable, conveyancing no more than a method of transferring land invented by lawyers for their own benefit. And deeds and written agreements are annoying and unnecessary formalities – after all, isn't a businessman's word his bond?

Yet the sad fact remains that, no matter how much you may wish it, you cannot do without lawyers. If you handle them with care, and even with a little of the intelligent respect which a knowledge of their craft inevitably brings, you may find the proceedings more profitable than you thought. You may save yourself trouble before it hits you – and not merely use the legal expert to get you out of trouble when it's too late. Why, you may even find that your business is better run, more profitable.

This volume presents the basic business law, which, whether you know it or not, surrounds your life and your work. It is intended as a guide, to be kept by your desk or your bed, as you wish. There is nothing to stop you reading from cover to cover, but each chapter is separate and deals with some specific aspect of business law. The carefully detailed index provides your guide to immediate access.

I hope that this book will help destroy your belief that the law is remote or dull. The majority of lawyers practise their ancient profession because they find it full of reality and fascination.

So this book offers a condensation, review and explanation of the law which you are most likely to meet in the business world. It explains the essential legal structures and rules and distils their essence in palatable form. May it bring you both profit and pleasure.

My thanks to all those who have helped in creating this book, and especially to my partner and friend, Paul Secher, to whom this book is dedicated with affection and respect; and to Antony Sendall, Barrister, for his research and assistance.

Greville Janner

Part One
Companies and Partnerships

1 Business Begins

Should you operate as an individual or in partnership, or through a limited liability company? The major joy of a company is that the liability of its shareholders is limited to any money unpaid on their shares (which is usually nil). A partner or an individual may be forced to pay business debts out of his own pocket. His own entire fortune (if that is not an overstatement) is available for the benefit of the business creditors.

Individual business people and partners generally pay less tax. There is no corporation tax to worry about, for a start. Legitimate expenses are normally easier to come by. So those who spurn limited liability are generally able to keep more profits for themselves. It is when the day of loss arrives that the individuals in business regret their short-term tax savings.

Again, company accounts must be filed and are available for the inspection of actual or potential creditors in particular, as well as the world at large in general. Personal and partnership accounts may be kept secret. However, if there is capital to be raised or shares to be doled out, company organization is simpler.

You may set up a private business without legal formalities. Partnerships may be created without even the benefit of a partnership deed or formal writing. Formalities are desirable, but neither essential nor particularly expensive. If you want a company, though, you may either buy one 'off the peg' which can cost you as little as £80 or you may wish to have one tailor-made to your requirements, probably by your solicitor or accountant. Either way, no memorandum and articles of association and no proper registration means no company.

Next, you must consider your capital. The main reason for the early failure of most businesses is lack of the money needed – not only to acquire and equip the premises and lay in stock or supplies but also to keep you in food while the business builds up, in those lean and early days. So you must consider the legal implications of fund-raising – problems of hire purchase; the rights of banks to call in money lent; and if you do run into serious debt, then how long your lawyer will be able to fend off your various debtors. Discuss this with him, and with your accountant, before you launch your venture.

Next, you will need premises. If you acquire a free-hold, you pay more initially but have no landlord and pay no rent. Remember, too, that you may sell your freehold (perhaps to an insurance company) and take back a lease – thus releasing the capital you need.

If you take a lease, remember that the length is not as important as you might think. You will be protected by the Landlord and Tenant Act 1954 as amended by the Law of Property Act 1969 – details in Chapter 23. So if you can buy up a 'fag end' cheaply, it may be well worth doing. Discuss the proposition with your solicitor. Ask him to advise you in particular about the repairing covenants. These may not mean what they appear to say. For instance, if you covenant to 'maintain' the premises in good repair, you may have to put them into good condition first.

If the lease contains an absolute prohibition against assignment, then you will only be able to sell the business with your landlord's consent. However, the law provides that where the tenant may only assign with the landlord's consent, that consent may not be unreasonably withheld. Also beware of the landlord who attempts to extract a premium from you for a licence to assign. This is illegal unless the lease contains an express provision allowing the landlord to do so.

Finally, if you are the first tenant under a new lease, even if you do assign you will retain your responsibility to your landlord. So make quite certain that you really want the term offered – and be especially careful before you personally agree to be a party to the lease and hence to guarantee the performance by the business of its obligations.

Then, you must choose a name for your business. If you use your own, the chances are that all will be well. But business names must not be misleading and your solicitor or accountant will discover whether the name you have in mind will be permitted (see Chapter 18).

Although registration of business names is no longer required, your solicitor should also ensure that your proposed business name does not infringe the Business Names Act 1985 or any of the regulations made under it.

However you trade, you must keep proper accounts. There are stringent regulations for companies (only an accountant can sort them out). Even the smallest, one-man (or -woman) shop must account to the Revenue. Cash 'fiddles' may pay in the short run, but apart from the grim possibilities of criminal prosecution, the day of reckoning arrives when you want to sell the business and the prospective buyers inspect the books.

Conversely, before you take over a business (of whatever size), make certain that the books are inspected by your accountant. Never take the sellers word for their turnover, receipts, profits. If they have any hesitation in letting you inspect the accounts once your deposit is paid, be on your guard. If in doubt, take your custom elsewhere.

If some misrepresentation is made to you before your purchase, you will be protected by the Misrepresentation Act 1967. If you can prove fraud, you will have a good claim in law. But by the time your case comes to court, you will wish that you had taken no risks. There is no substitute for the guidance of your accountant.

The Misrepresentation Act does not apply to Scotland but under the common law of Scotland if you are induced by an innocent misrepresentation to purchase the business when you would not otherwise have done so you are entitled to rescind the contract.

When acquiring your premises, you should employ a competent surveyor to warn you of wet rot, dry rot, subsidence and other defects in the structure of the premises which you yourself might miss. Obtain a written survey – and an estimate of the cost of putting the premises into proper order.

As for deposits, beware of 'the usual 10 per cent' – there is no such thing. As a token of goodwill, a small initial deposit is quite enough. Put it up to 10 per cent when contracts are exchanged – meanwhile do not tie up your own (or borrowed) money. And always ensure that deposits are paid 'subject to contract' – so that they are without doubt recoverable if the deal goes off, even through your own fault. And unless the vendor's estate agents are well known to you, pay your deposit to his solicitors as stakeholders not as agents.

Do not forget that if you are likely to have a turnover in excess of the currently prescribed limit then you will need to register for VAT purposes. Discuss your worries with your accountant.

Unless you plan to operate the business entirely on your own, you must plan to meet staff problems – in advance. These (once more) include tax provisions. Your accountant will help you to deal with PAYE, National Insurance and so on.

Thanks to the Employment Protection (Consolidation) Act 1978, your staff are entitled either to written contracts of employment or to written particulars setting out the main terms of their employment (see Chapter 26).

If you want to provide a home for your staff, get your solicitor to draw up the appropriate licence – making it clear that the employee is 'required to occupy the premises for the better performance of his duties'. Terms such as 'rent' and 'landlord' must be avoided: if you confer a tenancy – as opposed to a 'service occupancy' or licence – your employee will acquire the protection of the Rent Acts. You will then only get possession with grave difficulty, even when the employment ends. If you reasonably require possession for the occupation of a replacement employee whom you have actually engaged or who is ready to move in – and the County Court Judge thinks it 'reasonable' in all the circumstances to grant possession – all may be well, in due course. But if you may want a speedier eviction, plan for it in advance.

If you take over a business, you are not bound to buy stock, materials, plant or supplies at valuation or at all. If you agree to do so, make sure that you have a full and checked schedule, so that disputes do not afterwards arise. If you are to buy 'at valuation', agree on who is to do the valuing.

If you are buying in new stock, be very careful not to overstock in an excess of initial enthusiasm. Remember that unless you buy on sale or return you will not be entitled to return the goods ordered in a rash moment. Even on sale or return, it is up to you to reject or to 'give notice of rejection' within the agreed time or, if no time has been agreed, then within a reasonable time.

You will need cover against burglary, flood, fire, liability to staff, public liability, loss of cash and probably against many other forms of disaster. Find an experienced and reputable insurance broker and let him see what terms he can get for you. Remember that he normally gets his commission from the insurers with whom he eventually places your custom, so obtain a number of quotes. You should shop around for insurance in the same way as your customers do for the goods or service you provide.

When filling in your insurance proposal form, be careful to be absolutely accurate. Failure to make proper disclosure ... misleading or false statements in the proposal form ... these may give your insurers the right to repudiate liability on the happening of the very matters which you are paying your premium to cover. If your policy is to protect you, honesty is your only wise policy when taking on insurance.

To find out what cover you are offered, read the policy. It is a contractual document. It sets out what you are to receive in return for your premium. Beware of phrases like 'comprehensive' – a policy 'comprehends' the cover stated, that and nothing more, and if you run into insurance difficulties, take the policy to an expert to interpret.

Finally, make certain that any terms of the policy are complied with. For instance, if you are required to install a burglar alarm or to link one up with the police, make absolutely certain that this is done. Failure to comply with a condition may lead to entirely justifiable repudiation of the contract by the insurers.

Before you acquire transport make certain (a) that you will get adequate insurance cover at a price you can afford; (b) that the proposed driver is properly licensed for the class of vehicle concerned; and (c) that you will have somewhere to park. You have no greater right to station your vehicles on the highway outside your own premises than has any other member of the public. If in doubt, check with your local police.

It remains to wish you the best of good guidance from your advisers, and the most excellent luck available.

2 Problems of Partnerships

As any accountant or tax consultant will tell you, there is much to be said for the partnership. Apart from professionals, whose disciplinary or ethical rules forbid them to practise with the benefits of limited liability, modern legislation has put a premium on partnerships – or, for that matter, on trading as an individual.

First, the tax burden lies heavier on the company than on the firm. Corporation tax aside, the Revenue smiles far more upon the man who has to meet his debts and his expenses out of his own pocket than upon the company which can shrug itself into liquidation if disaster strikes.

On the other hand, of course, where your entire pesonal fortune rests upon the sucess of your business, you take added risks. But as partnerships are on the increase – and partnership ventures are even engaged in by companies – let us spare an informed thought, for the firm. Whether you are an actual or only a potential partner, it is well worth considering the laws on partnerships, most of which are in the Partnership Act 1890.

Unlike a company, which has no life without a formal memorandum and Articles of Association and due registration, no formalities are required for a partnership. 'Partnership is the relation which subsists between persons carrying on a business in common with a view of profit', says Section 1 of the Act, whether those persons know it or not. If you decide to embark on a partnership business or venture, you would be wise to set down the details in writing. The law will not insist that you do so.

In practice, it is sometimes difficult to know whether a partnership in fact exists. People who deal with the firm have no right to examine its accounts – unlike, of course, the company, which is required by the Companies Act 1985 to lay its cards on the Registrar's table. On the one hand, then, partners have the benefits of secrecy; on the other, those who deal with the firm have the security provided by the individual liability of each of its members.

Every partner is an agent for the firm and of his other partners 'for the purpose of the business of the partnership'. Each may bind the firm and all his partners, unless he has no actual authority to do so and the person with whom he is dealing knows that fact.

Equally, 'every partner in a firm is liable jointly with the other partners ... for all the debts and obligations of the firm incurred while he is a partner'. His liability is not confined to debts which he himself has incurred on the firm's behalf. If the partnership goes into debt, its creditors may enforce their rights against the property of any individual partner. Even a 'sleeping partner' may have a rude and expensive awakening.

Naturally, the partners are free to regulate their own rights and liabilities as between themselves. And a person who is admitted as a partner into an existing firm does not become liable to the creditors of the firm for anything done before he became a partner, unless he expressly agrees to assume that burden. But the converse does not apply. A retiring partner remains liable for partnership debts incurred before his retirement. His fellow partners may agree to discharge him from existing liabilities, but the creditors may still look to him.

It follows that while one partner may obtain an indemnity against another or make whatever arrangements he chooses with his fellow members of the firm, those who deal with the partnership and do not know of those special arrangements and are not party to them may still look to each individual partner for money due. 'The mutual rights and duties of partners, whether ascertained by agreement or defined by this Act,' says Section 19, 'may be varied by the consent of all the partners, and such consent may be either express or inferred from a course of dealing.' Equally, the normal rules regulating the relationship between a firm and its individuals and third parties may be altered by agreement between them.

In the absence of any agreement to the contrary, Section 24 of the Act provides that 'all the partners are entitled to share equally in the capital and profits of the business, and must contribute equally to the losses, whether of capital or otherwise, sustained by the firm.'

The firm must indemify every partner in respect of payments made and personal liabilities incurred by him 'in the ordinary and proper conduct of the business of the firm' or 'in or about anything necessarily done for the preservation of the business or property of the firm'. There is no right to an indemnity if a partner acts improperly, still less in respect of any outlay unconnected with the partnership business. As one judge put it: 'You could say that a member of a firm acts as a partner during his working day, but he does not take his partnership to bed with him at night.'

Unless some alternative agreement is made, the following important rules apply:

1 Where a partner makes any payment or advance 'beyond the amount of capital which he has agreed to subscribe', and he does so for the purpose of the partnership, then he is entitled to interest at the rate of 5 per cent (only), from the date of the payment or advance.
2 Before the ascertainment of profits, a partner is not entitled to any interest on the capital subscribed by him.
3 Every partner may take part in the management of the partnership business.
4 No partner shall be entitled to remuneration for acting in the partnership business.
5 No person may be introduced as a partner without the consent of all existing partners.

It follows that any partner who wishes to be paid for his efforts or to have the right to introduce his son into the business or to exclude another of the partners from the day-to-day management of that business or to claim interest on capital he subscribes (before profits are ascertained), must so provide in his partnership agreement (which, I repeat, *may* be made orally but *should* be set down in writing).

What of partnership disputes? 'Any difference arising as to ordinary matters connected with the partnership business may be decided by a majority of the partners, but no change may be made in the nature of the partnership business without the consent of all existing partners.'

Section 25: 'No majority of the partners can expel any partner unless the power to do so has been conferred by express agreement between the partners.'

So what happens if there is a dispute? Then we must see how the partnership can be dissolved.

First, the partnership may be for a fixed term or a specified object. If the term expires or the object is achieved, the partnership is automatically dissolved.

Next, where no fixed term has been agreed for the duration of the partnership, 'any partner may determine the partnership at any time on giving notice of his intention to do so to all the other partners'. Only where the partnership was originally 'constituted by deed', is a notice in writing essential. In all other cases, notice to dissolve may be given orally and may take effect forthwith. So if you do not want any partner to be entitled to put an end to the firm at any moment, you should make some agreement to the contrary.

Conversely, if you enter into a partnership for a fixed term and it continues after that term has expired and without any express new agreement, 'the rights and duties of the partners remain the same as they were at the expiration of the term, so far as it is consistent with the incidents of a partnership at will'. In other words, any partner may put an end to the partnership at any time, if he so wishes.

Meanwhile, the previous partnership arrangements will generally continue. As before, no partner may compete with the firm – and if he does so without the consent of the other partners and 'carries on any business of the same nature as and competing with that of the firm', then he may be forced to 'account for and pay over to the firm all profits made by him in that business'. He is bound to render true accounts and give full information 'of all things affecting the partnership', and is himself entitled to inspect and to copy the partnership books and accounts, as and when he sees fit.

Unfortunately, many partnerships break up in dispute and contention. If the partners cannot agree on the distribution of partnership property or upon the proper interpretation of the partnership agreement, or if there is a deadlock in the management of the business, what happens? As like as not, one partner will apply to the court to dissolve the business and to order that the proper accounts be taken and enquiries made, so that the rights of the parties can be ascertained.

Apart from cases where a partner is found to be of unsound mind or 'in any other way permanently incapable of performing his part of the partnership contract', the court may dissolve the partnership in four other circumstances. Here they are as set out in Section 35 of the Act:

(i) When a partner, other than the partner suing (for dissolution), has been guilty of such conduct as, in the opinion of the court, regard being had to the nature of the business, is calculated to prejudicially affect the carrying on of the business;

(ii) When a partner, other than the partner suing, wilfully or persistently commits a breach of the partnership agreement, or otherwise so conducts himself in matters relating to the partnership business that it is not reasonably practicable for the other partner or partners to carry on the business in partnership with him;

(iii) When the business of the partnership can only be carried on at a loss;

(iv) Whenever in any case circumstances have arisen which, in the opinion of the court, render it just and equitable that the partnership be dissolved.'

So if the partners cannot agree, the court may intervene. The law appears clear enough. But if doubts arise, you should consult your solicitor.

The Act lays down the rules for the distribution of assets on the final settlement of the accounts ... the rights of partners if there is fraud or misrepresentation ... the rights of outgoing partners to share profits made after dissolution ... and various other inevitable essentials. Where the parties have not made the rules for themselves, Parliament does so for them. 'What a pity we did not work out our own arrangements,' say the partners. But the time to have thought of that was when the partnership was first created.

3 The Director's Personal Liabilities

A company has no human existence. Its operations are directed by its board, controlled by its executives and managers and carried on by its staff and agents. The benefits of limited liability flow directly from the separation of private and corporate existence. But equally, the company as such may commit 'torts' – or civil wrongs. And those who administer the business may sometimes be held personally responsible.

An employer is 'vicariously liable' for the sins of his servant. If a director is negligent in the course of his duties and a third party suffers damage, the company can be made to pay. But when can the director be held personally liable? The higher your level in the company, the greater the mistakes you are liable to make – and the more important it becomes to know the legal answers to this major problem.

* * *

A Mr Feldman and a Mr Partridge were sued for damages resulting from an explosion caused by negligence, on land on which a company formed by them was manufacturing explosives. 'If the company was really trading independently on its own account,' said Lord Buckmaster, when the case reached the House of Lords, 'the fact that it was directed by Messrs Feldman and Partridge would not render these directors responsible for the company's tortious acts, unless indeed these acts were expressly directed by them.'

Then Lord Atkin: 'Prima facie, a managing director is not liable for tortious acts done by servants of the company unless he himself is privy to the acts – that is to say, unless he ordered or procured the acts to be done ... If the directors themselves directed or procured the commission of the act, they would be liable in whatever sense they did so, whether expressly or impliedly.'

So if a wrongful act is committed by one of the company's employees, you (as director, manager or executive) will only bear personal responsibility if you 'ordered or procured' the commission of the wrongful act. If you were the privy to it – if, in any sense, you expressly or impliedly authorized its commission – then you can be held personally liable.

A director, on behalf of his company, employed a band which performed a musical work in breach of copyright. The director knew absolutely nothing about their doing so. He was held in no way responsible for the wrong that was committed and could not personally be held to account for it.

Then there was the director who joined in an authority to brokers to obtain subscriptions. There were mis-statements of fact in a prospectus issued by those brokers. The director was held not liable in an action for deceit. He did not authorize or know of the mis-statements. A director is only liable in respect of false representations in a prospectus, even if this is issued by his co-director or some other agent of the company, if he expressly authorized or tacitly consented to its issue.

What, then, if one director commits a wrongful act with the knowledge of another? Both directors will be responsible. Judgment may be obtained against either of them, but each may seek a contribution or even an indemnity from his fellow. The chances are that each could be made to shoulder 50 per cent of the liability.

So, in so far as the 'torts' of company's servants are concerned, provided that you are never privy to any irregularity, even if wrongful acts are done in the name of your company, you yourself will not be held liable for them. Conversely, if you clap your corporate telescope to your blind eye ... if you deliberately avoid seeing the wrongs committed by others in the company's name ... if you direct the commission of a tort (expressly or by implication) ... then and only then can you be brought personally to book by those who suffer. Otherwise, they must look to the company.

Of course, if you yourself commit the wrongful act in the course of your employment, the situation is quite different. Then you may well get an indemnity from your company, but you will remain personally responsible.

In practice, the company's rights against its executives and employees are seldom exercised. The insurers pay up. The policy covers both corporate master and individual man, so no useful purpose is served by clutching at the private bank account. But make no mistake about it – the individual director is just as responsible for his own misdeeds as any other person by whom the company lives and earns its living.

4 A Director's 'Fiduciary Relationship'

An architect was managing director of a company which carried out construction services for large concerns, both private and public. His duties included the procuring of new business, especially in relation to the gas industry. He looked after the interests of industrial development consultants when negotiating with the Eastern Gas Board, who wanted to build four depots. Unfortunately for the company, the negotiations proved abortive.

Not long afterwards, the architect (says the Law Report) obtained his release from his employment by Industrial Development Consultants 'by representing dishonestly that he was in bad health'. It later transpired that he had been approached 'in his private capacity' by the Deputy Chairman of the Gas Board. He then obtained for himself the contract which his former employers had been after. This, we are told, resulted from work which he had done, unknown to them, while he was still their managing director.

The ex-employers sued the architect, claiming that he should account to them for all benefits which he had received under the contract, including all remuneration and fees. And even though it appears that the plaintiffs would not have got the contract in any event or at any time, they won their case.

Where an agent acts for a principal – or a director for his company or a partner for his firm – there exists a so-called 'fiduciary relationship'. There is a duty to exercise the utmost good faith.

If you sit on the opposite side of a bargaining table, you must not tell lies. You are not entitled to defraud the other contracting party. But you are not under any duty to disclose to him the profits which you may make from the deal, either personally or for your principal.

However, as between your company or firm or employer and yourself, you must (as one judge put it) 'disgorge your profits'. You must not make a 'secret profit' from the exercise of your duties.

Further, every principal is entitled to an account from his employee or other agent. Whether it is your partner, your manager, your fellow director or your foreman or secretary, he must account to you for any financial advantage which he obtains as a result of his employment with you.

Note. This duty does not cease along with the employment. The director had left his company before he made a penny out of the Gas Board. But the judge still ordered an account.

Note, too, even though the company itself would not have made anything out of the deal, the director was not entitled to benefit from the arrangement that he later made on his own account. A man who works for you is not entitled to turn that work to his profit merely because he cannot turn it to yours. He is not entitled to say to a prospective client or customer: 'Very well – you will not do the deal with the company – so why not do it with me personally?'

The same principle applies to a trustee, who must not make any profit out of his relationship with the beneficiaries. Unless there is some express provision to the contrary it is 'an inflexible rule' of court that a person in a fiduciary position may not make a profit out of his duties. Nor is he allowed 'to put himself in a position where his interest and his duty conflict'.

You are entitled to insist that your employees, your partners or the directors of your company give faithful service. Because of their 'fiduciary relationship', they are trustees for you (or for your firm or company as the case may be) of any money or goods, profits or benefits, which they receive as a result of that relationship. A court will force them, if necessary, to give an account of such money or benefits. And if the account shows any secret profit ... any benefit received as a result of work done as an agent but unknown to his principal ... then an order will be made, requiring payment.

Conversely, you (like the unfortunate architect) stand in a 'fiduciary relationship' towards your principals. So it is as well to appreciate the grim strictness of these legal rules.

5 A Director's Title

The title 'director' is an artificial creation. It leads to complications. On the one hand, a person who is not called a director, and, indeed, who does not even sit at the board, may bear responsibilites in law which are identical with those carried by an executive who has the name 'director' conferred upon him. On the other hand, people may be called 'directors' who are not on the board and may involve the company in exactly the same liabilities and responsibilities as if they were actually mighty board members.

The Companies Act 1985 defines 'director' as including 'any person occupying the position of director by whatever name called'. The affairs of the company may be conducted by 'trustees', 'members of the council' or 'governors'. A director, by any other name, will still come within the definition.

Once appointed (by the Articles or some alternative method provided by them or by the shareholders in General Meeting), the directors assume grave responsibilites. They must carry out their duties fairly and responsibly and in the best interests of the company. Their names must appear, in most cases, on stationery, trade catalogues, circulars and the like – and so must their nationalities, if they are not British. Their positions must be registered, so that anyone who makes the appropriate company search will know who is at the helm. They are directors in fact, even if they only take a nominal part in the running of the business.

Note that a director will be an officer but an officer will not necessarily be a director. 'Officer', says the Act, includes 'a director, manager or secretary'. And the liabilities of each (as we shall see) may differ.

What matters, though, is that 'the law looks at the reality and not at the form'. A court would be concerned with the function of the officer and not with the name which the company has seen fit to bestow upon him. You cannot appoint a man to your board and by calling him something other than a director remove his responsibilities and duties. Conversely, the mere fact that you deny a seat on your board to someone who in fact manages or directs the activities of your company will not mean that he can avoid playing the commercial game in accordance with the rules laid down by statute.

Now suppose that you call an official 'marketing director', 'merchandising director', 'director of personnel' or some other grandiose title which suggests that he is on the board, but you do not in fact admit him to your inner cabinet.

Anyone who is sufficiently curious can make a company search and discover that the employee is not a board member. But only if disaster strikes is anyone likely to take that sort of trouble. In fact, the 'director' will deal with third parties (including both employees of the company and outsiders) on the basis of the title given. And they will be entitled to accept the man's position at its face value.

It follows that a company is not entitled to squirm out of its responsibilities by saying: 'The man who made the arrangements or entered into the purported contract on our behalf was not a member of the board. And the board have declined to approve or to ratify his action.' Even if the man had in fact no actual authority, the company 'clothed him with its ostensible authority'. It saw fit to give the man its apparent authority to act on its behalf in the capacity of director and anyone with whom he deals in that capacity may take the company's action at its face value.

If you wish to dignify an employee with the title of director, the fact that you do not put him on your board will restrict his powers, authority and status within the company itself, but it will not prevent him from exercising the power which third parties are entitled to presume that he has by virtue of his title.

So if you dub a man director, you must take the consequences. The company will normally be bound by his contracts whether or not he is on the board. If he is negligent, the company will be liable to pay for his carelessness. And, of course, looking on the profitable side, the company will also be entitled to benefit from his good work. For better or for worse, the man who directs normally assumes the burdens and responsibilities of a director. And the man called 'director' is given responsibilities and status which the company must honour.

6 Must You Supervise Your Colleague?

'It is not the duty of each director to supervise the running of a company,' said the Lord Chief Justice in the case of *Huckerby v. Elliot*. He is not even bound 'to exercise some degree of control over what is going on'. Nor is he bound to supervise his co-director, whom he has no reason to mistrust. With those wise words, the learned judge lifted at least part of the burden that rests upon the bowed shoulders of the director of the industrial concern.

The Windmill Clubs Limited ran a gaming club in Leeds called the New Embassy. Chemin-de-fer was played by the guests. The company did not hold the appropriate licence.

At that time, the Customs and Excise Act 1952 provided that where a company did not hold the correct gaming licence and the offence was 'proved to be attributable to any neglect by a director' then the director as well as the company was to be 'deemed guilty of the offence'. Mrs Mavis Huckerby, one of the directors of the Windmill Clubs, was charged with an offence and convicted by the Leeds Stipendiary Magistrate. She appealed. The case came before a Divisional Court of three judges of the Queen's Bench Division, presided over by the Lord Chief Justice, Lord Parker.

The judge first set out the facts. Then he said this: 'At the trial, no evidence was offered other than agreed statements of fact ... which disclosed that although the appellant was a director of the company, she knew little about the conduct of the club. This she left to her co-director and to the manager.' Mrs Huckerby took no active part in the running of the club. Her co-director and the manager were in charge.

When the case had come before the Stipendiary, said Lord Parker, he had held 'that it was for a director of the company to exercise some degree of control over what was going on'. These words were 'too wide. It is not the duty of each director to exercise some degree of control over what is going on, nor is it right to say that there is a duty on a director to supervise the running of the company and, in particular, to supervise a co-director who is secretary.'

I repeat that magic formula because it may work wonders if ever you (or your spouse) get prosecuted for the sins of others on the board. The fact that your name is on the notepaper or even that you attend board meetings will not of itself make you responsible for exercising control over the running of the company – or, to be more precise, over the way in which others run it.

Or suppose that you decide that you want to get a distinguished name on to your board. You approach a man well known in the City? You tackle a titled gentleman, whose breeding and lineage exceed his knowledge of industrial affairs? He is unwilling to join you because he is afraid that he may be responsible if you go off the rails? Then read him the words of the Lord Chief Justice.

Anyway, Lord Parker continued as follows: 'I know of no authority which says that it is a director's duty to supervise a co-director or to acquaint himself with all the details of running the company. The prosecution evidence disclosed that the appellant was leaving matters such as licences to a co-director and to a secretary who was fully acquainted with the business.' So the prosecution had not proved their case and the appeal was allowed.

Mr Justice Ashworth said: 'I cannot accept that there is a duty on a director to see that the law is observed.' The Section concerned does not create 'an absolute offence'.

There are some offences which you commit even if you did nothing negligent or improper. If, for example, you fail to give preference to a pedestrian on a zebra crossing, you break the law. Even if the pedestrian ran out under your wheels, giving you no opportunity to stop, you have still offended, because the offence is 'absolute'. Of course, the fact that you could not avoid an accident, and that the pedestrian was in fact at fault, will provide your solicitor or counsel with marvellous material for a plea in mitigation. But it is no answer to the charge.

What matters to directors, though, is that unless an offence is absolute, we know that one director cannot be made criminally liable merely because his colleague failed to carry out his obligations. We have a loophole through which directors may leap if charged with offences (for instance) under the Trade Descriptions Act, the Health and Safety at Work etc. Act, or the Factories' Act. If you are charged and are a director in name alone – or a boardroom director, with no control over the day-to-day running of the factory or works – then do not plead guilty. Thrust the case of *Huckerby* v. *Elliot* before the eyes of your solicitor. And then let him fight for your good name. With fortune (and the facts) on his side, he should win.

Anyway, prosecuting authorities learn their lessons. So we can hope that inactive or boardroom directors will avoid prosecutions for company offences which were in no way caused by their neglect. And it is not 'neglect' to leave the job of complying with statutory obligations to those whose business it is to do so.

So the court has placed a benevolent limit on the ancient rule that each director is his brother's keeper. The case of *Huckerby* v. *Elliot* should bring joy to many an anxious boardroom.

7 Take-overs, Mergers – and Self-protection

When take-over time arrives, heads may roll – for executives as much as people on the shop floor. But a director is in a better position to see the blow coming and to try to feather his nest in anticipation of possible redundancy. How far can he go before personal interest conflicts with company responsibilities?

* * *

A company, of course, is a separate legal entity. So even if a director owns a substantial proportion of the shares, his first duty is to act in its best interest.

To prepare a new and long term service contract for himself shortly before a take-over – so as to ensure a handsome golden handshake if and when the take-over materializes – is not an act likely to benefit the company. On the contrary; the company will not have to pay, and there is rarely any good reason why it should do so.

Conversely, the director is fully entitled to make appropriate arrangements with the acquiring concern for his own protection. He can join its board or enter into a contract of service. He can do a deal with that company whereby he is to be paid compensation when the take-over occurs – as long as the payment comes from the coffers of the acquiring concern and not from those of the company which is to be swallowed. But if there is any such arrangement, it must be revealed to the shareholders, as it is one of the factors to be borne in mind when deciding whether or not to vote in favour of the take-over.

An extremely useful guide to conduct during take-overs and mergers is contained in 'The City Code' prepared by the Issuing Houses Association in co-operation with the Accepting Houses Committee and various other bodies. This code, written at the suggestion of the Governor of the Bank of England, was revised most recently in April 1985 and, although it relates primarily to companies whose shares are publicly held, it is also relevant to transactions in respect of private companies.

'The boards of an offeror and of an offeree company and their respective advisers', the Code says, 'have a duty to act in the best interests of their respective shareholders ...'. A basic principle of law.

When approached with an offer, the board of the offeree company must obtain 'competent independent advice ... and the substance of such advice must be made known to its shareholders'. Above all, 'directors of an offeror or an offeree company must always, in advising their shareholders, act only in their capacity as directors and not have regard to their personal or family shareholdings or to their personal relationships to the companies. It is the shareholders' interests taken as a whole, together with those of employees and creditors, which should be considered when the directors are giving advice to shareholders.'

To ask a man to put on one side 'personal or family shareholding' or 'personal relationship with the companies' is feasible for the director who is wealthy, but for the individual whose daily bread depends either upon his position on the board or his shareholding it is often an impossibility.

There may be good reasons for a board preferring a lower offer or rejecting an attractive offer. Nevertheless, where acceptance of the lower of two offers is recommended or a controlling board accepts such a lower offer or rejects a more attractive one – frequently forcing the minority shareholders to act similarly – it must be prepared to justify its good faith.

'Good faith' are the operative words. A director has a 'fiduciary duty' in law towards the company to exercise his powers honestly and in the interests of the company and the shareholders.* In practice, of course, conflict often arises when there is a take-over. It is because directors owe a fiduciary duty that they are not permitted to make a secret profit out of their position.

Where directors (and their close relatives and related trusts) sell shares to a purchaser, as a result of which the purchaser is required by Rule 9 of the Code to make offers to all of the remaining shareholders, the Code provides that the directors must ensure that as a condition of the sale the purchaser undertakes to fulfil his obligations under the Rule.

'Directors whose shareholdings, together with those of their families and those held on trust, effectively control the company, or shareholders in that condition who are represented on the Board of a company, who contemplate transferring control,' says Rule 10, 'should not, other than in very exceptional circumstances, do so unless the buyer undertakes to extend a comparable offer to the remaining shareholders.'

In such very exceptional circumstances the panel on take-overs and mergers set up at the request of the Bank of England should be consulted in advance.

A take-over bid is made for a company where the directors have only six months to go before expiry of their contracts of service. They know perfectly well that if the company remains independent, with themselves in control, new contracts on improved terms will be made. But if the small company is to be embraced in the grasp of a larger outfit, their services may not be required. Alternatively, they may be retained on sufferance, for a limited period, to ensure a smooth change over. Or maybe they will not want to remain as subordinates. Naturally, the first reaction is to move the clock forward – very fast – and enter into new contracts with the company.

'The take-over is still far away and may never transpire ... If the company remains independent, as seems likely, it will need our services and if we are not to be enticed away by other concerns, the company must be competitive in the remuneration and conditions and security it provides ... We would have made these arrangements, even had there been no question of take-over ... It would have been stupid for us to wait until the last minute.'

Some or all of these excuses may be justified. But the odds are that they are nothing more than a mask for what is, in strict theory, an improper practice to ensure that if there is a take-over or merger the golden handshake will be a firm one.

What protection does a director have? Section 303 of the Companies Act 1985, states: 'A company may by ordinary resolution remove a director before the expiration of his period of office notwithstanding anything in its Articles or in any agreement between it and him.'

With certain exceptions such as life directors of private companies a simple majority is enough to shift a director, provided only that special notice is given of the resolution to remove them, giving the individual concerned the opportunity to reply.

If removed before his or her period of office expires, the director has the same rights as any other servant or agent of the company when it comes to claiming damages for wrongful dismissal.

In general, this means compensation for loss of office by a tax-free golden handshake. The longer the period of office lost, the higher the pay which would have been received and the more the company will have to contribute. It will be the director's company and not the acquiring company which will do the paying.

Section 314 of the Act provides that where, in connection with the transfer to any persons of all or any shares in a company, being the result of an offer made:

a to the general body of shareholders;
b by or on behalf of some other body corporate with a view to the company becoming its subsidiary or a subsidiary of its holding company;
c by or on behalf of an individual with a view to his obtaining the right to exercise or control the exercise of not less than one third of the voting power at any general meeting of the company;
d conditional on acceptance to a given extent

a payment is to be made to a director of the company by way of compensation for loss of office, or as consideration for or in connection with his retirement from office, it is the director's duty to take all reasonable steps to secure that particulars of the proposed payment (including its amount) are included in or sent with any notice of the offer made for their shares which is given to any shareholders. If a director fails to take those steps or if any person who has been properly required by the director to include those particulars in or send them with the required notice referred to above fails to do so, they are liable to a fine.

Worse, if the director does not comply with the duties of disclosure, any sum received will be held in trust for any persons who have sold their shares as a result of the offer made. Indeed, the expenses incurred in distributing that sum amongst those persons shall be borne by the director and not be deducted from the sum.

Still, practice tends to be far removed from theory. There appears to be no report of any case where Section 314 has been put into effect. Moreover, it has been held that the Act fails in its attempt to ensure that the amount paid to a dismissed director by way of compensation is to be approved by the general meeting because the section applies only to compensation for loss of office as director (as opposed to, say, employment as managing director) and to compensation to which the individual is not legally entitled under the contract. But there are case reports which throw light on these vital rules.

In *Lindgren and Others* v. *L. & P. Estates Limited* the question of the fiduciary duty of a director was considered by the Court of Appeal.

'A trustee cannot in general deal with himself or obtain an advantage himself in a transaction in which he is on both sides of the table,' said Lord Justice Harman, pointing out that a director must 'consider the interests of the company' before taking a decision.

Lord Justice Winn held that on the particular facts there had been no 'breach of an equitable duty' by the director to the company. The director had 'independently considered the commercial merits' of the agreement in question. That is all that the law requires – that, and proper disclosure.

In *Selangor United Rubber Estates Limited* v. *Cradock* – a case which was argued before Mr Justice Ungoed Thomas for over four months, the judge considered the alleged misapplication of the plaintiff company's monies by a director 'in bad faith and in breach of his duty as director and in furtherance of an arrangement' with another defendant. The complications which can arise from such arrangements emerge as the most frightening moral of this massive, legal tale.

If your company is to be taken over, mind what you do for your own protection – and preferably do it on the advice of your lawyers, as well as your accountants. Ignore the rules and you may get away with it. At worst, you may find yourself in the midst of a High Court legal battle.

Finally, the Transfer of Undertakings (Protection of Employment) Regulations 1981. They are intended to safeguard employees' rights when a business or undertaking or any part of it is transferred to a new owner. They are complex: your solicitors will have to know their details but their two main provisions are these:

1 When an undertaking changes hands, people employed by the old owner automatically become employees of the new one, on precisely the same terms and conditions of employment. So when you take over the other business, you will automatically acquire the employees of the other business; they will preserve their continuity of employment; and they will also keep all their previous employment rights, except occupational pension entitlements.
2 However: You may dismiss your newly acquired employees, provided that you do so for an 'economic, technical or organizational reason' which requires changes in the workforce. But even then, a dismissed employee who is entitled to unfair dismissal protection may take the case to a tribunal claiming that you have applied the rules unfairly.

Note: If the previous employers recognize an independent trade union for collective bargaining, the union representatives of employees affected must be informed about the transfer and consulted about measures which the old or the new employers intend to take and which would affect employees.

Note that these rules only apply when the undertaking is transferred and not merely where shares in a company are bought and control taken over.

8 Battles in the Boardroom

A large industrial concern recently sacked its managing director. Sensibly, he consulted his solicitor. 'We quarrelled over policy,' he said. 'I want to expand ... to modernize ... to build for the future.... The rest prefer to sit back on their uninspired haunches. "Consolidation", they called it. "Stagnation" was my word. Anyway, they conspired to sack me. I want to sue for conspiracy.'

Now, it is a civil offence ('tort') to conspire to defraud. Damages may be obtained against those who put their heads together in an attempt to rob you or your business of its money. But if an act is lawful, it does not become improper because several people combine to do it.

Suppose, for instance, that Mr X decides that the head of his department (a Mr Y) should be elbowed out of the way. Mr X hints to the chairman that Mr Y is inefficient. He lets it be known that he (Mr X) would do the job much better. And he says quite openly that some of the recent disasters have been caused through Mr Y's dereliction of duty, advancing senility or galloping incompetence. The chairman sacks Mr Y.

Now, if Mr Y gets his proper notice or pay in lieu, he will probably have no lawful complaint except a possible claim for compensation for unfair dismissal (see Chapter 39) – even if he happens to be on the board. However immoral the behaviour of Mr X and however ungrateful the sacking by the chairman, Mr Y has got his desserts – the money to which he was lawfully entitled under his contract of service. He would therefore recover no further damages either against the company or (still less) its chairman or against Mr X.

Now suppose that Mr X was not alone in sharpening the knife which he was to drive into Mr Y's back. He was ably assisted by Mr Z and Mr A, who both felt that the elbowing out of Mr Y would make room for their advancement. The three men conspired against the fourth. But there was no question of fraud. Mr Y would get no damages. As a judge once proclaimed, 'The Dirty Tricks Act is not yet on the statute books'.

He could then sue the company for damages for wrongful dismissal. And if he happened also to be a shareholder and could show that Messrs X, Z and A (and possibly the chairman) had put their crafty heads together in order to defraud him of the value of his shareholding then a claim for conspiracy might arise.

'A conspiracy consists in the agreement of two or more to do an unlawful act, or to do a lawful act by unlawful means,' said Mr Justice Willes. The real purpose of the conspiracy must be 'the inflicting of damage on A as distinguished from serving the bona fide and legitimate interests of those who so combine', with the result that A suffers damage. This view was approved by the House of Lords in the case of *Lonrho Ltd v. Shell Petroleum Co. Ltd.*

So to succeed in a conspiracy action, the dismissed director (or other executive) must show that former colleagues or superiors combined to cause him or her an unlawful injury.

Of course, if you can prove fraud by one person, that should be quite enough. And remember that fraud consists of the making of a false statement either in the knowledge that it was untrue or 'recklessly, careless whether it be true or false'. Commercial fraud does not necessarily involve knowledge of the untruth. Recklessness is quite sufficient.

So now put yourself in the unhappy position of an industrial executive or director shown to the door. The first question to ask is – have I been lawfully wronged? The fact that there has been a moral injury is normally irrelevant. There are many injuries for which the law provides no recompense.

Next, is there a good claim for damages for wrongful dismissal? If so, then remember to mitigate your loss.

If the removal was from the board of the company, was it in accordance with the company's Articles – or in compliance with the Companies Act? Directors who have become bankrupt or of unsound mind or who have committed an indictable offence against the company will have no complaint if they are sacked.

Then what about fraud or conspiracy? Could this provide the level for the extraction of a sensible compromise settlement?

They say that you may judge a man by the company he keeps and the books he reads and the executive by the subordintes whom he employs. You may also judge the wisdom of an industrial executive by the experience and sagacity of the solicitor he employs. If disaster comes your way, then the sooner you get to your lawyer the better.

Conversely, if you are considering ousting an executive or a colleague, then ask yourself: Will I give him any rights against the company or myself? And if you are not sure of the answer, then you too should make your way with speed to your legal adviser – before you take an irreversible step in the wrong direction.

9 Oppressed Minorities

The world of industry is beset with strife. The chairman of a great complex is fired by his colleagues on the board. The managing director of an industrial giant is consigned to the scrap heap. One of the three founders and shareholders in a manufacturing company is turfed off the board. So what happens? The miserable outcast rushes hotfoot to his lawers. 'I am an oppressed minority,' he says. 'They have conspired against me. I want my rights.'

What rights has the member of the board ousted from his seat of office? If you are in that unhappy non-position, what can the law do to help you? Conversely, what are the risks for you, if you heave an aggravating rival or a non-productive fellow director out of office?

* * *

First, the dismissed director may have rights as an employee. They may work under a contract of service, in the same way as any other servant of the corporation. If their dismissal is in breach of their contract of service, then they are entitled to damages. Just because the board are mighty, they do not lose their rights as servants.

Conversely, a director who misbehaves may be sacked in the same way as anyone else. Board members who persistently fail to turn up for meetings ... who neglect their duties ... who enter into competition with their own company ... who 'repudiate' their contract of service ... are asking for the sack. If they get it, the law will give them no special rights.

So the dismissed director's first duty to himself (or herself) is to attempt to obtain compensation for loss of office. This (says the Companies Act 1985) must be disclosed to the members and approved by the company. If it does not exceed £25,000, it is a golden handshake and free of tax. So the clouds of fraternal disapproval may have a golden lining.

But what about 'oppression of minorities'?

This protection (which is not very powerful) applies to shareholders and not to board members. In theory at least, a board is a democratic body and the minority must bow, if necessary. But what of the shareholders?

For the smooth functioning of a company, says one expert, 'a proper balance of the rights of the majority and minority shareholders is essential'. The law 'attempts to maintain that balance by admitting on principle the rule of the majority but limiting it, at the same time, by a number of well defined minority rights'. If you hold shares in the company which employs you, then you should know these rights. Equally, if you are thinking of evicting a director who is also a shareholder, pause and consider.

First, there are occasions when the act of a company must be approved by the members – and sometimes special resolutions must be passed, requiring a three-quarters majority. For instance, in general the Articles of Association (which govern the internal regulations of the company) can only be altered by special resolution.

Next, there are occasions when individual shareholders may be able to recover the company's property from those who have taken it and who, by their voting power, have prevented the company itself from suing. This is an example of a 'fraud on the minority'. Majority shareholders must not milk the company for their own benefit in a fraudulent manner.

Next, under Sections 459–61 of the Act, a member can petition the court for relief where the company's affairs are being conducted in a manner which is 'unfairly prejudicial to the interests of some part of the members', including the petitioner. The mere fact that you don't like the way that the company is being run is not sufficient. If, however, the court is satisfied that the company is being run in an unfairly prejudicial manner, then it has very wide powers to give relief.

If you can gather together 200 members or the holders of one-tenth of the issued shares, you could apply to the Department of Trade and Industry for an investigation of the company's affairs or of the ownership of the company. Again, if there is an attempt to alter the objects of the company, dissentient holders of 15 per cent of the issued shares could apply for cancellation of that alteration. But generally the majority rules.

In practice, though, the director who is also a contributory to the company holds one major card, which may be withdrawn from the sleeve at any time. They may apply to have the company wound up. Even if this application fails, the moment it is advertised the company is likely to be in trouble. Its creditors will become restive and its credit may dry up. Even if the petition is thrown out by the court, it may cause very great harm.

10 Winding up the Company

There are many reasons for winding up a company, some a good deal more laudable than others. As we have seen, the threat of winding up may cause chaos on the board. So whether you are yourself a director with a massive shareholding or a more minor executive who has seen fit to acquire a share or two in the business, you should know the basic grounds for thrusting a company out of business.

The grounds on which a company may be wound up will be set out in Chapter 24. Two of these grounds call for special attention. By far the most common ground for compulsory winding up is inability to pay debts. The five situations in which a company will be deemed to be unable to pay its debts are also set out in Chapter 24. It should be noted, however, that if there is a bona fide dispute over a debt, the fact that it has not been paid will not give rise to a presumption that the company is unable to pay its debts. But where the company is commercially insolvent in that it does not have assets presently available to meet its current liabilities, it is in trouble. And just think how many industrial concerns would be unable to meet their current liabilities if their credit were to dry up.

The fact that your company is carrying on a business which is losing at the moment will not make it 'unable to pay its debts', if its assets exceed its liabilities. But even where assets do exceed liabilities, if those assets are not 'presently available to meet its current liabilities', the company may be insolvent.

The disgruntled director dismissed from his post may well know the state of the company's finances. If these are presently shaky even if there are great hopes for the future, the director may have to be assuaged, if only to stave off a petition.

The second ground which calls for special attention is the so-called 'just and equitable' ground. But this ground is not as wide as it sounds. In the course of time courts have defined what is 'just and equitable'.

Where there is deadlock in the management, it may be 'just and equitable' for the company's business to be wound up. But deadlock usually applies only where the company is in substance a partnership and there are grounds for dissolving a partnership.

In one case, a director behaved in a thoroughly irregular manner, excluding other directors from the management of the company and acquiring complete control of its operations. As there was a fairly even holding of shares amongst the directors, and as the business was in reality a partnership even though it was cast in the mould of a company, winding up was ordered.

In another case there was an unjustifiable exclusion of a working director from the 'partnership' business. A winding up order was made.

Two men were the sole shareholders and directors of a company, with equal rights of management and voting power. They quarrelled bitterly. They could not agree on the appointment of important executives. They communicated through the company secretary. Although the company made large profits in spite of a disagreement, it was held that there was a complete deadlock in the management. It was a proper case for a winding up.

Then there was the private company which consisted of three shareholders only. They held all the issued shares and were the original allottees. The shares were fully paid in equal proportions. One shareholder was resident in America and the other two were the present directors of the company. They could not agree. The affairs of the company were now in deadlock and there were pending actions between the shareholders of the company.

The Articles of Association provided that when a shareholder wished to withdraw from the company he should offer his shares to the others; in the event of neither of them purchasing those shares the shareholder who wanted to withdraw should be entitled to have the company wound up. One of the directors offered his shares to the two other shareholders. Neither of them agreed to buy. He presented the petition for the compulsory winding up of the company, which the other two shareholders opposed. The court held that it was 'just and equitable' that the business should be brought to an end.

The managing director of a company had 'a preponderant voting power'. He failed to hold meetings or to submit accounts or to recommend dividends. He 'laid himself open to the suspicion that his object in so doing was to acquire the minority shares at an under-value'. The judge made a winding up order.

In other cases, companies have been wound up where they were held to be 'bubbles' – to have had no business or assets; or where the company was 'formed to carry out a fraud' or to 'carry on an illegal business'.

So the court does have wide powers. But these will not be exercised merely because a director is dismissed or a shareholder is disgruntled. Still, the director spurned may be in a stronger position than he realizes. Next we consider ways in which he can prevent himself from being removed from the board.

11 Removing a Director

The vast bulk of modern businesses are operated through limited liability companies. Every company is run by directors – and a seat on the board is the ambition of most executives. But once you are appointed to a chair at the table of power, what are your prospects of staying there? When and how may a director be removed?

The Companies Act 1985 says that (with very few exceptions) any director may be removed by an ordinary resolution passed at a general meeting of the company. A simple majority is enough to shift a director, even if his period of office has not expired. And this applies notwithstanding anything in the Articles or in the agreement between him and the company. Provided that special notice is given of such a resolution, it will be upheld by the courts.

The director is entitled to receive a copy of the notice of the intended resolution. He may have his own representations set out in writing at reasonable length and sent to the members of the company. Only if he sees fit to use his right to make written representations for the purpose of 'securing needless publicity for defamatory matter' may he lose it. But in any event, he must be given the right to speak out at the company meeting.

The Articles of Association of one family company provided that each of the three directors was to have one-third of its shareholding. But on any resolution to remove a director from office, that director's votes were to treble in power. So instead of having one vote for this purpose, he would have three – and hence he could keep himself permanently in office.

The family quarrelled. Two of the directors wished to oust their relative. And they maintained that the Article which prevented them from doing so was unlawful and contrary to the rule in the Companies Act that any director could be removed by an ordinary resolution.

Unanimously, the Court of Appeal upheld the right of the company to provide special weight to its members' votes. So if you wish to ensure that you cannot be thrown off the board, you should create (or amend) your Articles accordingly. Until the law is changed, the Court of Appeal has provided a safety belt for directors with sufficient power to install it.

In practice, of course, general meetings normally vote on resolutions placed before them by the board. The board itself operates on a majority system (subject only to the chairman's casting vote). If you wish to remain in power, then you should pack the board with as many of your own supporters as you can decently muster.

Now suppose that you are heaved out of the boardroom. What can you do? You may claim damages for breach of your contract of service. But you must mitigate your loss by trying to find suitable alternative employment. Your damages will be the amount which you would have received had you retained your job for the specified period, minus anything wich you actually managed to earn during that period. And a further deduction will be made in respect of the tax which you would have paid had you not been removed.

If a director receives a golden handshake, then the first £25,000 is tax free. He is better off, then, with compensation than he would be with damages. So the Revenue has provided one of the most satisfactory ways of settling this sort of claim. The ex-director drops his action. The company votes him a golden handshake. He receives more than he would have got had he won his case.

Apart from removal, a director must retire at the end of the first annual general meeting after he reaches the age of 70. There are exceptions. First, if the company is a private company which is not the subsidiary of a public company, this rule does not apply. The articles of the company may themselves otherwise provide. Or the director may have been appointed or approved by the company in general meeting by a resolution of which special notice stating his age was given.

In practice, if a director does have to retire because of age, he may be reappointed by a resolution stating his age. And the rule that the articles may alter the age limit or provide that the director shall not be obliged to retire on reaching any age enables many a wise beard to hobble into the boardroom supported by arthritic shoulders.

Normally, a company's articles provide for directors to vacate offices on the happening of certain specified events. Table A of the Companies (Tables A–F) Regulations 1985 provides draft articles which are commonly incorporated into those of a company. Article 81 of Table A provides that the office of director shall be vacated not only if he is dismissed but also in the following cases:

1 if he ceases to be a director by virtue of any provision of the Companies Act 1985 or he becomes prohibited by law from being a director; or
2 if he becomes bankrupt or makes any arrangement or composition with his creditors generally; or
3 if, in certain circumstances, he is suffering from mental disorder; or
4 if he resigns his office by notice to the company; or
5 if, without permission of the directors, he has been absent for more than six consecutive months from meetings of directors held during that period and the directors resolve that his office be vacated.

If a director is ill and unable to travel, then his office is not automatically vacated. But in one case a director was advised by his doctor that his health 'would be benefited by going abroad'. He was away for over six months and his office was held to have fallen vacant.

So directors should not regard themselves as appointed for life. They may be removed for bad behaviour – or for no reason at all. In the former case, they may still receive compensation for loss of office – but if the company tightens its fists, the law cannot help. In the latter case, the director's scorn may unleash a legal fury.

12 The Protection of Depositors and Investors

'Fifty per cent interest per annum – and your money back at any time on demand!' The impossibility of this sort of advertiser living up to his promise ought to be obvious to everyone. It is not. From the days of the South Sea Bubble to the present day, greed, or gullibility, has continued to overcome good sense. Investors and depositors still tumble over themselves to lose their money.

From time to time Parliament has stepped in to try to protect the unwary. First came the Prevention of Fraud (Investments) Act 1934. Then there were sections in the Companies Acts of 1947 and 1948. In 1958, these provisions were consolidated into the Prevention of Fraud (Investments) Act 1958. Following the fiasco of the State Building Society, The Building Societies Acts 1960 and 1962 and the Protection of Depositors Act 1963 (subsequently repealed and replaced in part by the Banking Act 1979) tightened up the law still further.

However, there was still thought to be considerable room for improvement. In particular, over the last ten years or so there has been an increasing demand to widen the scope of the legislation to include investment advisers and consultants. In 1981 after the collapse of four licensed dealers in securities including Norton Warburg, Professor L.C.B. Gower was appointed by the Secretary of State to conduct a review of the existing legislation and advise on reform. The Stock Exchange's 'Big Bang' accelerated matters even more.

As a result, the Financial Services Act 1986 effected a complete overhaul of the existing legislation for the regulation of investment business. A new regulatory body has been set up, the Security and Investments Board (SIB), which is intended to incorporate the best aspects of self-regulation and statutory regulation – 'practitioner based, statute-backed'. Also, the Act is not limited to the area of securities; it extends to investments and the carrying on of an investment business. Perhaps most important, the criminal and administrative sanctions are backed up by a civil remedy given to investors who have suffered loss by reason of contravention of the Act.

The Act prohibits the carrying on of investment business without authorization or exemption. Authorization can either be by the SIB or indirectly by certification by a recognized professional body. Authorization may be suspended or withdrawn for failing to comply with the obligations imposed by the Act. There are several important exemptions from the Act, in particular, the Bank of England, Lloyd's and listed money market institutions. Provision is also made for the recognition or exemption of investment exchanges and clearing houses.

The Act renders illegal misleading statements and practices. S.47 of the Act provides that:

' 1 Any person who –
    a makes a statement, promise or forecast which he knows to be misleading, false or deceptive or dishonestly conceals any material facts; or

    b recklessly makes (dishonestly or otherwise) a statement, promise or forecast which is misleading, false or deceptive,
is guilty of an offence if he makes the statement, promise or forecast or conceals the facts for the purpose of inducing, or is reckless as to whether it may induce another person (whether or not the person to whom the statement, promise or forecast is made or from whom the facts are concealed) to enter or offer to enter into, or to refrain from entering or offering to enter into, an investment agreement or to exercise, or refrain from exercising, any rights conferred by an investment.
2. Any person who does any act or engages in any course of conduct which creates a false or misleading impression as to the market in or the price or value of any investments is guilty of an offence if he does so for the purpose of creating that impression and of thereby inducing another person to acquire, dispose of, subscribe for or underwrite those investments or to refrain from doing so or to exercise, or refrain from exercising, any rights conferred by those investments.
3. In proceedings brought against any person for an offence under subsection (2) above it shall be a defence for him to prove that he reasonably believed that his act or conduct would not create an impression that was false or misleading as to the matters mentioned in that subsection.'

A particularly welcome provision is contained in S.56 of the Act, which makes it a criminal offence to make unsolicited calls and in the course of or in consequence of such a call to enter into, by way of business, an investment agreement with the person upon whom the call is made. Indeed, it is also made an offence to make an unsolicited call to procure or endeavour to procure a person to enter into such an agreement. This is intended to put an end to so-called 'cold calling'.

The Act also attempts to deal with advertisements. Section 57 of the Act makes it an offence for a person other than an authorized person to issue or cause to be issued an investment advertisement in the United Kingdom unless its contents have been approved by the authorized person.

Further, from now on the Secretary of State has the power to direct that an individual shall not be employed in connection with investment business without the Secretary of State's written consent if it appears to the Secretary of State that the individual is not a 'fit and proper person to be employed in connection with investment business'.

You will now also be able to check up on any person involved in investment business because the Secretary of State has to keep a register giving details of all authorized persons and this register is open for public inspection free of charge.

The Financial Services Act 1986 promises to be a significant step towards protecting the increasing number of private investors who, by the sale of British Telecom, British Gas, the TSB and British Airways shares have been lured into the investment market by the prospect of large gains at low risk.

13 Company Meetings

What meetings must a company call? What meetings may it call? And when may members of a company themselves requisition a meeting – either directly or with the help of the court?

* * *

Section 366 of the Companies Act 1985 provides that every company shall in each year hold an annual general meeting and shall specify it as such in the notices calling it. Not more than 15 months may elapse between the date of one annual general meeting and the next – subject only to the proviso that a new company has 18 months from the date of its incorporation within which to hold its first AGM.

If a company in which you are interested has not held its AGM, and you can get satisfaction no other way, you should (either directly or through your solicitor) contact the Department of Trade and Industry. The DTI may then itself call or direct the calling of a general meeting 'and give such ancillary or consequential directions as the DTI think expedient . . .'.

Suppose, now, that a member wishes to call a special meeting of the company to discuss some particular matter. To get results, he must either himself hold at least one-tenth of the paid-up capital of the company or must be able to get the backing of enough shareholders to make up that proportion. Under Section 368 of the Companies Act 1985 (which we shall call 'the Act'), 'the directors of a company shall, on a members' requisition, forthwith proceed duly to convene an extraordinary general meeting of the company.' A members' requisition is a requisition of members of the company holding 10 per cent of the voting rights in the company.

The requisition must state the objects of the meeting and must be signed and deposited at the registered office of the company. The requisition itself may be in a single document or it may 'consist of several documents in like form each signed by one or more requisitionists'. The directors then have twenty-one days from the date of the deposit of the requisition in which to convene the meeting. If they fail to do so, the requisitionists or any of them who represent more than one-half of the total voting rights of all of them may themselves convene a meeting. But this may not be held after the expiration of three months from the date of the deposit of the requisition.

The Act lays down the length of notice which must be given before meetings are called. Twenty-one days' written notice is required for the AGM. Meetings other than the AGM, or those called for the passing of a special resolution, require fourteen days' written notice.

If insufficient notice is given, the meeting may still be valid. If, in the case of a meeting called as the AGM, all the members entitled to attend and vote agree that the meeting shall be treated as validly convened, all will be well. And in the case of any other meeting, if there is a majority who together hold not less than 95 per cent in nominal value of the shares giving a right to attend and vote at the meeting and if they resolve that the meeting was properly convened, then once again the irregularity is waived.

So if ever a shareholder wishes to call a meeting, he should check the articles of the company to see what provision they make as regards procedure and voting. In the absence of anything to the contrary in the articles, he should look at the 'Table A' clauses, which are usually made to apply where there are no special, contradictory articles. For instance, 'two or more members holding not less than one-tenth of the issued share capital ... may call a meeting ... In the case of a private company two members, and in the case of any other company three members, personally present shall be a quorum. ... Any member elected by the members present at a meeting may be chairman thereof ... In the case of a company originally having a share capital, every member shall have one vote in respect of each share or each £10 of stock held by him, and in any other case, every member shall have one vote.'

Suppose, now, that the company will not call a meeting which a member believes is necessary, though he cannot himself muster sufficient share power to requisition it. All is not necessarily lost. Under Section 371 of the Act, 'if for any reason it is impracticable to call a meeting of the company in any manner in which meetings of that company may be called, or to conduct the meeting of the company in the manner prescribed by the Articles or this Act, the court may, either on its motion or on the application of any director of the company, or of any member of the company, who would be entitled to vote at the meeting, order a meeting of the company to be called, held and conducted in such a manner as the court thinks fit. Where any such order is made, the court may give such ancillary or consequential directions as it thinks expedient ... Any meeting called, held and conducted in accordance with an order under the foregoing sub-section shall for all purposes be deemed to be a meeting of the company duly called, held and conducted.'

It is not often that the court can be convinced or cajoled into calling a meeting. But there is a powerful, residuary right given to investors who feel that otherwise they are not going to have the opportunity to ventilate their grievances.

Finally, a word about voting at meetings. If a member believes that a proper poll ought to be taken, then he is entitled to demand one. 'Any provision contained in a company's articles shall be void,' says the Act, 'in so far as it would have the effect either of excluding the right to demand a poll at a general meeting on any question other than the election of the chairman of the meeting or the adjournment of the meeting; or of making an effective demand for a poll on any such question which is made either by not less than five members having the right to vote at the meeting or by a member or members representing not less than one-tenth of the total voting rights of all the members having the right to vote at the meeting, or by a member or members holding shares in the company conferring a right to vote at the meeting, being shares on which an aggregate sum has been paid up equal to not less than one-tenth of the total sum paid up on all the shares conferring that right.'

Five members with the right to vote at the meeting may demand a poll. So may those holding one-tenth of the total voting rights or one-tenth of the paid-up share capital.

Parliament, then, has done its best to see that company meetings are properly conducted and members' grievances properly aired. But that is hardly surprising. Who does not wish to encourage self-imitation?

14 Changing Your Line of Business

We are all agreed that the object of a business is to make a profit. But how to do it, that is the question.

'Well,' you say, 'first you decide what your line's going to be ... and then you follow it. Too simple. And if you're a partnership or a one-man firm, you can do what you like, and if things don't go well, you can just change course and head for something better. But if you're a company, all your objects have to be written into its Memorandum of Association – and once that's done, you've had it. Those are your objects and you've got to stick to them.'

Nonsense. You can change them any time you like.

'Really? Still, I would like to know just how broadly a company's objects clause is interpreted, and whether and how it can be altered.'

The acts of a company only have legal effect if they are *intra vires* – that is, if they come within the scope of the objects clause of its Memorandum of Association. That is its charter. That document gives it life and a purpose for its existence. Outside the bounds of that purpose, it is quite ineffective.

'Does that mean that if my company is empowered to engage in the sale and manufacture of clothing and it enters into an agreement to take over a colliery, then that agreement is so ineffective that even if the objects clause is amended later on to include a power to purchase and operate collieries, that won't bring my contract to life?'

Absolutely.

'Which explains why this clause is so important?'

Quite so. The objects clause should be most carefully drafted, to incorporate in the most specific terms possible all the lines of business in which the company intends to engage. But even then, not everything can be thought of, and so most of these clauses end with words like this – 'and to do all such other things as are incidental or conducive to the attainment of the above objects, or any of them'.

'And that could mean anything or nothing. What does it mean?'

'That is a very difficult question. Some lawyers believe that it means very little. In the case of *Rolled Steel Products Limited* v. *BSC* the Court of Appeal reaffirmed the commonly held view that a company has an implied power to do any act which is reasonably incidental to the attainment or pursuit of any of its express objects, unless such act is expressly prohibited by the memorandum. Slade LJ said that 'whether a particular transaction, carried out in purported exercise of an express or an implied power contained in a company's memorandum of association, is within the capacity of the company must still depend on the true construction of that memorandum.'

So a company formed to carry on the business of a colliery proprietor might no doubt acquire and work collieries; have a banking account; for the purpose of its business borrow money on mortgage or otherwise, and draw, accept, and endorse bills of exchange, compromise claims made against it; remunerate its employees; pay dividends to its shareholders; advertise its products; establish branch offices; acquire rolling stock, and machinery, and vessels for conveying its coal – for all these things and many others are reasonably implied by the words used.

Of course, the difficulties arise when the directors want to know what is 'reasonably incidental' to the objects. It is much more convenient for businessmen not to leave to implication powers with which it is clearly desirable specifically to invest the company.

'All of which really means, I suppose, that if a particular operation is not specifically mentioned in the objects clause as coming within the powers of the company, then you must look carefully to see whether or not it is "*intra vires*", i.e. within the company's powers. You must ask yourself, using your common sense, whether that particular operation is "reasonably incidental" to the main purposes of the company. Having asked yourself, if you don't give yourself a clear answer you'll have to ask a lawyer!

And to avoid having to do that, you're much better off if you draw your objects clause in the widest way in the first place.'

Yes, indeed. But 'widest' is not the same as 'vaguest'. If a clause is too vague, the Registrar of Companies can refuse to register it.

'Suppose that my company was incorporated for the manufacture of ladies' clothing, would I need a special power to take over a similar business – to buy out someone else in the same line?'

Yes. But that's the sort of additional clause that's normally in a Memorandum.

'And could I use my machinery to manufacture men's clothing if I felt like it?'

Again, no – unless your objects clause provided for it. But why should it not do so?

There is no point in not putting it in. If your objects clause specifies that you may make men's clothing, this does not mean that you have to do so if you don't want to.

'What about extending or altering the objects clause? When can that be done?'

In the old days, it could not be done at all. Later, it could only be effected by applying to the court. But today a company may alter the objects clause of its Memorandum by special resolution.

'Always?'

Always – in so far as the changes are required to enable the company:

1 To carry on its business more economically or efficiently.
2 To attain its main purpose by new or improved means.
3 To enlarge or change the local area of its operations.

4 To carry on some business which under existing circumstances may conveniently or advantageously be combined with the business.
5 To restrict or abandon any of the objects specified in the memorandum.
6 To sell or dispose of the whole or any part of the undertaking of the company.
7 To amalgamate with any other company or body of persons.

Item (4) is the main one. You can now alter your objects so as to carry on almost any other trade or business. But you must remember to make the alteration before and not after you branch out into fresh fields of commerce, or you may find that the grass is greener where you were.

A reminder. Application can be made to the court by shareholders with a big enough holding to have the alteration cancelled (for details, consult your solicitor). This application must be made by petition, within 21 days after the date when the special resolution concerned was passed. But if 21 days go by and no such petition is filed, then you have just 15 days to deliver to the Registrar of Companies a printed copy of your Memorandum as altered.

If you do not, then you, your company and every one of its officers are liable to be fined.

15 Checklist for Closing Down

Call it 'rationalization', 'consolidation' or disaster – when you close a branch or a business, there are legal complications to be recognized in advance. Check the list, before taking your decisions.

There are four main areas of potential trouble: premises, employees, suppliers and creditors.

1 Are you a freeholder or a tenant? If you own the freehold, then you are fully entitled to sell it, as and when you wish, provided that you can find a buyer. If you are short of cash, you may still be able to sell and then to lease back the premises from the buyer. But there is no legal reason why you should not dispose of your asset.
2 Are you a tenant? If so, then carefully examine your lease or tenancy agreement to see whether there is any term affecting assignment or sub-letting. These may be absolutely forbidden – in which case you are in the hands of your landlords. They may waive the prohibition, probably in return for payment, but possibly with

some relief if your business is in trouble and you can find an assignee or sub-tenant in a stronger business position.

3 Do you need your landlord's consent to assignment or sub-letting? If so, the law implies a term that such consent shall not be unreasonably withheld. If you find a responsible and solvent assignee or sub-tenant who can provide adequate references, you should be in the clear.

4 Have you given any personal guarantees? If you are the original tenant under a lease, the landlords may have a comeback against you if your assignee does not comply with the covenants. So *you* may need a personal guarantee from an individual before you assign to a limited liability company.

5 Check the curious rules on redundancy. For instance, if you make an employee redundant, then you will have to find 65 per cent of any statutory redundancy payment to which he is entitled out of your own business pocket (or, in the case of an individual trader, out of your assets). Since the Wages Act 1986, employers of 10 or more employees must pay all statutory redundancy payments out of their own resources – rebates are now only available to the tiniest employers. If you put your company into liquidation, then the entire redundancy pay comes from public funds – and the Revenue provides in the liquidation for the 65 per cent which the company ought to have paid – but its claim goes into the pool with other non-preferential creditors. Also under the Employment Protection Act (Part 5) you must (if possible) give prescribed warnings of redundancies or face potentially massive penalties.

6 Have you outstanding orders with suppliers for goods or for equipment? If these are already purchased, you may dispose of them as you wish (subject to any retention of title clause imposed by your supplier). The closing of a business does not give any right to cancel orders already placed with suppliers.

7 All contractual documents should be handed to your solicitors. They may find loopholes – maybe some element of a binding contract was missing. Perhaps your unconditional order was not 'accepted' by the supplier, who only agreed to deliver on terms substantially different from yours (hence making a 'counter-offer').

8 If a deal is firm, you have no right to cancel because you have decided to go into a different line of business, to move your premises, to sell or to close down. If you refuse to accept delivery, you will have broken the contract and your supplier will be entitled to damages. Therefore:

a Can you induce your supplier to let you off the hook – for the sake of goodwill; because you can promise further orders in the future; or because of your difficulties in paying for the goods if they are delivered?
  b If you are selling, can you get the assignee to take over your obligations?
  c If you are going to have to pay damages, then check on the profit which your supplier will not now make on the deal. But can he mitigate his loss by selling elsewhere? If so, then he must do so. Note: there is no need for a term in your contract with the supplier giving him the right to damages. Such a term is inevitably applied into a contract for the supply of goods or services of any sort, in the absence of some agreement to the contrary.
9 Have you consulted your solicitor and your accountant, so as to sort out all the legal and tax angles (including possible tax losses)? It is vital that you should know both the strength and the weakness of your position.
10 Anyone who considers buying your business will wish to inspect the books and to know the precise trading position. Are your records in order?
11 If you close down the business, then you will have to make your peace with the creditors. Among factors affecting the strength of your bargaining position will be the following:
  a Liquidity of the business.
  b Whether it has been trading as a separate company or as part of a major enterprise.
  c The extent of the limitation of its liability – as opposed to the existence of personal guarantees from you, your family or others.
  d The reasonableness of any offers which you can make to those who are owed money.
  e The answers to the problems posed in points (1) to (10) above.

16 Confidential Information

The son of a well known company director is said to have emerged from college with a degree in business administration. His father asked him to replace a light bulb in the hall chandelier. The son duly climbed up a ladder and was about to change the bulb when his father gave the ladder a shove and the son fell to the ground.

'Why did you do that?' the son protested, rubbing his bruises.

'So that you will learn that in business you must trust no one – not even your own father!' he replied. 'Business studies are excellent in their own way. But the practical realities are rough.'

Still, you have to trust – your colleagues, your subordinates and, on occasion, complete strangers. But what help does the law give you, if that trust is betrayed?

An employee owes a duty to give faithful service and he may be sacked on the spot if he hands over secrets. If he is paid for the betrayal, then he may be prosecuted under the Prevention of Corruption Acts – corruption is a crime for both briber and bribed (see chapter 91). Industrial espionage as such is no offence, but if the confidential information is given by stolen document, the taker is a thief.

An employee's obligations depend on the contract with his employer. If there is no express term, those concerning the use and disclosure of information depend on implied terms.

An employee owes a duty of good faith to his employer. The extent of that duty varies according to the nature of the contract. Suppose, for instance, that your employee makes or copies a list of your customers for use after his employment ends, or deliberately memorizes such a list. This is a breach of his contract.

The implied term which imposes an obligation on the employee as to his conduct after the determination of the employment is more restricted in its scope than that which imposes a general duty of good faith. It is clear that the obligation not to use or disclose information may cover secret processes of manufacture such as chemical formulae, or designs, or special methods of construction and other information which is of a sufficiently high degree of confidentiality as to amount to a trade secret. The obligation does not extend, however, to cover all information which is given to, or acquired by, the employee while in that employment, and in particular may not cover information which is only 'confidential' in the sense that an unauthorized disclosure of such information to a third party while the employment subsisted would be a clear breach of the duty of good faith.

To decide whether any particular item of information falls within the implied term so as to prevent its use or disclosure by an employee after the employment has ceased, it is necessary to consider all the circumstances of the case. In the Court of Appeal case *Faccenda Chicken Ltd* v. *Fowler* the Court held that the following matters were among those to which attention must be paid:

a The nature of the employment. Thus employment in a capacity where 'confidential' material is habitually handled may impose a high obligation of confidentiality because the employee can be expected to realize its sensitive nature to a greater extent than if he were employed in a capacity where such material reaches him only occasionally or incidentally.
b The nature of the information itself. Information will only be protected if it can properly be classed as a trade secret or as material which, while not properly to be described as a trade secret, is in all the circumstances of such a highly confidential nature as to require the same protection as a trade secret.
c The fact that the circulation of certain information is restricted to a limited number of individuals may throw light on the status of the information and its degree of confidentiality.
d Whether the employer impressed on the employee the confidentiality of the information. Thus, though an employer cannot prevent the use or disclosure merely by telling the employee that certain information is confidential, the attitude of the employer towards the information provides evidence which might assist in determining whether or not the information can properly be regarded as or is equivalent to a trade secret.
e Whether the relevant information can be easily isolated from other information which the employee is free to use or disclose.

The Court of Appeal also emphasized that the above principles cannot be circumvented simply by putting a restrictive covenant in the contract of employment. A restrictive covenant in relation to the disclosure of information by an ex-employee will not be upheld unless the information sought to be protected is a trade secret or the equivalent of a trade secret.

One type of knowledge is peculiarly secret. It involves new inventions, ready for sale. If you create an idea in the course of your normal duties as an employee, or in the course of duties falling outside your normal duties, but specifically assigned to you, then that invention or idea belongs to your employer (see Chapter 29). But if you have a bright idea which belongs to you, you may decide to sell it – quite properly.

A Mr Seager invented a hidden carpet grip which he called the 'Invisgrip'. He took this to an executive of Copydex Limited and tried to sell him the idea – obviously in complete confidence.

At the time Copydex were not interested but later they themselves applied for a patent in respect of a carpet grip very similar to that dreamed up by Mr Seager. They maintained that the grip was their own idea, but Mr Seager sued for damages 'for breach of confidence'. The case reached the Court of Appeal.

Lord Denning referred to 'the broad principle of equity that he who has received information in confidence shall not take unfair advantage of it. He must not make use of it to the prejudice of him who gave it, without obtaining his consent.'

Mr Seager had told Copydex 'a lot about the making of a satisfactory carpet grip which was not in the public domain. They would not have got going so quickly except for what they had learned in their discussions with him ...' True, Copydex 'were quite innocent of any intention to take advantage of him. They thought that so long as they did not infringe his patent, they were exempt. In this, they were in error. They were not aware of the law as to confidential information.'

Ignorance of the law is no excuse, say the judges. And innocence of any wicked intent is no answer, in a case like this. All the judges agreed that the employees of Copydex acted honestly. But the fact that they could not be convicted of any offence in a criminal court did not free their company from an obligation to pay damages.

Later, the Court of Appeal had to consider the basis upon which damages in a case like this should be assessed. They held that Mr Seager was entitled to 'reasonable compensation for the use of the confidential information, assessed on the market value of that information as between a willing buyer and a willing seller'.

Happily for Copydex, the judges said that once the damages were both assessed and paid, the company acquired ownership in the confidential information which became 'vested' in them and they had right to make use of it. Naturally, had they been dishonest and stolen the information, they would have acquired no right whatsoever. A thief can never acquire 'property' in that which he has purloined.

In *Fraser* v. *Evans and Others*, the Court of Appeal (again presided over by Lord Denning) considered another branch of the law on confidential information. The plaintiff was a public relations consultant, employed by the government of Greece to make reports to them. He specifically undertook 'never to reveal to any person or organisation any information related to the work in the areas where it was operating, or information which comes to his knowledge during the course of the contract'. This sort of term often finds its way into contracts of service of industrial managers and other executives.

A translation of one of the reports was 'obtained surreptitiously' and came into the hands of a journalist employed by the defendants, the proprietors of *The Times* newspaper. Mr Fraser attempted to get an injunction, to prevent publication of the confidential information. He maintained that it was defamatory – and this the defendants admitted, although they alleged that in so far as it contained statements of fact, it was true and in so far as it represented opinions, these were 'fair comment on a matter of public interest'.

The court held that the plaintiff had no right to prevent publication as there was no breach of confidence as against him. The people entitled to the information were the Greek government and they were the only ones who could prevent the publication.

If you work for a company, then any information you obtain on behalf of the company belongs to your employers and not to you, and if anyone can take action to prevent its publication, it is your employers.

More interesting: 'There is no confidence as to the disclosure of iniquity ... It is an instance of just cause or excuse for breaking confidence. There are some things which may be required to be disclosed in the public interest, in which event no confidence can be prayed in aid to keep them secret ... '.

If you find out that a crime or some other 'iniquity' has been committed, even though the disclosure would be defamatory, you will not be forced by law to keep the evil news to yourself.

Even if the statement is defamatory, you will be allowed to publish it provided that you intend to plead 'justification' or 'fair comment'. And although in Fraser's case the court doubted whether there was such 'iniquity' as to justify publication, *The Times* was entitled to proceed because any defamation action would be defended.

'The right of free speech is one which it is for the public interest that individuals should possess and, indeed, they should exercise without impediment, so long as no wrongful act is done.'

It is a wrongful act to give away your company's secrets or those which have been imparted to the company in confidence. It is both right, proper and necessary that citizens should speak freely, when no wrong would be done.

In *Hubbard* v. *Vosper*, the founder of the Church of Scientology attempted to obtain an injunction to prevent the publication by the defendants of a book highly critical of Scientology and containing many extracts from the books and other writings of Mr Hubbard. The application was made before trial (at a so-called 'interlocutory stage') – and was refused.

Lord Denning said this: 'I think there is ground for thinking that Mr Vosper may have used information knowing that Mr Hubbard claimed it to be confidential. Nevertheless, he may have a good answer ... the Court will, in a proper case, intervene to restrain a defendant from revealing information or other material obtained in confidence, such as trade secrets, and the like. This depends upon the broad principle of equity that he who has received information in confidence shall not take unfair advantage of it ...

'But information must be such that it is a proper subject for protection ... there are some things which may be required to be disclosed in the public interest, in which event no confidence can be prayed in aid to keep them secret ...'.

Pointing out that the court could not decide on the facts at that stage, the judge added: 'I think that, even on what we have heard so far, there is good ground for thinking that these courses contain such dangerous material that it is in the public interest that it should be made known'.

Lord Justice Megaw added: 'Counsel for the defendants is more than abundantly justified in his proposition that there is here evidence that the plaintiffs are or have been protecting their secrets by deplorable means ... and, that being so, they do not come with clean hands to this Court in asking the Court to protect those secrets by the equitable remedy of an injunction'.

Suppose that your company had been engaged in a tax or customs fiddle. You come across the information and decide to reveal it – to the authorities, perhaps, or to the press. However confidential the information, the court will not force you to keep it to yourself. There is no confidence in an iniquity – and if the company wishes the court to exercise its discretion and to grant an injunction – a so-called 'equitable' remedy, available to ensure that justice is done – then it must come 'with clean hands'.

A worker's hands may be physically dirty through contact with your machinery or equipment. A company's hands may be metaphorically dirtied, throught contact with 'iniquity'. It then loses its right to have its confidences kept secret.

17 Banking

The next time you are on your knees before your bank manager, bolster yourself with the remarkable thought that his employers make their living through granting loans, not refusing them. But it would be more tactful to keep this thought to yourself. Naturally, you are in need. A client seldom makes an appointment with his manager to announce that he is paying off his overdraft. You have either come for more money today or to postpone payments until tomorrow. Either way, you must manage your manager. To do so, you must appreciate the nasty legal niceties of your situation.

When you are granted 'facilities' by the bank, it is making you a loan. And like most other loans, in the absence of some agreement to the contrary the money lent is repayable on demand. The moment the creditor requires the return of his cash, he may ask for it. You are then bound to pay up. Refuse to do so and you are in breach of the contract of loan – with all the miserable legal consequences to which contractual breaches may give birth.

If, then, you require facilities for a specified period, you should say so when you make the initial arrangements. 'All right,' says the manager. 'I'll mark a £5,000 limit on your overdraft.' Fine. But as the facility was not for any specified period of time, the bank may terminate it at any moment. 'Regretfully, we must ask you to clear your overdraft within the next seven days. . . . ' Alas.

Alternatively: 'We'll let this run for an initial six months and then the situation will have to be reassessed.' The loan cannot be called in for six months. Any attempt to force you to reduce the amount of the borrowing before the period has expired would be a breach of contract on the part of the bank. But once the half-year has gone, so has your right to refuse payment.

Incidentally, just in case you are thinking of trying to convince the bank that their oral agreement was for a longer term than they say, remember that every manager is required to note every lending limit and the period for which it is to run either before payment or up to review. If ever you have to do battle with your bank, these records will be powerful evidence – probably against you.

Suppose, now, that you are required to reduce or to liquidate your overdraft – and the money is simply not available. What can the bank do about it?

First, like any other creditor, the bank may sue for its money. Presumably you would have no defence to the claim: judgement would be given against you – and swiftly, at that: and the bank (now a 'judgment creditor') would be entitled to 'levy execution' on your goods and chattels ... to take out a judgement summons, to show cause why you had not complied with the order of the court to pay the money ... or to tip you into bankruptcy or your firm into dissolution. In a word, failure to comply with your manager's 'request' may spell ruin.

Next (or alternatively) the bank is entitled to 'realize' the securities which you have lodged as collateral. That, after all, was the object of requiring security. If circumstances have arisen under which the bank is entitled to sell your shares ... cash in your life insurance ... sell your house – then you must rely upon the benevolence of the bank not to exercise those rights.

A much earlier disaster tends to arise, of course, when the bank 'bounces' your cheque. A cheque is no more than an order to the bank to pay money from your account and if the cupboard is bare and there is no agreement under which the bank has agreed to restock it from its own resources, it is fully entitled to decline to accept your instructions. On the other hand, mistakes are sometimes made. Cheques are occasionally dishonoured in error. If this happens to you, you may well have a good claim against your bank, which is in effect saying to the person to whom the cheque is addressed: 'We regret that our client's credit will not come up to the sum specified.' And that is a highly defamatory statement.

Of course, if you 'stop' your cheque – countermand your instructions to pay – the battle will probably be joined between the payee and yourself. In that case, the bank simply stands in the sidelines. It has carried out its instructions and that is all that you can demand of it.

In practice, millions of satisfied customers have their cheques honoured when the bank is under no obligation to do so. We may all be grateful that the powers of the mighty are so seldom used. We sleep comfortably in our beds, confident that before our securities are sold, we will be given plenty of notice ... that when the manager says that he will 'speak to Head Office', he will succeed in putting our case to them better than we have to him ... that he will not drive us into ruin by keeping to his word regarding the reduction of our loans – even if we have been unable to keep to ours.

However: This reticence or kindness cannot be guaranteed. Too many businesses have been driven into ruin by bankers unwilling to continue their support.

Meanwhile and in any event, remember that you should shop around for the best terms you can get from your own or from other banks. Interest rates vary from the most modest, granted to the best customers, to the entirely horrific, charged to the (often unsuspecting) recipient of what is (or is regarded as) an 'unarranged' advance.

18 When Your Name's the Same

Sentiment apart, you may be as attached to your name as your name is to you. It represents your goodwill and that means money. An invented or adopted business or professional pseudonym, or firm or company name, may symbolize your life's work. It may even be your most valuable capital asset. So consider how far it is yours to use as you please. If you use it unlawfully, then you may be restrained from doing so. You must not use your name in such a way as to 'pass off' your goods or business as those of someone else.

It is an 'actionable wrong' for anyone 'so to conduct his business as to lead to the belief that his goods or business are the goods or business of another'. This may be done not only by copying the name.

You have no absolute right to use your own name for the purposes of your trade, business or profession or as part of your business name. If confusion or deception would be likely to arise, then you may be banned from using your name. Still, 'the sole right to restrain a person using any name he pleases in his trade or business', as one judge put it, 'is when the name adopted, whether fictitious or real, is calculated to do injury to any other person by representing that such business is the business of that other person.'

On the face of it, the use of your own name will not be taken as 'evidence of intention to misrepresent your goods'. But if, in addition to using your own name, you 'do other things which show that you intend to represent, and are in point of fact making your goods represent, the goods of another person', then the courts may step in and protect the good name and goodwill of the other. 'The court will not restrain a man for trading in his own name except where he uses his name in such a way as to pass off his goods as the goods of another.' But the converse applies.

Suppose that you have built up an excellent business. You have done so under your own name, William Jones. Another William Jones opens up in the same line of country (and possibly in the same immediate neighbourhood), proudly displaying his name (and hence yours) on his notepaper, publicity or fascia. What are your chances of restraining him from using that name?

You must try to show that besides using his own name, he is doing 'other things which show that he is intending to represent, and is in point of fact making his business represent' the business you carry on. Alternatively, you may be able to establish fraud. In one old case, Mr Burgess Snr had for many years sold 'Burgess's Essence of Anchovies'. He fell out with his son, who sold a similar article under the same name. No fraud was proved and the court refused to restrain the son from cashing in on the family name.

But in another case Messrs Wright, Layman & Umney Limited succeeded in obtaining injunctions restraining a Mr Wright from 'causing his goods to be passed off as theirs'. The plaintiffs 'had a wide reputation' under the name 'Wright's' in certain goods. Mr Wright called his similar goods 'Wright's'. Although he was found guilty of no dishonesty whatsoever, two injunctions were granted against him; he was restrained from trading under a name containing 'Wright' or 'Wright's' and further from using the name 'Wright' or 'Wright's' on his goods without sufficiently distinguishing them from the plaintiffs.

The Law Reports record battles between Vallantine and Ballantyne, Steiner Products and Willy Steiner, Valentine Meat Juice Company and Valentine Extract Company, Rodgers (Joseph) and Joseph Rodgers. Then there was the Mr Sidney Lyons, who changed his name to Joseph Lyons and had notepaper printed, headed: 'J. Lyons, Food Specialists'. The court held that he 'intended to deceive and had deceived the public into buying his goods as and for those of the famous J. Lyons & Company'. He was restrained from so doing in the future.

While you may trade in your own name or use it as part of your business name, provided that you do so honestly, if your use of the name 'is calculated to deceive the public unless precautions are taken', you will be given the choice: either take precautions or else cease using the name. For instance, just as you may 'pass off' your goods by marketing them in the same wrapping or 'get-up' as those of some more famous competitor, so you may be able to distinguish them by using a contrasting 'get-up'. If your competitor cannot establish that he is carrying on a business with which others 'will be led to associate' your activities, then all will be well.

So while in most cases you are fully entitled to make use of your name for whatever business purposes you see fit, if your real intention is to cash in on the goodwill of your namesake, you may find yourself in trouble with the law. Where the name's the same, very often the first to use it gets the right to keep it.

19 Laws of Copyright

For professional architects, surveyors, draughtspeople, writers, artists, photographers ... or any other professionals who put their talents on to paper ... there is no branch of the law more important than that concerned with copyright. And every businessperson who creates ideas in any artistic form – or who would like to purloin the ideas of others – should study this branch of the law with equal care. Here are the main rules, as found in the Copyright Act 1956.

* * *

Copyright (you will be pleased to hear) is a right to copy – or, to be more precise, the ownership of that right. It can subsist in 'an original literary, dramatic or musical work' or in an 'artistic work'. 'Artistic work' includes 'works of architecture, being either buildings or models for buildings' (Section 3). 'Drawings' are regarded as 'artistic', and by Section 48 these now include 'diagrams, charts, plans and maps'. So the plans of a projected factory are the subject of copyright. But who owns that copyright?

In general, 'the author of the work' is entitled to any copyrights subsisting in it. The individual who makes the drawings, produces the designs, prepares the plans – has the right to say who may or who may not copy his or her work. They may 'license' the use of their ideas ... grant permission to reproduce them ... or refuse that permission, if they see fit.

'But when I commission someone to do the drawings for me, do I not get copyright?'

If you commission someone to take a photograph, to make a painting or engraving or to draw a portrait, you become entitled to the copyright in the work. Section 4(3) of the Act says so. But commissions not coming within Section 4(3) leave the copyright with the author. What you are acquiring is the right to make use of the commissioned work for the specified purpose. When you employ an independent architect, surveyor or designer to prepare plans or drawings for you, you in general acquire the right to use them only for the specified purpose.

Of course, all this is subject to agreement to the contrary. If your architect is prepared to allow you to use his design for all purposes, for ever and ever – that is a matter for him. If you want that privilege, negotiate for it. You may have to pay more heavily – but it may be worth it. Otherwise, to use the 'work' for some purpose other than that contemplated may involve you in paying for the right all over again. Alternatively, you may find yourself restrained by an injunction of the court from continuing to make use of the other's 'artisitic efforts'.

'Does this apply if the architect or designer is on my staff?'

No. If the work is made 'in the course of the author's employment by another person under a contract of service or apprenticeship, that other person shall be entitled to any copyrights subsisting in the work'. If your employee in the course of his or her employment by you produces the masterpiece in question, and you employ him or her for the purpose of creating such masterpieces, you may use it as you see fit.

But note: where the work is done in your employees' own time and not in the course of their employment, the copyright vests in them. They may perhaps be prevented from using their spare time working for their own purposes or those of others. But nonetheless, the copyright is theirs. If you want to make use of the material produced in their spare time, you may have to pay them extra for it. But assuming that the work was done 'in the course of their employment', you are entitled to make use of it in the course of your business.

There is one interesting corollary to all this. While you cannot use the drawings for a second building without the architect's consent (which you should have been able to obtain fairly cheaply, because the work would not have to be redone), the architect would be entitled to use those drawings again. Assuming no breach of some express or implied term in the contract with another client, the architect could reproduce the drawings for that other client. Just as you get no exclusive right to wear the copy of the Paris model, so you cannot prevent the owner of the copyright in the design of the premises you have built from exploiting that ownership for his or her own benefit and that of others.

Naturally, these rules are capable of alteration by consent. For instance, suppose that you are an illustrator. Publishers offer you payment on an all-in basis, full copyright to go to them. Then make sure that the price is sufficiently lucrative before you accept.

Authors are often prepared to accept a fee for full copyright instead of selling book rights only. That is a matter for them.

Journalists (particularly of the freelance variety) seldom specify what rights they are selling. In the absence of any agreement to the contrary, the answer is: 'First British serial rights' – the publisher acquires the right to reproduce the work once only, in a British journal or newspaper. So what do you do if you receive a receipt or a cheque which purports to acknowledge that you have sold all copyright? Refuse to sign.

Artists, too, should take care to retain their copyright. If the man who commissions the portrait wants to do as he will with it, reproducing it where and when he sees fit, then he must pay for that privilege.

Or take the architect, who prepares a plan for one building and may be scandalized if it is used for 300 identical copies on other estates. This branch of copyright law is complicated. You should make your deal as clear as possible from the start and there will be no expensive misunderstandings at the end.

So copyright law spills over into the law of contract. If you have a deal to be done which involves the right to copy or reproduce, by all means know the basic copyright laws. But the more money that the arrangement involves, the more important it is for you to let a lawyer draw up your contractual documents. Whether you are a buyer or a seller of copyright material – or both – you are venturing into a field so narrow and so complicated that even amongst the gentlemen and ladies of the Bar there are only half a dozen who are acknowledged experts in the field.

One final, happy thought. 'Reproducing the work of one person,' it is said, 'may be a breach of copyright. Reproducing the works of many, in a suitable amalgam, is research!' Which suggests, does it not, the most common way to avoid copyright troubles? You then create an 'original work' out of the ideas of others – and the law (kindly creature that it is) bestows the copyright in your new, mongrel creation upon you.

Note: Following the Copyright (Computer Software) Act 1985, the 1956 Act now extends to cover computer programs.

20 Registration of Trade Marks

There is nothing like an inventive mind to propel a professional person into success or an employed executive into starting his or her own business. First, you will probably want an invention – the rules on ownership are in Chapter 29. Then you will need your own trade mark. The Trade Marks Act 1938 lays down the rules on registration. Here is what it says.

For a mark to be registrable, it must contain or consist of at least one of the following essential features:

1 The name of a firm, individual or company, represented in a particular or special manner.
2 The signature of the applicant for registration, or of some predecessor in their business.
3 An invented word or words.
4 A word or words having no direct reference to the character or quality of the goods.
5 A word or words not being according to its ordinary signification a geographical name or surname, unless sufficient distinctiveness can be shown.
6 Any other distinctive mark.

If you want to register a mark which contains one of these features, then you must still come within Section 11 of the Act – and, in particular, you must ensure that the mark would not be 'calculated to deceive'. It must not be too near some other mark, or you will not get it registered.

'Suppose that I cannot have a mark registered. If I use it anyway, what extra risks do I run?'

That all depends on the reason for non-registration. There are many brand names which are not registered, but which are jealously preserved. Non-registration will prevent you from taking proceedings for an infringement of a trade mark, but will not rule out 'passing off actions' if you consider that some other product is being marketed under a name so similar to your own as to suggest that your competitors are trading on your goodwill and trying to 'pass off' their goods as yours.

Finally, some examples from industry, of registration allowed and disallowed. The following have been held registrable – 'Solie' for photographic printing paper; 'Savonol' for soap – but not 'Absorbine' for an absorbent product or 'Lactobacilline' for a lactic ferment.

The former words were held to be 'invented' – but the latter were not. Which shows that the borderline between invention and actuality is a narrow one indeed.

Next, once you have registered your mark, what are your rights?

Everyone knows that it is an infringement of someone else's trade mark to use it to describe one's own product. If you were to market goods under the name of 'Q Brand', then Q Limited could doubtless obtain an injunction, to restrain you from doing so, plus damages, to compensate it (as registered proprietor of the brand name) for any damage suffered. But what is not obvious (and what few people realize) is that it is also an infringement of a trade mark simply to quote it when making comparisons with one's own product. There was a case in the Court of Appeal not so long ago in which a manufacturer of a famous chemical successfully restrained a competitor from publishing a circular which named that chemical under its brand name and pointed out that its quality in no way justified its price. The mere use of the other man's registered trade name was itself a breach of the proprietor's rights.

'But I thought that the object of giving the proprietor of a trade mark his rights was to prevent anyone else from passing off other goods as those of the registered proprietor ...'

That may be. But on the proper interpretation of the relevant section of the law, it has been decisively established that even if there is no question of passing off, there can still be an infringement of the registered proprietor's rights.

The let-out? There seems to be no reason why a manufacturer should not make a true and favourable comparison between his product and that of another producer, simply by saying, 'Our product is better and cheaper than the equivalent line manufactured by Q Limited.' Do not mention the other man's registered trade name and all will be well.

For the rules on the protection of your own marks, apply the above – in reverse.

The Trade Marks (Amendment) Act 1984 (effective October 1986) amended the 1938 Act to enable the registration of service marks for the first time in Great Britain. The 'services' covered include: Advertising and Business; Insurance and Financial; Construction and Repair; Communication, Transport and Storage; Education and Entertainment and others. Full details are available from the Trade Marks Registry in London.

21 Data Protection

Modern business involves computerizing a mass of personal data. This concerns not only employees but also, and especially, individual customers and suppliers. So here are the basic rules on 'Data Protection' as you need to know them – now.

The main object of the Data Protection Act 1984: To ensure that the UK is not excluded from various trade deals through non-ratification of the European Convention for the Protection of Individuals with regard to Automatic Processing of Personal Data. The Act creates a Data Protection Registrar and requires 'personal data users' to register. It sets out 'general principles' for ways in which personal data must be held and used. And it gives 'data subjects' legal rights, including access to their personal data and claims to compensation for inaccuracy or improper disclosure.

A 'data subject' is an individual in respect of whom personal data is held by some automatic process – in your case, your employees and possibly your actual or potential individual customers, clients or suppliers. You are the 'data user' because you collect and store the data for your use. The Act regulates your behaviour as a 'user' for the protection of those people whose personal data you computerize.

The eight principles are set out in the first Schedule. They are:

1 The information to be contained in the personal data must be obtained and the data processed 'fairly and lawfully';
2 Personal data must only be held for one or more *specified* and lawful purposes. So in each case you must decide the purpose for which the data is to be held; register that purpose; and stick to it;
3 Personal data held for any purpose or purposes shall not be used or disclosed in any manner incompatible with that purpose or those purposes;

4 Personal data held for any purpose or purposes must be 'adequate, relevant and not excessive' in relation to that purpose or those purposes;
5 Personal data must be accurate and, where necessary, kept up to date. So you will have to review and update personal data, as necessary;
6 Personal data held for any purpose or purposes must not be kept for longer than is necessary for that purpose or those purposes;
7 An individual data subject will be entitled –

   a at reasonable intervals and without undue delay or expense –
   (i) to be informed by any data user whether he holds personal data of which that individual is the subject;
   (ii) to access to any such data held by data user; and
   b where appropriate, to have such data corrected or erased.

   This is the key 'principle'. An individual may ask you whether you hold personal data of his; and you will be required to provide a copy in writing of such information, with an explanation where otherwise it would not be 'intelligible'.

   If application is made for data, you will be entitled to a modest, approved fee; to proper identification of the applicant; and to a written request.
8 The final principle applies both to data users and to computer bureaux – which means those who provide others with computerized data services. All users and bureaux must take 'appropriate security measures against unauthorised access to, or alteration, disclosure or destruction of, personal data and against accidental loss or destruction of personal data'.

Suppose that an employee or ex-employee, a tenant or other individual whose personal data you hold claims either that you have not given proper access to his or her personal data; or that they are wholly or partly inaccurate or out of date; or that you have improperly disclosed them. The complainant may require that the information be (where appropriate) corrected or erased; and may claim compensation for any damage they can prove that they suffered as a result of your non-compliance with the rules.

There are exemptions on grounds of national security; crime and taxation; health and social work; judicial appointments and legal and professional privilege. In general, there is no access to personal data held only for payroll and accounting purposes.

22 Travel Costs and the Tax Inspector

If you travel for fun, you cannot expect the tax man to foot the bill. But if you are dragged out of bed to attend to the needs of a patient or client or customer, what then? In the past, you would probably have been in the same unhappy position as the famous recorder of Portsmouth, whose claim for expenses incurred in travelling from home to court was disallowed. Work began in Portsmouth. That was his place of employment. And just as his secretary could not claim the cost of her season ticket nor his clerk the running expenses of his car, incurred on the way to trial, so the learned judge had to pay his travel costs out of his taxed income.

But now? The case of *Owen* v. *Book* (Inspector of Taxes) reached the House of Lords. By a majority of three to two, Dr David Owen – who held part-time appointments as obstetrician and anaesthetist at a hospital – was held entitled to deduct the expenses incurred by him in travelling from his home. At home, he carried on practice as a general practitioner. In hospital, he dealt with emergency cases. He had two places of work – and just as the barrister may charge for travelling from court to court ... the businessman from shop to factory or from supplier to customer ... so the doctor won the day.

Dr Owen was on stand-by duty at home at certain specified times. He had to be accessible by telephone. When a telephone call came through, he gave instructions to the hospital staff, and either waited for a further report or set out immediately. 'His responsibility for the patient began as soon as he received the telephone call.' The committee in fact paid his travelling expenses at a fixed rate a mile between home and hospital, up to a single journey of ten miles. The remaining five miles were paid out of the doctor's own pocket. He sought to deduct the whole cost of travelling – between two and three pounds a week – from his taxable income.

Now, where you are employed by a hospital (or anyone else), you are taxed under Schedule E. For expenses to be deductible, it must be shown that they were incurred wholly, exclusively and necessarily in the performance of your duties. But where you operate as a one-man band, you are taxed under Schedule D. You must then show that the expenses were 'wholly and exclusively' incurred in the course of your work. But, whatever the schedule, you must prove that you travelled in the course of your work, and not simply in order to get to the place of work.

The basis of Dr Owen's case was that he had two places of work. There was his home consulting room, where he dealt with his general practice and also received emergency calls. Then there was the hospital. The Court of Appeal held (as Lord Donovan later put it), 'that Dr Owen had one place of employment ... the hospital ... When he answered the telephone and gave any necessary preliminary instructions, of course, he was performing the duties of his office. But when he got into his car and drove to the hospital, he was not performing such duties. He incurred the expense of so travelling because he chose to live in one town when the hospital was in another.'

But happily for the doctor (and for all like him – probably including the other professional people who work both at home and elsewhere) a majority of the House of Lords thought otherwise.

Lord Guest: 'Dr Owen's duties commenced at the moment he was first contacted by the hospital authorities ... His responsibility for a patient began as soon as he received the telephone call ... He sometimes advised treatment by telephone. There were therefore two places where his duty was performed, the hospital and his telephone in the consulting room. If he was performing his duties in both places, then it was difficult to see why, on the journey between the two, he was not equally performing his duties. But the travelling expenses were necessarily incurred in the performance of the duties of his office.'

Lord Wilberforce: 'Dr Owen had two places of work. The expenses were incurred in travelling from one to the other in the performance of his duties.' So the expenses were deductible.

The name of Dr Owen, then, has become beloved of those who must travel in the course of their work. But there are still limits to the new and merciful doctrine. Your accountant will doubtless still have to haggle with the Revenue over the percentage of your expenses which should be allowable ... or whether you attended that congress in Hawaii, Hong Kong or Hungary 'in the performance of your duty' – a question which may not be so easy to answer, if your spouse came with you. And anyway, what of their travel expenses? Can you prove as a matter of fact that they actually worked with you?

You are only entitled to deduct those business expenses which were incurred wholly and exclusively (if you are an employed person) in the actual performance of your duties. So travel between office and site, site and factory, factory and supplier and so on is all properly deductible. Travel from home to work is not. Like the cost of obtaining a post, it is incurred prior to and not in the course of your duties.

A bricklayer and labour-only sub-contractor named Horton made a benevolent dent in this rule – which is well worth knowing, if you happen to be a peripatetic person – and particularly if you, like Mr Horton, are self-employed.

Mr Horton supplied the labour of a three-man team, of which he was the leader. His team worked exclusively for one employer, travelling according to that employer's requirements for labour, from one site to another through the South of England.

Mr Horton lived in Eastbourne and used his car to take his men to the sites and back again. He was assessed for income tax as a self-employed man, under Schedule D. Question: Was he entitled to set off his travel costs against his earnings?

The Revenue maintained that while expenses in travelling from site to site were allowable, those between home and site were not. They relied on the famous case of *Newson* v. *Robertson*, in which it was said that the place of business of a London Barrister was his Temple chambers, so that his travelling expenses between home and chambers could not be allowed.

Mr Horton maintained that he carried on 'business activities' at home. His employer used to come round to negotiate labour-only sub-contracts and his house contained his tools and his business books. Still, the home business was described by Lord Justice Stamp as 'very small ... involving exiguous office equipment and no doubt only a very few tools'.

Still, Mr Horton was allowed to set off a proportion of his household expenses against tax and as he received the part-time secretarial services of his wife, he paid her a modest salary and she got her own allowances.

The case eventually reached the Court of Appeal which unanimously held that Mr Horton's home was 'the locus' (or place) of his trade, 'from which it radiated as a centre'. It followed that his travel from home was indeed tax deductible.

Mr Horton won an important victory. Mr Barnes was less successful. Mr Barnes was a dentist who maintained a laboratory for the purposes of his practice. Every morning on the way to his surgery he picked up finished work from the laboratory, and every evening on his way home he stopped off to deliver dentures and new work to be done. He claimed that his working day began and ended at his laboratory and that accordingly, he ought to be entitled to deduct his expenses for travelling between the laboratory and the surgery. Oliver, J. refused to allow the deduction, and held that the expenditure was incurred: 'if not exclusively then at least in part, for the purposes of enabling the taxpayer to get from his private residence to the surgery where his profession was carried on. The fact that it served the purpose also of enabling him to stop at an intermediate point to carry out there an activity exclusively referable to the business cannot, as I think, convert a dual purpose into a single purpose.' Nevertheless, if you can show that your business or profession 'radiates' from your home as a central point, then travel to and from your home will be tax deductible. So when the next unhappy accounting season arrives, remind your advisers accordingly.

Unfortunately, it is very unlikely that the kindly rules will help you, if you are employed by a company – even if you and your spouse happen to own all the shares. You will be taxed under Schedule E, and your expenses will be 'perused' with far greater care by the tax inspectors. Unless your company operates from your own home, you would hardly be able to show that the company's business 'radiates' from your study. Even if you have a home office, it is the company's HQ that forms the centre of its undertaking.

Of course, the company may if it wishes pay you all your travelling expenses. But the sum you get will be lumped together with your taxable income, in the same way as any benefit in kind, including the appropriate proportion of the use of the company car, if you take that back and forth to your home.

One day, I suppose, the unfair advantage gained by 'independent contractors', self-employed and travelling tax free, will be nullified. Meanwhile, just as home buyers are much better off from the tax angle than home renters, independent, self-employed people should be grateful for a mercy which may be small if they work in many places, or near home, but which will be proportionately much larger if their efforts take them far afield.

The law, then, has been clarified and made more merciful. But the facts upon which a court would base its decision would still have to be considered with care. If in doubt about the tax chargeable on your travel, you should see your accountant, who should certainly have studied the rise to victory of Dr David Owen of Fishguard.

23 At Your Lease's End

No business or professional person can operate without premises – and most premises are on lease. So consider the protection given to the tenant by the Landlord and Tenant Act 1954 which was heavily amended by the Law of Property Act, 1969.

* * *

The 1954 Act applies 'to any tenancy where the property comprised in the tenancy is or includes premises which are occupied by the tenant, and are so occupied for the purposes of a business carried on by him or for those and other purposes'. Provided that you yourself occupy and carry on a business in the premises, then, even if you live there as well, the Act is designed for you. But if you are a property owner and rent out flats, you do not normally 'occupy' them, so your tenancy will not be protected.

A business tenancy does not come to an end, unless either the landlord or the tenant takes some step which determines it. The landlord can do so by serving notice on the tenant not less than six, nor more than twelve months, before the date when the tenancy would otherwise determine, specifying the date at which it is now to come to an end.

This notice must require the tenant, within two months of its being received, to tell the landlord in writing whether he will be willing to give up possession. It must also state whether or not the landlord would oppose an application to the court on the part of the tenant for a new tenancy, and if so, on which of the specified grounds.

If you are a tenant and the landlord has not served such a notice on you and you wish to remain in the property, then say nothing and do nothing. Of course, you won't have any absolute certainty of security. If you want that, then you yourself must give notice to the landlords, requesting a new tenancy. Within two months of your request, he is entitled to give notice to you that he would oppose an application to the Court for the grant of a new tenancy, and, once again, this notice must state which of the grounds specified by the Act he intends to rely upon.

Consider these grounds. If the landlord can satisfy the court of any one of them, no new lease can be granted. They are seven:

1 That the tenant has not kept the property in good repair.
2 That the tenant has been persistently late in paying his rent.
3 That there have been 'other substantial breaches' by the tenant 'of his obligations under the current tenancy'.
4 That the landlord is willing to provide alternative accommodation suitable for the tenant's requirements.
5 That the landlord wishes to let off the property as a whole, and the tenant's current tenancy was created by sub-letting only part of it.
6 That on the termination of the current tenancy, the landlord intends to demolish or reconstruct the premises. Note that a landlord cannot now resist a tenant's application for a new business tenancy on this ground if the tenant is prepared to accept a new tenancy of all or part of the premises, and the landlord can do the work 'without interfering to a substantial extent or for a substantial time' with the tenant's business. The tenant must agree to the new

tenancy containing a term which would give the landlord reasonable 'access and other facilities for carrying out the work intended'.
7 That the landlord, not having acquired his interest in the property less than five years ago, intends to occupy the premises himself.

Now note Section 6 of the 1969 Act: 'Where the landlord has a controlling interest' in that company, then 'any business to be carried on by the company shall be treated ... as a business to be carried on by him'. If he has power over a majority of the directorships or holds (in his own right) over one-half of the share capital, then he will be able to control not only the company but its business premises.

Suppose the landlord fails to prove his contention and a new lease has to be granted. The next questions are what will be its terms, what rent will the tenant have to pay and how long will it be for?

In most cases, landlord and tenant indulge in some hard bargaining, either in person or through their solicitors, and the terms of the new tenancy are hammered out between them. But if no agreement can be reached, the Act provides that the court shall decide all these points.

The tenancy shall be such as is 'reasonable in all the circumstances' but not for more than fourteen years. The rent generally speaking is 'that at which ... the holding might reasonably be expected to be let in the open market by a willing lessor'.

In practice, the parties arrive in court, backed by expert estate agents or valuers. The landlord's agent will say, perhaps, that the rent should be £15,000 a year. He will justify this by giving examples of recent lettings of similar property in the neighbourhood.

The tenant's valuer, using the same criterion, will possibly suggest that £11,000 per annum would be a rent reasonably obtainable in the open market.

And the judge, who must decide between them, like as not will chop the difference in half and award £13,000. However, there's no guarantee of this – in some cases judges accept in its entirety the evidence of one or other of the experts.

Next, how long a term will the tenant get? Obviously, in most cases he will wish for the longest possible term and will try for the fourteen years maximum. He will tell the court how long he has been there, how he has built the place up, how his need is a great one whereas the landlord will lose little by the grant of a long term – and so on. The judge must consider all the circumstances and decide what is reasonable.

As for the other terms in the tenancy – such as the covenants as to repair of the property – normally no alteration is made. Judges do not like having to settle the terms of new leases any more than they can help and it is rare, in the absence of agreement between the parties, that terms other than rent and duration are altered.

Section 2 of the 1969 Act: 'Where the rent is determined by the Court the Court may, if it thinks fit, further determine that the terms of the tenancy shall include such provision for varying the rent as may be specified in the determination.' So the judge may order that a rent revision clause be included in the new tenancy – whether or not there was one in the tenancy which has expired.

Section 8 of the 1969 Act extends the power of the court when fixing the terms of a new tenancy. The fact that the tenant had certain rights in the past does not mean that a judge is now bound to grant him the same privileges under a new lease.

As for the landlord, assuming that his tenant has served the appropriate counter-notice within the time limit laid down by the Act, he will only be successful in opposing the grant of a new lease if he can bring himself within one of the statutory exceptions. If he can prove to the court that he really does intend to demolish or reconstruct the place, for instance, then he will get possession. If he really does want to use the premises for his own business, or even as his home, then again he will be entitled to possession. But the onus of proof lies on him. So it is important for him to prove, for instance, that his Minute book shows that the company really is resolved to take the proposed steps.

Suppose now that the tenant can get no new lease and has to leave the premises, what compensation will he be entitled to for his loss of goodwill? In the old days, tenants like him got compensation for lost goodwill, under the Landlord and Tenant Act 1927. Unfortunately for businessmen – in this respect, at least – this was superseded by the 1954 Act. In its place comes a provision which provides compensation on a much lower scale.

First, the tenant must prove that the only reason that he has not got a new tenancy is because the court is precluded from granting him one through the landlord bringing himself within one of the last three exceptions. In other words, if he cannot get a new lease and this is entirely in order to suit the landlord's convenience and not through any default on his own part, then he is entitled to compensation.

The extent of the compensation depends on how long the tenant has been in business in the premises. Roughly speaking, if he or some predecessor in his business has been in occupation for fourteen years or more, then he will be entitled to twice the rateable value of the premises. If he has been there for less than this time, the compensation is the rateable value of the holding.

Section 1 of the 1969 Act provides that business tenants are not to be penalized for improving their property. If an improvement was carried out by the tenant, he cannot afterwards be forced to pay a higher rent because he has seen fit to spend money on his premises. Exception? If the work was done to comply with a covenant in the lease.

The 1969 Act recognizes that the delays of the law may prejudice landlords. They may be forced not only to keep their business tenants, but also to allow them to pay rent at the old (and often highly uneconomic) rate, until the court fixes a new rental. The landlord may apply to the court to fix a reasonable rent during the interim between the date specified in the landlord's notice, or the tenant's request, or the date of the application to the court (whichever is the later), and the commencement of the new tenancy (and rental).

Section 4 sews up one possible landlord's loophole in the 1954 Act. Tenants were sometimes required to hand their landlords their notice to quit before their tenancies began. Such a notice is invalid if given or executed before the tenant has been in occupation for one month. But landlord and tenant may make joint application to the court, asking that the 1954 Act protection be excluded from a particular tenancy. There are times when both parties agree that it would be fair for the tenant to remain un-protected. If they can induce the judge to agree with them, then the tenant may 'contract out' of his rights.

Still, the surest and the most popular way to lose your rights is to delay when you receive notice under the 1954 Act.

If you have missed your chance, you will never get it back. There is no prospect of getting leave from the court to serve your notice late. If you are late, you are finished. But if you have the good sense to put the matter in the hands of your lawyer in good time, the Act can bring you enormous benefits. The end of your lease need not bring disaster after all.

24 The End of a Business

Solvency is an art – and so is insolvency. You must know how to put a business on its feet but it is sometimes useful to understand how best to lay it to rest. It's not clever to leave it to others to cremate your hopes, in their own time and in their own way. If business is bad, then you may have to understand the best ways of putting it to a decent end. And even if business is good, it is pleasant to analyse the way in which your

The End of a Business

competitors come to a sticky termination – if only so as to appreciate when not to give them credit. So here they are – the basic rules on insolvency, corporate and incorporate, personal and impersonal.

Many a business person with creditors howling hungrily around the door has considered bankruptcy as a possible solution. And many have rejected it because of the effects of the Bankruptcy Acts, carefully designed to make it unpleasant for anyone who too readily attempts to rid themselves of their liabilities. Quite apart from the stigma attached to a bankruptcy, an undischarged bankrupt is forbidden to obtain credit for £250 or more without revealing that they are an undischarged bankrupt – so there goes any hope of sloughing off one hungry heap of creditors so as to start right in accumulating another. It isn't so easy to get rid of your bankruptcy, either. You will have to apply to the court for an order of discharge, but there is no saying that you'll get one. And if you do, it may be made conditional – and the court has an absolute discretion.

Of course, while you can voluntarily throw in the bankruptcy towel, others may count you out whether you like it or not. If you fraudulently convey your property, conceal yourself or abscond to avoid paying your debts, fail to satisfy the judgment of the court – in fact, commit any 'act of bankruptcy' – then you may have a bankruptcy petition served on you. A receiving order will be made and an official receiver placed in control of your property – all of it. You may treasure secrets from your wife (or your husband), your lover or your private secretary – but the Official Receiver will know all.

The job of the Official Receiver is to get in as much as possible for your creditors. As for your debts, they are paid according to strict and settled priorities.

Top of the list come funeral and testamentary expenses. This may prove troublesome to your widow or widower, but is unlikely to make you turn over in your grave any faster than your stock managed to during your lifetime.

Next come a series of so-called 'preferred debts', which 'rank equally' – if there is money enough to pay them all, then well and good – if there is not then they share in the proceeds in the same proportion.

If and when all the preferential creditors are paid off, the rest of the world's lenders can queue up for the crumbs.

'Aha!' you exclaim. 'But how naïve can one get? The law may choose the preferred creditors – but I will get there first. And then it is woe betide the mean and nasty people who have trodden me down, and the best of luck to the kindly folk who have picked me up. The latter will get paid before I go down the drain – and the others can gurgle for their money.'

'We've thought of all that,' replies the law. 'If you attempt to favour one creditor at the expense of the others and go bankrupt within six months of any such preferential payment, the payment will be void as being "a fraudulent preference" and your effort will have been entirely in vain.'

'But suppose that one creditor threatens to sue me if I don't pay up, while the others don't bother me – will it be a fraudulent preference if I pay the one applying pressure?'

'No, it won't. You are not then voluntarily preferring anyone – you are submitting to pressure which you cannot be expected to resist.'

All of which goes to show that kindness to prospective bankrupts just doesn't pay.

So much, then, for the downfall of individual, business brilliance. What now of two penniless genii in concert? How can one terminate an unhappy or an unsuccessful partnership? The rules are in Chapter 2.

When the firm is dissolved, its assets are used first for the paying of partnership debts, on similar lines to those governing payment of creditors in a bankruptcy. If the assets exceed the liabilities, then well and good – the debts are paid off and the partners share the balance. But if the liabilities exceed the assets, then it's heaven help the partners – they have to share the losses in the same proportion as they share the profits and each one of them is liable for the partnership debts to the full extent of all his worldly possessions – if any.

Which leaves companies. Assuming that they are not extinguished by being struck off the register, they can be wound up in any one of three ways. First, there may be a voluntary winding up, secondly, there may be a winding up under the supervision of the court – and third, the court may order a compulsory winding up.

If the shareholders decide by special resolution to dissolve the corporation, then they voluntarily put an end to their own association. If the directors deliver to the Registrar of Companies, not more than five weeks before the passing of the resolution, a statutory declaration confirming that the company will pay all its debtors in full within twelve months of the start of the winding up, then it is described as 'a members' voluntary winding up'. The advantage of this is that the liquidator will be appointed and controlled by the shareholders who will, in effect, control the passing of their own, corporate legal entity.

If the directors cannot make the statutory declarations, the winding up is described as 'a creditors' winding up'. The day following the resolution, a creditors' meeting is called and a liquidator appointed – but if the shareholders and creditors disagree, it is the creditors' representative who will do the job.

Mind you, even where there is a voluntary winding up the court is entitled to step in. It may order that the winding up proceed under its supervision. And it will then appoint an additional liquidator to keep an eye on the proceedings.

A compulsory winding up is much more unpleasant. A court can wind up the company for any of seven reasons. They are these:

1. the company has by special resolution resolved that the company be wound up by the court;
2. being a public company which was registered as such on its original incorporation, the company has not been issued with a certificate under section 117 (public company share capital requirements) and more than a year has expired since it was so registered;
3. it is an old public company, within the meaning of section I of the Companies Consolidation (Consequential Provisions) Act 1985;
4. the company does not commence its business within a year of its incorporation or suspends its business for a whole year;
5. the number of members is reduced below 2;
6. the company is unable to pay its debts;
7. the court is of the opinion that it is just and equitable that the company should be wound up.

The most interesting of these grounds is 'inability to pay debts'. This is divided up by the Companies Act 1985, and comes under five heads. Here they are:

1. if a creditor who is owed more than £750 has served a written demand for payment on the company – but has gone three weeks without being satisfied;
2. if, in England and Wales, execution or other process issued on a judgment, decree or order of any court in favour of a creditor of the company is returned unsatisfied in whole or in part;
3. if, in Scotland, the induciae of a charge for payment on an extract decree, or an extract registered bond, or an extract registered protest, have expired without payment being made;
4. if, in Northern Ireland, a certificate of unenforceability has been granted in respect of a judgment against the company;
5. if it is proved to the satisfaction of the court that the company is unable to pay its debts (and, in determining that question, the court shall take into account the company's contingent and prospective liabilities).

It is not really as complicated as it sounds. If it looks to the court as if there is a good chance of the company getting back on its feet, it won't be wound up. But if it seems that extra time would only lead to further and deeper wallowing in the mire, the company will have to go.

A company's creditors are paid off on much the same basis as those of a bankrupt – but the shareholders will only be liable for debts to the extent of any unpaid portion of their share capital. And – unless they are shareholders, or have committed some fraud or other – the directors will not be liable at all. Which is certainly a great advantage. Their families can rest easy in their beds – no one will spring a surprise and remove the sagging springs from under them. The reason? An individual is a legal entity. The partners in a firm are separate legal entities – but the firm is not. But a company, while it has life, exists in law – and has an existence entirely separate from those of its shareholders. And that is why limited liability is the greatest boon to business ever invented by fertile legal minds.

Finally, note that in one High Court appeal the judges all agreed that one partner could be found guilty of stealing the partnership assets or property. It was held that: 'In relation to partnership property, the provisions of the Theft Act 1968 have the effect that ... one partner can steal the partnership property, just as a stranger could commit the theft of the property of another.'

There are three provisos. First, there must be 'the basic ingredient of dishonesty'. If there was no 'dishonest intent', the partner would be acquitted.

Next, there must be 'no question of there being a claim of right made in good faith'. If your partner honestly believes that he is entitled to help himself as he has done, then he is not a thief.

Third, there must be 'an intention permanently to deprive'. If, for instance, the partner was 'only borrowing', he might get away with it.

25 Retirement – Voluntary and Otherwise

Whether or not the economists call the particular commercial era one of 'depression' or 'recession' is almost irrelevant. Every day in every year brings top level unemployment. Maybe the cause is bad business, bringing economies at the whim of imported management consultants or home grown economists, seeking economies in the salary list. The reason may even lie in business boom, accompanied by merger, take-over, boardroom battle – and the shifting of the mighty from the corridors of commercial power. Whatever the season or the reason, someone is hurt.

Thanks to the law, those who depart in peace and those who leave after battle are both accompanied, in the main, by financial hand-outs. Severance pay, redundancy pay, pay in lieu of notice ... call it what you will. Those who leave for any reason other than provable misconduct are likely to take company money with them. This chapter attempts to make sure that its readers make the best of this sort of bad situation – at least by consulting top-notch lawyers, before they accept less money than they might properly claim.

The corporate goose generally lays a golden egg which is taken away by the dismissed industrial executive. How, then, can other geese be bred, to produce equally satisfactory results? There are other board-rooms to be staffed, to be sure – and other jobs to fill. But there are always too many top hats for the racks available. And the older the wearer the longer and more desperate the search is likely to be. Every industrial executive who values their future should provide some sort of home-produced alternative to their current work, to be available in time of emergency. Consider some typical cases.

Mr X resigned from his board after a take-over. He did so upon the (later fulfilled) promise of a handsome golden handshake. He immediately set himself up as an industrial consultant in the field in which he was an acknowledged expert. He used the available capital for advertising, and to live off while he acquired his clientele.

Legal problems? Practically none. No staff; no licence; no planning permission required. He had no need to consult his lawyer – only his accountant, so as to set up a proper system of bookkeeping. And by keeping adequate records, he would have some accumulated losses in his early days which could probably be set off against his profits as time marched on.

Mr Y decided to invest his redundancy money and accumulated savings in a South Coast lodging house. He had always intended to retire to that district. His wife was a former nursery school teacher and she would open a school on weekday mornings in the living room and conservatory.

First problem? Planning consent. They were changing the use of an ordinary residential dwelling to that of a boarding house and school. Then there were bye-laws and fire regulations to be considered. These problems were sorted out at the town hall.

Next, the property was leasehold. Like many leases, that of Mr Y contained a clause restricting the use of the property to the residence of one family only. The landlord was prepared to waive this clause in return for a modest increase in rent – such waiver being restricted to Mr Y, and not intended for his successors in title. In order to allow successors to have the benefit of the change, and hence to ensure that the business (as opposed to the remainder of the lease) would be saleable in due course, the rent went up still further.

Still, if Mr Y had simply charged ahead and opened his business without knowing the legal snags, he might well have seen his entire investment go down the legal drain. As we said, the time to consider the legal implications is before you leave one living for the next.

Incidentally, quite apart from the law, Mr Y learned that he misjudged his district and his site, as much as his market. He discovered that in the summer months there was a shortage of staff but plenty of money. In the winter, there were plenty of men and women looking for work, but very little money to pay them with. You do not leave business complexities behind you when you depart from the company and strike out on your own.

Mr Z was happy to retire to his converted country cottage. He signed a lease just a month before he moved out of the boardroom.

Unfortunately, Mr Z tried to save money on his purchase. He begrudged solicitors' fees, and did not know enough to make the necessary searches. So he did not discover that there were plans for driving a motorway through the countryside just a few hundred yards from his peaceful retreat.

Worse, Mr Z had learned to trust the evidence of his own eyes, and he did not employ a surveyor to check the property on his behalf. To his horror, he discovered after exchange of contracts that the place was riddled with wet rot and dry rot and suffered from a substantial subsidence. There was nothing he could do except pay to have the place put right and made habitable.

Mr A had his eye on a small antique shop. He was not altogether sorry to leave the board. He collected his tax-free severance pay; he sold his house; and he bought the shop, with living accommodation up above.

Unfortunately, the vendor refused to complete the sale on the agreed date. Mr A was therefore forced to delay completion of the sale of his own home. The proposed purchaser started raising the legal roof. 'Notices to complete' flew in all directions. Legal costs increased. Eventually, everything was sorted out – but after more time, delay and expense than Mr A had reckoned on.

Then the unfortunate executive found that trade was not all that he had expected. The stock took a long time to move. And, anyway, although he and his wife were knowledgeable people, they found that retail trade is just as cut-throat in its own way as any industrial business – and requires just as much knowledge, experience and good fortune before much money is made.

So Mr A was guilty of the most common error of all – he was heavily under-capitalized. He had not allowed enough money in his reckoning for his own and his wife's living expenses during the lean years, nor had he made sufficient allowance for legal and other expenses, which cropped up so unexpectedly. His new business crashed. He staved off bankruptcy but was left living on his retirement pension – if 'living' was the right word.

Mr A also learned that it is not only a big business which should have the benefits of limited liability. In these days of corporation tax and careful perusal of directors' expenses, there is much to be said for operating as an individual or a partnership. But the individual trader or the partner may be made liable for the debts of the business, almost up to the last penny that he personally owns in the world. The shareholder of a company will only be liable for the corporate debts up to any amount which he has left unpaid on his shares – and that is normally nil.

Mr A could have bought a ready-made company. He could have created his own tailor-made corporation (with the help of his solicitor or his accountant). His failure to do either cost him (almost literally) his shirt.

The trouble is that far too many executives leave their business acumen behind them when they retire (willingly or otherwise) from their industrial companies. To operate on your own account is an intelligent and potentially worthwhile move. But there are legal and financial angles which require careful study and preparation. And whether you are planning to spend your (voluntary or enforced) retirement running a hotel or restaurant, a sweet shop or car hire concern, a business or property or investment consultancy – or any other sort of commercial enterprise – look with a legal, eagle eye before you leap, or you may land in a mire of disaster from which you are too old to emerge unscathed.

Mr B was determined to retire into an independent future. He decided to take on a franchise for a particular business. In return for an investment of £X,000, he was assured – assuming that he worked hard – of an annual income of at least £Y,000. He noticed, in passing, that the sales literature was carefully worded to indicate that there was no absolute guarantee of success. Still, he said to himself, you cannot go far wrong with the guidance, experience and success of the main company behind you.

Unfortunately, he forgot that the people who were anxious to obtain his capital were concerned primarily with their own living. They helped him to select a site and to acquire the necessary equipment. They even trained him in the necessary techniques. But when it turned out that he had chosen an unsatisfactory site and that trade fell way below expectations, they shrugged and said how sorry they were – and he lost his precious nest egg.

The shoemaker, we are told, should stick to his last. There are some great captains of industry who make the world of commerce their stage and can step with ease and an apparent Midas foot from one industrial enterprise to the next. But these men are rare. Far more common is the self-confident executive who knows one business or trade well and thoroughly and fancies that he can step merrily into another. He may be right. But if he is wrong, the law can do nothing to assist him.

The unfortunate Mr B soon found that he could obtain no damages from the sellers of the franchise. They had been guilty of no fraud and no misrepresentation. Neither was there any breach of contract. His own eagerness and enthusiasm combined with his inexperience in the field in which he ventured cost him his savings. And no lawyer in the land could help him. He had learned the hard way that successful and lucrative retirement requires quite as much acumen, knowledge and caution as any other commercial venture. So when you retire, mind how you go.

Part Two
Employment Law

26 Your Contracts of Employment – a Checklist

Not later than thirteen weeks after the beginning of employment, an employee must be given a written statement of his main terms of service. Some terms are obvious; others often get left out.

First, the basic requirements. Make sure that you include them all:

1 the identity of the parties to the contract;
2 the date when the employment began and, if the contract is of fixed duration, the date on which it will come to an end;
3 the date on which the employee's period of continuous employment began (taking into account any employment with a previous employer which counts towards that period);
4 the scale or rate of remuneration, or the method of calculating remuneration;
5 the intervals at which remuneration is paid (eg weekly or monthly);
6 hours of work, including normal working hours and any required overtime;
7 holiday entitlement, including public holidays and holiday pay;
8 provisions in respect of incapacity for work due to sickness or injury, including entitlement to sick pay;
9 pensions and pension schemes;
10 the length of notice which the employee is obliged to give and entitled to receive to terminate his contract of employment;
11 the title of the job which the employee is employed to do.

If there are no particulars to be included under paragraphs 7, 8, or 9, above, that fact must be stated.

The written statement of terms must also include a note –

a specifying any disciplinary rules applicable to the employee or referring to a document which is reasonably accessible to the employee and which specifies such rules;
b specifying by description or otherwise –
 (i) a person to whom the employee can apply if he is dissatisfied with any disciplinary decision relating to him; and

(ii) a person to whom the employee can apply for the purpose of seeking redress of any grievance relating to his employment, and the manner in which any such application should be made;

c where there are any further steps consequent upon any such application, explaining those steps or referring to a document which is reasonably accessible to the employee and which explains them; and

d stating whether a contracting-out certificate is in force for the employment in respect of which the statement is given.

In addition to the *required* information and terms, every businessman or professional should *consider* including the following terms in each contract:

1. A restraint clause, ie a term restraining the employee from competing against the business when his employment ends. No restraint clause means no restriction on competition. But these clauses are complicated and if you wish to insert them you should consult your solicitor.
2. A mobility clause. If your employees' contracts of employment do not contain a clause permitting you to move them from place to place it may be a breach of contract for you to attempt to move them. A clause which expressly permits you to require them to work at any of your establishments, wherever they may be, could save you a lot of problems in the event that you want to redistribute your workforce.
3. A confidentiality clause. Recent cases have emphasized the need to impress upon employees the confidential nature of any confidential information which they may be required to handle in the course of their employment. Your ability to prevent them from passing such information on to your trade rivals after they have left your employment depends in part upon the contract making it quite clear what information is confidential. However, only information which can properly be described as confidential can be protected – see Chapter 16.
4. Office, business or works rules. Incorporating these into the contract of employment may provide a useful means of avoiding misunderstanding. On the other hand, you may find that it unduly restricts your flexibility as an employer and may inhibit necessary changes in working practices. This matter should be given careful consideration.
5. Right to search. To search a suspect's person without his consent is an assault; to search his property is a trespass. Many employers

include a term in contracts of service saying: 'The employee agrees to submit to the search of his person or property at the request of the management.' If an employee then refuses to be searched, you should refer him to his contract of service – but if he persists in his refusal, call in the police.

6 Moonlighting – which becomes more frequent as times grow tougher. Are you prepared to allow your employees to take other jobs in their spare time or at weekends – if not, then specify that the employee shall not engage in other employment without your consent. There is an implied term in any event that the employee will not compete against you; but include an express one which leaves the decision as to what is or is not competitive to you.

7 No employee is entitled to 'stationery or other materials', franking facilities for private mail or anything else as a 'perk', without his employer's consent, express or implied. Do your employees, though, take certain privileges for granted? Are they likely to help themselves to unauthorized 'perks'? Then why not set out precisely those privileges to which they are entitled – and those which are forbidden. If your employee has a company car, you should set out his entitlement (if any) to use the car for private mileage as well as upon whom the liability to tax, insure and maintain it rests.

If you find on checking this list that there are items that you have not included in the contracts of present employees but which you would like to insert, here is how to do it:

1 You must vary the present contracts.
2 Variation is only lawful with the employee's consent.
3 If the term is not to the employee's benefit, he is likely to agree to the variation only as part of a larger deal which is beneficial to him.
4 So when you grant an increase in pay, inform your employees; 'We are taking this opportunity to revise our employees' terms of service. Please read the enclosed documents; if you have any questions about it, Mr ——— will be pleased to discuss them with you; and please sign at the foot of the document, to indicate your agreement'.
5 Signature is not necessary – but once an employee has signed, he cannot then successfully claim that he did not read or understand the revised terms; he will be bound by them.

Note: A contract of service – or written particulars of main terms – may be contained in a number of documents – or even may be partly oral or partly in writing. The fewer the documents and the more complete the writing, the less the chance of disputes.

Care should also be taken not to confuse the written statement of terms with the contract of employment. The written statement is only evidence of the terms of the contract, being of its nature a post-contractual document. Where the written statement differs from the terms which were in fact agreed between the parties, the employee can compel the employer to amend the written statement. Such confusion is now often avoided by incorporating into a written contract of employment all of the terms which are required to be set out in the written statement of terms. Section 5 of the Employment Protection (Consolidation) Act 1978 provides that where this is done the employer is freed from his obligation to provide a written statement of terms.

27 Varying Your Contract

There are many reasons why you may wish to vary the terms under which you serve your company. Maybe there is to be a merger or takeover, so that the company will no longer be under your control and you wish to protect your future. But equally, you may simply wish to better yourself ... to improve the conditions under which you work ... to raise your pay, secure your future, make up for underpayments in the past whilst the business was being put on its feet.

So let us consider how, when and where these happy ends may be lawfully achieved – and when any contract, in fact, may be varied.

* * *

The ordinary rules for the variation of a contract may be stated simply: With the consent of the parties, any variation is possible at any time. Suppose, for instance, that you are a purveyor of goods or services and have agreed on a price. It turns out that your expenses rocket sky high. In theory you could be held to your price. But in practice you might well say to the other party: 'Look, if I have to abide by the agreed price, there is no question about it – I shall have to skimp ... it would be most unfair, under the circumstances. ... I would be grateful if you would agree to increase the rate for the job, to make it an economic proposition. ...'

The other party may decline to oblige. He is fully entitled, within the terms of his contract, to do so. But then he may not wish to see your company become insolvent in the middle of doing a job for him. He may think that your request is reasonable. He may agree to the variation of the contract, so as to comply with your wishes. In that case, the parties having consented, the changes can be made.

Again, you may have agreed on a date for delivery. Time of delivery may be 'of the essence' of the deal. You may be entitled to call off the entire arrangement if the goods do not arrive on the due date, and then to sue for damages, to compensate you for any loss that you may have suffered as a result of the breach of contract. But you may decide to stay your hand ... to give the other party additional time, to carry out his obligations. ... You may waive the right to obtain delivery on due date – and, in the process, vary the contract.

Of course, unilateral variation of a contract, without the consent of the other party (or contrary to his wishes), is a breach of contract. It may amount to a repudiation of the entire deal. The other party may be entitled to regard the agreement as at an end. Just as no original contract can be made without agreement, so no lawful variation may be achieved otherwise than by consent.

Now apply these ordinary contractual principles to those extraordinary contracts – agreements for service or employment. There is normally no reason whatever why these should not be varied, by agreement between employer and employee.

Suppose, for instance, that your assistant asks for a rise. 'I know that I am on a sliding scale,' he says, 'and my next rise is not due for another twelve months. But I have had to do a vast amount of additional work ... to assume responsibilities never contemplated between us ... and my finances are in a bad way. ...' You may well oblige him and put forward his rise.

Alternatively: 'I am afraid I can no longer cope on the salary you are giving me. I appreciate that I must give you six months' notice – but I cannot survive that long without receiving better pay.' You have the choice. You can either tell the man that you insist upon his keeping to the terms of his contract – in which case, he will doubtless walk out on you and you will be able to do nothing whatsoever about it (other than to enforce any binding restraint clause which may exist in his contract – see Chapter 31 – or you can agree to a variation.

Now look at your own contract – the agreement under which you serve your company. This may have years to run – but there is no reason, in law, why it should not be varied in order to comply with your wishes – provided, of course, that no one is going to be defrauded and that you are not using your position so as to take unfair advantage of the shareholders.

'No man can ... acting as an agent,' said a Lord Chancellor, many years ago, 'be allowed to put himself into a position in which his interest and his duty will be in conflict.' So under Section 317 of the Companies Act, a director who is in any way interested in a proposed or actual contract with the company is bound to declare the nature of his interest at the board meeting at which the question of entering into the contract is first considered – or otherwise at the first meeting after he becomes interested in the contract in question. And the company's articles usually provide that he shall not vote on any such contract or that, if he does vote, the vote shall not be counted.

Again, he must not take a secret benefit as a result of his office. He may not accept (for instance) any money, shares or other benefit from a promoter, either while negotiations between the promoter and the company are still going on or after they have been completed. Nor can a director obtain some benefit for himself and then authorize himself to retain it as a result of the use of his voting power.

But what about a contract of service? No secrecy arises here – and the director's interest could not be more direct, declared or apparent.

Article 82 of Table A provides that: 'The directors shall be entitled to such remuneration as the company may by ordinary resolution determine ... '. Usually, then, any variation in remuneration to be paid must be as a result of a vote at a general meeting. If you want a variation, you must call your general meeting – and vote yourself your money. In any event check the articles.

Note too that Section 311 of the Companies Act 1985 prohibits tax free payments to directors – the only way to achieve that sort of happy result is through a 'golden handshake' of up to £25,000. This too, can be voted to you – even if it forms no part of your original contract. Indeed, it is almost certainly a variation. In consideration of your being paid the money in question as compensation for loss of office, you agree to shake the company's hand and depart.

Subject, then, to the rules which (in theory at least) require a director to make a clean breast of any benefits which he will require as a result of a merger or take-over, variations of the original contract are perfectly in order – provided that they are made in accordance with the articles and with the Companies Act.

My advice? Have the varied contract of service tailored to your needs, in the same way as the original – and this time, make sure that you have it properly vetted by a solicitor fully instructed by you as to your requirements. That is very often the only way to make certain that you are getting what you want in a thoroughly lawful (and hence enforceable) manner.

28 Attachment of Earnings

The Attachment of Earnings Act 1971 consolidates all previous enactments under which wages and salaries could be 'attached' for the payment of debts. But it also added new and important rules which every office proprietor and manager ought to know.

In the past, if a debtor failed or refused to meet his obligations when he was in a position to do so, a judge would eventually send him to prison. There was no alternative. The result? The man was rendered at least temporarily incapable of meeting his obligations, even if he would otherwise have been prepared to do so. No one benefited – least of all the public, who had to provide the debtor with full board and lodging.

The Act enables creditors to lay hold of at least part of a person's earnings. Because the appropriate deductions are made at the source of his income, the debtor will not have the opportunity to avoid his obligations.

The Act applies to civil debts resulting from judgments in the High Court or the County Court. However, the jurisdiction to make such orders in respect of judgment debts (as opposed to maintenance orders) is vested in the County Court. There must be a judgment debt in excess of £15 before an attachment of earnings order can be made.

A Magistrates' Court, too, may make an order in respect of 'fines, costs, compensation or forfeited recognisances'. But most important of all, in practice, any court may make an order attaching an employee's earnings, to secure payment 'under a maintenance order' – and that means not only an order for alimony or maintenance payable to a wife, but also one to provide maintenance for children.

If an Attachment of Earnings order is made, it will be 'directed to a person who appears to the court to have the debtor in his employment'. If you are the employer, it will 'operate as an instruction' to you, to make periodical deductions from the debtor's earnings. And at such times as the order may require, you will have to pay the amounts deducted not to the creditor but to the collecting officer of the court.

Once an order is served on you, then you must comply with it within seven days. And you may also deduct the sum of fifty new pence 'or such other sum as may be prescribed by order made by the Lord Chancellor', towards your clerical and administrative costs. You must also give to the debtor a statement in writing of the total amount of the deduction, although this may be included in your ordinary wages slip.

The order will specify 'the normal deduction rate, that is to say, the rate (expressed as a sum of money per week, a month or other period) at which the court thinks it reasonable for the debtor's earnings to be applied to meeting his liability under the relevant adjudication'. It will also specify a so-called 'protected earnings rate'. This will be the rate below which 'having regard to the debtor's resources and needs, the court thinks it reasonable that the earnings actually paid to him should not be reduced'.

If an employee's earnings are the same each week, all this will present little difficulty. Assuming that when you deduct the appropriate money at 'the normal deduction rate', the balance left to be paid to the employee is at least as great as 'the protected earnings rate', there are no problems. But if earnings fluctuate and you find that by deducting the 'normal deduction' you would leave the employee with less than his 'protected earnings', the judgment debtor will get less than the 'normal deduction' for the week in question.

So you take the employee's 'attachable earnings' – that is, the gross sums payable by the employer to the debtor as wages or salary – including overtime pay, bonus, fees, commission 'or other emoluments payable in addition to wages or salary or under a contract of service' – plus 'pension, or periodical payments by way of compensation for loss of office'.

You deduct PAYE and National Insurance and Health Service contributions as usual, and also contributions to any 'regular superannuation scheme'. You do not take off any other sums which you may ordinarily deduct from the debtor's earnings, such as National Savings contributions.

From the 'attachable earnings' you deduct the employee's 'protected earnings'. If the balance does not exceed the 'normal deduction' you ship off that balance to the court. If there is a surplus, you pay that to your employee, along with his 'protected earnings'. If the balance is less than the 'normal deduction', then the judgment creditor is out of luck – all they will get is the balance.

If there is an underpayment one week, you will have to make it up in a future week which produces a surplus. And if the debtor's 'attachable earnings' are less than his protected earnings, he must be paid the full amount – and you are not even allowed to deduct your fifty pence. Well, you have made no deduction so you incurred no clerical expenses.

So you now have an outline of the rules as you need to know them. Even if their operation comes within the domain of the company accountant, you will probably have to explain the rules to your employees – in which case, it is a very good idea to know them yourself.

29 An Employee's Inventions

Employees with inventive minds are a blessing to their bosses. But who owns the inventions they make during the course of their employment? And how far are servants entitled to use the skill, knowledge and technical know-how obtained in your service when they leave to work for someone else? These questions are answered by the Patents Act 1977. An invention made by an employee belongs to the employer if –

- *a* it was made in the course of the normal duties of the employee or in the course of duties falling outside his normal duties, but specifically assigned to him, and the circumstances were such that in either case an invention might reasonably be expected to result from the carrying out of his duties; or
- *b* the invention was made in the course of the duties of the employee and, at the time of making the invention, because of the nature of his duties and the particular responsibilities arising from the nature of his duties, he had a special obligation to further the interests of the employer's undertaking.

In any other case, the invention belongs to the employee. This is so notwithstanding any term in the employee's contract of employment to the contrary.

Even if the invention belongs to you as the employer, your employee can apply to the Comptroller General of Patents (or Patents Court) for an award of compensation. Such an award may be made where the invention patented is of outstanding benefit to you when regard is had to the size and nature of your business and it is just that your employee should receive compensation. The amount of compensation payable should be a fair share of the benefit which you have derived from the patented invention. In assessing the amount of compensation regard must be had to the following factors:

- *a* the nature of the employee's duties, remuneration etc.;
- *b* the effort and skill which the employee has devoted to making the invention;
- *c* the effort and skill of any other person involved in the making of the invention and the advice and assistance of any other employee who is not a joint inventor of the invention; and
- *d* the contribution which you yourself may have made as the employer in the making, developing and working of the invention, by the provision of advice, facilities and other assistance, by the

provision of opportunities and by your managerial and commercial skill and activities.

Where an invention belongs to one of your employees, you may be able to persuade him or her to assign their interest to you. However, they will still be able to apply for statutory compensation if they can show that the financial return they have received is inadequate in relation to the benefit which you have derived from the patent, and it is just that compensation should be paid. Such compensation will amount to a fair share of the benefit which you have derived from the assignment, taking into account inter alia:

a any conditions granted in respect of the invention or patent;
b the extent to which the invention was made jointly by the employee with any other person; and
c any contribution which you have made as mentioned in (d) above.

However, no award of compensation can be made if there is in force a relevant collective agreement which provides for the payment of compensation in respect of employees' inventions. A collective agreement is only 'relevant' if it is made by a trade union to which the employee belongs and by you as the employer or an employers' association to which you belong, and is in force at the time the invention is made. Non-unionists therefore, may still apply for statutory compensation.

30 Is Moonlighting Legal?

Times are tough and many employees are prepared to work evenings, weekends and holidays in order to make both ends meet. 'Moonlighting' is becoming increasingly common. But is it legal? If you 'moonlight' and your employers find out about your activities, are they entitled to dismiss you?

Conversely: if you discover that your employees are making an honest outside living, are you entitled to insist that they either give up that activity or leave your service? And what difference does it make if a contract of service contains the sort of clause that is common in contracts of service of many people: 'You will be expected to devote your full time to the service of the company ... '. Or 'You will not engage in any other employment during the subsistence of this contract ... '?

* * *

All contracts – including contracts of service – contain two types of term: 'express' and 'implied'. A term specifically banning alternative or additional employment is 'express'; a term preventing an employee from competing with their company or firm is invariably implied.

A term in a contract for personal service that places an unreasonable restraint on the individual's freedom to earn a living is usually void and 'contrary to public policy'. A clause in your contract, for instance, preventing you from competing with your company or firm on leaving its service will only be upheld if it is reasonable in all respects. But there is nothing 'unreasonable' – in law at least – in saying: 'We employ you full time and object to your engaging in any other lucrative employment. We want you to be free to do your work for us, as and when required. ... We do not wish to run the risk of your engaging in other gainful activities ...'.

Naturally, you do not have to agree to this term. It is open to negotiation, in the same way as any other. And even if you have an express term in your contract which forbids 'moonlighting', your employers may turn a blind eye, if they wish. If in doubt, ask. They will recognize the problems of keeping up your standards when cash is tight and may even be glad that you can earn money elsewhere so that they do not feel that they are bound to increase your pay – a step which they may or may not be able to afford.

So much for the express term. What of the more common case where nothing is said?

Employers do not buy their employees' time, twenty-four hours a day, three hundred and sixty-five days a year. So we start from the basis that employees are free to spend their spare time as they wish. And if they prefer to take on additional lucrative employment – instead of playing with their children or watching television – then (says the law): 'Good for them'. But they must not compete with their full time outfit.

Obviously, you would not expect to be entitled to take business from your company. You cannot use your contacts and knowledge in order to acquire for yourself work that should go to your employers. You must not compete with those who provide your daily bread by your activities on behalf of others who provide you with some extra cake.

In practice, difficulties arise in the borderline cases. There is no direct competition – but could problems arise in the future?

Some years ago, a company of instrument makers employed six men at weekends who worked as glass grinders for a different company during the week. Their full time employers obtained an injunction restraining the employment of the men at weekends. The court recognized that there was no direct or immediate competition because the companies were in different lines of business. But competition could arise in the future. One day, the employee might have to say: 'I'm sorry, I cannot answer your question because to do so I would have to reveal a process or a secret which came to me in the course of my part time working'.

The court granted the injunction with obvious reluctance. It said, in effect, the lower down the scale the employees come, the less likely it is that the court would interfere with their freedom to use their spare time as they wish. Conversely: The more experienced, skilled, professional, responsible and highly paid you are, the more readily the court would intervene to prevent any conflict between your full time and your spare time working – even if that conflict is future and potential rather than present and immediate.

As usual, these general rules are subject to agreement to the contrary. There is nothing to prevent you, for instance, from saying to potential employers: 'I will gladly come to work for you, but only provided that you do not object to my carrying on my own, private business in my own spare time.' If they are prepared to take you on upon that basis, then so be it – provided, of course, that even then you do not abuse your position as an employee for your private benefit. There is all the difference in the legal world between honest 'moonlighting' and making secret profits as a result of your privileged position in your firm or company.

The same rules that apply to you apply in reverse to those whom you employ. They may not compete with you, dishonestly steal your goodwill, or make secret profits – and the fact that they may be doing so in their own spare time will in no way make the practice lawful. They must not break express or implied terms in their contracts – however rough their financial weather.

31 Restraint Clauses – and Unfair Competition

The competition most to be feared is that from a former employee, partner, assistant or fellow executive. They (literally) know your business. Conversely, if you switch jobs, what can you take with you when you go? Are you entitled to use the knowledge and know-how, skills, specialities and contacts that you acquired in your present post, for some competing outfit – or for yourself?

* * *

In general, ex-employees may compete to their hearts' content. They may set up in exactly the same line of business, in adjoining premises, the day after they leave. Only if there is a valid, binding restraint clause in their contract of service can they be prevented from doing so. And as the law seeks to preserve people's freedom to earn their living where, when and how they see fit, restraint clauses are, on the face of them, void as 'contrary to public policy'.

A restraint clause will only be upheld if it is reasonable from everyone's point of view. It must not be more extensive than reasonably necessary for the protection of the employer's business. It must not put an unreasonable restraint on the employee's freedom to earn a living. And it must not be unreasonable from the viewpoint of the public.

Some restraint clauses are a nullity because they are too wide in time. Others cover too wide an area. Yet others are worthless because they include too wide an area of business activity.

Normally, a restraint clause that is too extensive can seldom be 'severed'. Like every egg except that of the renowned curate, a restraint clause is usually either all good or all bad. A restraint clause *will* be severed, however, provided that the following conditions are satisfied:

a The parts to be severed are independent of one another and are substantially equivalent to a number of separate restrictions;
b The severance can be affected without affecting the part remaining; and
c The excess to be severed is not a part of the main purport and substance of the clause.

For instance, it was held that a restriction imposed upon an estate agent's clerk and negotiator which prevented him from carrying on or working in a similiar business within five miles of the branch office which he managed or the head office, at which he had not worked, was severable. The restriction regarding the head office was deleted from the clause.

But suppose that the clause simply provides that the former partner will never solicit business from the firm's clients. This is undoubtedly too wide. Had it been restricted to those people who were clients during the period whilst the partner was in the firm's service, then it would probably have been binding. As it is, the clause need have no effect.

The drafting of these clauses, then, is a highly skilled occupation. Only someone with specialist knowledge of the sort of clauses which courts have upheld in similar circumstances will be able to judge the chances of a particular restraint being upheld. If you want to prevent competition from those whom you employ today when they leave you tomorrow, you should get your solicitor to draft a restraint clause tailored to your particular needs. And have it incorporated into the service contracts of your employees.

Conversely, if you wish to compete with your present or former outfit, look at your contract of service. If there is no restraint clause at all, then all is well. If there is such a clause, all is not lost – take it to your solicitor to see whether a court would be likely to enforce it. You may be luckier than you think.

Even if you discover that you are free to compete with your ex-employer do not forget that there may well be confidential information which you are not free to disclose because it is covered by an implied term in your contract (see Chapter 16).

32 Who Gets a Share in the Bonus?

Bonus, commission or profit sharing schemes are common in the business world – and so is the unnecessary misunderstanding and ill will created by that most common question: What are the rights of employees who leave (for whatever reason) during the course of the year? Are they entitled to a pro rata share, or to nothing?

The manageress of a travel business was employed on the basis of a letter of appointment that set out her annual salary, holiday arrangements and duties and added: 'You will be entitled to participate in our profit sharing scheme'.

Six months later she was offered a better post elsewhere and she handed in her proper notice, which was duly accepted. But when she was paid off, she received no commission. She wrote to complain.

The employers replied: 'As we explained to you at the interview, profit is shared among the staff with us at the end of March, when the year's accounts are done. We cannot know our profit before that date.'

The legal position depends upon the contract made between the parties. What was agreed – expressly or by implication?

Contracts of employment or of service (like any other contract) may be made orally or in writing or partly orally and partly in writing. To spell out the agreement, a court would look first at any written terms.

The travel agent's letter of appointment made it plain that the employee was entitled to participate in the profit sharing arrangement. But it left open the question: What was that arrangement? On the face of the letter, the employee could reasonably expect to obtain a share in the profits. In the absence of some other express term, a court would be likely to hold that once you have given service, you are entitled to a share; and if your service does not last a full year, then you should get a proportionate amount.

After all, otherwise a person might serve 51 weeks and then be dismissed, perhaps as redundant. Why should the law put a bonus on employers' engaging in dismissal operations immediately before their accounting year comes to an end?

Still, the law will not *require* employers to give any commission or bonus at all, nor any share in the profits – and if employees have agreed (however unwisely) to limit their rights, then they cannot afterwards obtain a legal remedy.

The travel agents maintained that they explained the details of the profit sharing arrangements to their prospective employee when they interviewed her for the job. They said that they told her that only those staff who were actually on their books when those books were totted up would be entitled to a share in the profits shown. They argued that no one who leaves before the profits are assessed can obtain a share because the firm will not know what profits (if any) are available for sharing; that employers cannot be expected after the profits are made up to check on each employee who left during the course of the previous accounting year (even people who may have served only a few days, at the start of that year) and send them a share in the money; and that the arrangement was not only agreed but one which is common practice and extremely reasonable.

Once again, a court would not be concerned at the *reasonableness* or otherwise of the arrangement, except in so far as it might shed light on the likelihood of the employee having agreed to it. The question that a judge would, if necessary, have to determine is this: In the light of the letter of appointment of all the circumstances of the case, what probably happened at the interview?

The employee will undoubtedly say that it was not made clear to him or her that they had to serve a full year or would get no share in the profits; the employer's representative would (with equal certainty) say that they told the prospective employee of the circumstances and moreover it is their invariable practice so to do.

The employee will retort: 'I am not interested in your invariable practice – you did not follow it in this occasion – otherwise I would not have worked for you. The salary on its own was not enough ...'.

This would probably receive the retort: 'We would not have employed you on any other basis than that now stated. Nor have we ever employed anyone else on any other basis than that since our profit sharing scheme was initiated.'

After looking at the documents and considering the evidence, the judge would have to piece together the probabilities of the past in order to do justice in the present. And no lawyer, however wise, can guarantee the outcome of that battle.

Like most cases of this sort, the travel agent's dispute was compromised. Neither side wanted to get involved in the miseries or the expense of litigation which is uncertain in its outcome. But the morals of the tale are clear – for employed business and professional people and those who employ them alike.

Make your agreement sufficiently clear at the beginning and you will avoid miseries at the end. When dealing with profit sharing or bonus schemes, make it plain that only employees on the books on a specified date will be entitled to the money – or that bonus, commission or a share in the profits will (like holiday money) be paid on a pro rata basis.

It is precisely to avoid this sort of frequent dispute over holiday pay that the Employment Protection (Consolidation) Act 1978 provides that written particulars of holiday entitlement should specifically set out the manner in which holiday pay is to be calculated. There is no similar law applying to profit sharing and the like. There should be; no doubt in future there will be; but meanwhile, it is for the parties not only to make their deal but to be sure that they can prove it in case of dispute. A little care in specifying the terms in writing at the start of the relationship will make the ending of that relationship a lot less harrowing.

33 Sick Pay

Broadly speaking, as an employer you are obliged to pay statutory sick pay ('SSP') to any employee who falls sick. SSP is essentially a part of the social security system. The employer is in effect the agent of the DHSS for administering sickness benefit: you pay the sick employee and then claim a refund from the DHSS. The scheme was established by the Social Security and Housing Benefits Act 1982, but in order to apply it you must delve into a dreadful morass of barely intelligible regulations.

Most employees are unable to claim any sickness benefit from the DHSS during the first 28 weeks of sickness. Instead, they claim SSP from you as their employer. However, after 28 weeks of sickness an employee will normally transfer from SSP to state sickness benefit; and state sickness benefit is usually available for any employee who is ineligible for SSP for some reason. An employee cannot claim SSP for the first three days of sickness, but after those three days you must pay SSP at the stipulated rate to the equivalent of 28 weeks' pay in any period of incapacity for work (including linked periods not separated by more than 8 weeks). You then recover from the state the amount of SSP paid by deducting it from the National Insurance contributions you would otherwise make – and an extra 7 per cent towards the employer's National Insurance payments.

What is the position if your employees are covered by a private, company sick pay scheme? SSP does not directly affect and is not affected by such a scheme. However, your employees are not entitled to what would otherwise be double payment. The Act provides that payment under one scheme decreases any entitlement under the other by the amount of the payment. The majority of employees nowadays are covered by a company sick pay scheme. These schemes commonly take the form of a 'top-up', that is, entitlement is calculated to make up the difference between SSP or state sickness benefit and the employee's normal pay for a specified period. Details of any such scheme must be set out in the employee's written statement of terms and conditions of employment and, if there is no contractual entitlement to sick pay, this must also be stated (see Chapter 26).

It should be noted that an 'employee', for the purposes of SSP, is not identical to the definition for the purposes of other statutory rights. The Act defines an employee as a person over sixteen who is gainfully employed under a contract of service or in an office and who is liable to be taxed under Schedule E for income tax purposes. This definition is modified by the regulations, so that, if the person is not taxable under Schedule E, but is an 'employed earner' for social security purposes, they are to be treated as an employee, provided they are over sixteen, and if they are taxable under Schedule E, but are not an 'employed earner', they are not an employee under the Act. The broad effect of this is to bring into the definition of employee under the Act:

a office cleaners;
b some temporary workers supplied by agencies;
c a person employed by his or her spouse for the purposes of the spouse's employment;
d certain lecturers and teachers;
e some ministers of religion.

There are a number of categories of persons excluded from entitlement to SSP. These are:

a employees over state pension age;
b short term employees (under a contract for 3 months or less);
c persons whose pay is below the level at which national insurance contributions have to be paid;
d persons who within the last 57 days have claimed certain other state benefits;
e strikers;
f persons who have already received the maximum of 28 weeks' pay in the relevant tax year;
g pregnant employees (within the maternity pay or maternity allowance period);
h prisoners;
i employees abroad, outside the EEC.

If you intend not to pay SSP because an employee falls within an excluded category, you must notify the employee of that fact within 7 days in the prescribed form. It is an offence to fail to notify the employee.

The precise conditions of entitlement are beyond the scope of this book. However, it is very important, in order that entitlement can be clarified, and in order to comply with the statutory requirements, that you keep in relation to each employee a record of:

a every day of sickness in a period of 4 or more consecutive days;
b any of those days of sickness in respect of which SSP was not paid;
c why SSP was not paid;
d all the qualifying days in that tax year, including also any qualifying days in a period of entitlement which straddle the year.

34 The Stealing of Staff

What can the law do to prevent your competitors from stealing your staff? Conversely, if you prefer to acquire your skilled help ready trained, are there any legal limits on your right to fish them out of your competitors' pool? Every business person needs to know the legal rules on the poaching of staff. Here they are.

*   *   *

The law insists on people's right to improve themselves. They are entitled to change jobs as often as they see fit, so as to improve their pay or conditions of work. Provided that they give proper notice. the law wishes them the best of good fortune in their climb to the top.

Conversely, every employer is entitled to attract the best staff available. If, in the process, they strip competitors' businesses of their most valued employees, well – that's business, isn't it? If you cannot offer sufficiently attractive pay or conditions to keep your staff happy, that will be your misfortune.

It follows that there is no law against the poaching of staff. You are entitled to fish in any waters you please, to hook for yourself the finest, best trained, most efficient employees. And if the treasures from your payroll are slipping into other people's pockets, what can you do? Usually, your only hope will be to meet the competition by raising levels of pay and/or by improving conditions of work. You must be as competitive in the labour market as in any other, if you are to administer an efficient business.

But there is one major exception to this rule. Would-be employers must not induce prospective staff to break their contracts of employment. They must not entice new employees to leave their old employment without giving proper notice. Failure to give due notice is a breach of contract. Procurement of such failure is a 'tort' – a civil wrong, giving rise to a good claim for damages.

Suppose, then, that you cast covetous eyes upon your competitor's office manager, personal assistant or sales director. By all means invite them to join your ranks. Inveigle them away from their present post with higher pay for now, better prospects for later, grim comments on the lack of future in their current employment. But do not let your need or greed for their services induce you to encourage them to leave without giving and serving due notice.

Of course, the mere fact that an employee does not give the notice required will not of itself give the jilted ex-employer any rights against the new boss. It is not enough to show that your employee broke the contract. You must also prove that the breach was procured.

If, then, you set out on a staff-hunting foray, there are two rules to remember. First, if you can snatch staff from another's table, the law allows you to help yourself. Law and morality are seldom synonymous. Second, provided that you do not procure a breach of contract by your new employee, the law will give the former boss no remedy whatsoever against you.

On the other hand, if you are losing employees, here are two rules for you. First, to staunch the flow of the lifeblood of your business, you will almost certainly have to apply greater quantities of cash. But second, if you can prove (*a*) that an employee has left you without giving proper notice; (*b*) that an employee has taken another job with a particular employer; and (*c*) that the employee did not break the contract of their own volition but as a result of some procurement or enticement by the new boss – then and only then will you have a good 'cause of action' against your successor. The difficulty, in practice, of proving these cases explains their rarity.

Incidentally, you may find your competitors actually coming on to your premises to seduce (metaphorically in most cases) your staff. Ask them to go, and if they refuse, then throw them out. They are trespassers and you may use reasonable force to eject them. But if they rendezvous with your executives in the local bar, restaurant or hotel, you had best rely on the loyalty of the latter, and your excellence as an employer, to keep them on your payroll.

35 Go – in Good Health!

Executives tend to be no more static than the products their businesses produce or sell. Problems of dismissal and redundancy arise from the highest level downwards. One way or another, the law on the subject is well worth some careful thought.

* * *

'It was a good job, as good jobs go,' said the executive on the street, 'and as good jobs go, it's gone.' Maybe he should have gone first. One tactic if you suspect that your position is likely to be taken away is to hang on as long as possible. The other is to choose your own time to move. There are, as usual, legal considerations to be weighed in the balance before making your decision.

Just as your employer is bound to give you proper notice to terminate your contract of service, you must do the same by him or her. If you have been continuously employed for four weeks or more, then Section 49 of the Employment Protection (Consolidation) Act 1978 says that you must give not less than one week's notice. But your contract may itself provide for a longer period of notice. Or if it is silent on the point, then you are bound to give 'reasonable notice' – which may be far more than the statutory minimum.

That is the theory. The practice is very different. If an employer wrongfully dismisses, then the employee's loss is reasonably simple to calculate. But what is the employer's damage if a manager or assistant leaves without giving proper notice? How much money does the company lose if a director, research chemist, accountant or operative leaves without any notice at all? What is the firm's financial loss if a salaried partner, a bookkeeper, a clerk or a secretary simply fails to return from holiday? 'Incalculable,' you say. Precisely. It may be large or small, but either way you cannot tot it up in terms of hard cash. And no calculation means no effective legal claim.

Suppose, then, that you are offered a better post at a higher salary. But they need you now. If they induce you to break your present contract of service by not giving proper notice, then (once again in theory) your present employers may have a good claim against the procurers of your contractual breach. But their chances of getting any money out of you are remote in the extreme. However great the chaos caused by your departure ... however much harder your colleagues may have to work to make up for your absence ... however scandalous your behaviour ... the odds are that your foul play will not give rise to any penalty.

'But surely my employers could get an injunction, requiring me to serve out my period of notice or at least not to work for others during that period?' you say.

Not so. Courts dislike making orders which they cannot enforce. And who is to judge whether the employee who is forced back to the grindstone is bringing his nose anywhere near it?*

The sad fact (for the employer at least) is that the theory and the practice of this branch of the law are completely at odds. An employee who is both knowledgeable and unscrupulous can probably walk out at any time without fear of legal retribution. But maybe this is not as unfair as it seems, in a world in which almost any employee may receive notice or pay in lieu at any time to suit the employer.

So if you decide to beat the boss to the draw, the law usually says: 'Go – in good health.' But there are hazards. Naturally, you must be sure not to leap into the fire or you may be homesick for the frying pan. Perhaps a negotiated withdrawal might produce some form of golden handshake. Maybe your employers have some hold over you through your overdrawn commission account. And have you checked your contract of service to ensure that there is no binding restraint clause (Chapter

---

* Note, however, the exceptional case of *Evening Standard Company Limited* v *Henderson* (1987) in which the *Standard* obtained an injuction to prevent Mr Henderson leaving to join a rival newspaper, albeit on the special terms that the *Standard* undertook to continue to employ and pay him for the twelve month period of required notice.

31) to prevent you from taking on the new post you have in mind?

Above all, make sure that you are not going to lose your redundancy pay or pension benefit without adequate return. In one recent case, a company warned its staff that a particular section of the factory would have to be closed down before too long. An executive who saw his job going up in smoke found an alternative appointment. He left and then requested his redundancy pay. As an employee of very long standing, this would have amounted to some hundreds of pounds. But because he had left before he was actually dismissed, he completely lost his entitlement to redundancy pay. You are only entitled to redundancy pay if you are actually dismissed because of redundancy (as defined by the Employment Protection (Consolidation) Act 1978). You normally get no redundancy pay if you leave prior to dismissal. So more haste may mean less money. If you've got to go, you've got to go – but do try to wait until you are actually dismissed.

Once you are dismissed, then you may give written notice to your employer that you want to terminate your contract on a date earlier than the date on which your employer's notice is due to expire. Then, unless your employer gives you a counter-notice in writing within the specified time you will normally be entitled to your redundancy pay even if you do not work out your notice. Redundancy is a complicated concept. So words with your solicitor before you take the plunge are unlikely to be wasted. If you must leave, then mind how you go, won't you? A false step may prove extremely expensive.

36 References – and the Cost of Free Advice

What are the real risks in giving a reference? Are you liable to be sued for libel? What if the reference is incorrect? Are you bound to give a reference? How can you protect yourself? Important questions these for the commercial employer – but even more personally vital to anyone deciding to seek fresh outlets for their talents. What, for instance, are your rights if your company declines to supply a reference? Or maybe you are in line for a series of posts, and each time something goes wrong. You suspect that you are getting bad references. What should you do?

Finally, if you want a reference – either for an employee, or, perhaps, for a business concern to which you are considering giving credit – how best should you handle the situation, from both a legal and a tactical viewpoint?

* * *

No one is bound to give or entitled to receive a reference. There is no law which requires people to oblige by helping each other to decide whether to grant employment or loans. References, in the main, are commercial courtesies. But, once given, they carry legal consequences in their wake. Their two main sources? Defamation and negligence.

Naturally, there is nothing defamatory about a good reference. But as soon as you give a bad one, you speak ill of your fellow. You tend to 'lower him in the eyes of right thinking people' or 'to bring him into hatred, ridicule or contempt'. If the unkind words are written, they are libellous; if spoken, slanderous. In either case, they are defamatory.

The fact that the bad reference is true will provide a defence to a defamation action brought by the person named and defamed. But if a plea of 'justification' fails, the damages will be far greater. After all, you have then repeated the defamatory statement, before another (and probably much wider) audience. If you stand your ground and the law pushes you into retreat, the result may be extremely expensive.

Quite apart from defamation, the reference giver must take care. *If, for instance, you say that James Smith was an honest clerk or bookkeeper who left of his own accord – whereas in fact you muddled him with another man of the same name who was sacked for 'fiddling the books' you may be in trouble.

In a House of Lords case, Lord Reid put the rule like this; 'A reasonable man, knowing that he was being trusted or that his skill and judgement were being relied on would, I think, have three courses open to him. Keep silent or decline to give the information or advice sought; or he could give an answer with a clear qualification that he accepted no responsibility for it or that it was given without that reflection or enquiry which a careful answer would require; or he could simply answer without any such qualification. If he chooses to adopt the last course, he must, I think, be held to have accepted some responsibility for his answer being given carefully, or to have accepted a relationship with the enquirer which requires him to exercise such care as the circumstances require.'

Lord Morris of Borth-y-Gest, in the same case, said: 'If A assumes her responsibility to B to tender him deliberate advice there could be a liability if the advice is negligently given. I say "could be" because the ordinary courtesies and exchanges of life would become impossible if it

---

* The *Lawton* v *BOC Transhield Ltd* (1987) seems to extend the liability of employers when giving references about former employees. Appropriate 'disclaimers' are important – see pages 99 and 100.

were sought to attach legal obligations to every kindly and friendly act. But the principle of the matter would not appear to be in doubt. If A employs B (who might, for example, be a professional man such as an accountant or a solicitor or a doctor) to give advice, and if the advice is negligently given, there could be a liability in B to pay damages. The fact that the advice is given in words would not, in my view, prevent liability from arising.

'Quite apart, however, from employment or contract there may be circumstances in which a duty to exercise care will arise if a service is voluntarily undertaken. A medical man may unexpectedly come across an unconscious man, who is a complete stranger to him, and who is in urgent need of skilled attention: if the medical man, following the fine traditions of his profession, proceeds to treat the unconscious man he must exercise reasonable skill and care in doing so.'

Whether dealing with references or with ordinary advice, the law may be summed up like this: 'In the ordinary course of business or professional affairs, a person may seek information or advice from another who is not under contractual obligation to give that information or advice. If the circumstances are such that a reasonable person so asked would know that they were being trusted – or that their skill or judgement was being relied upon – and they choose to give the information or advice ... then the person replying accepts a legal duty to exercise such care as the circumstances require in making his reply.'

Note that this applies not just to the giving of free references about people or the financial status of business concerns, but any other sort of advice. If you choose out of kindness to confer the benefit of your wisdom upon others, take care. That bad tip on the stock exchange ... those unwise words on the building of a business or the liquidation of an enterprise ... may cost you dear.

So we start with the proposition that the reference giver is a risk taker. Why, then, should you extend your commercial neck? Because you wish others to do the same for you. You must do as you would be done by. And the law recognizes that commercial wheels would cease turning if business people were to find it too potentially expensive and perilous to cooperate through exchanging information and advice.

So the law provides, first, a special and splendid defence to proceedings arising out of defamatory references. It says that these references are given on occasions of 'qualified privilege'.

Judges, advocates and witnesses in court or parliamentarians speaking in the Lords or Commons are blessed with 'absolute privilege'. Whatever they say, however defamatory, unfair or malicious, cannot result in successful defamation proceedings. It is regarded as so important that

Courts and Parliament should both operate without this sort of constraint that those who speak in either are highly privileged persons.

Similar privilege is granted to the givers of references. But it is 'qualified'. If it can be shown that the reference was given not out of a desire to assist the receiver but out of a wish to damage the person named, then the defence is destroyed. If the reference was given out of 'malice' it will fail. But even if the reference is unjustified and cruel, the non-malicious giver will be fully protected in law.

So the risks of defamation proceedings arising from unfavourable references are, in fact, quite small. And in practice, the person defamed seldom sees the document concerned – so even if malice exists, the chances are that they will not even be able to start to prove their case.

Note, in passing, that the subject of the reference has no right to see it. They are not entitled to a good reference, nor can they bring action against former employers who decline to give any reference at all. And if they lose jobs because the references are both untrue and to their discredit, they are generally powerless.

In practice, quite senior people often leave companies or firms after a splenetic row and then find it difficult to get another post, particularly if they were with the previous concern for a considerable period and can get no references elsewhere. My advice, if you are faced with this situation? Be completely frank with your prospective employers. Tell them the circumstances in which you left the other company. Point to your long period of loyal service with them. Say that it is hopeless to ask for a reference – or, if one comes, that it is unlikely to be favourable. Produce such references as you can (private ones, if necessary) showing your integrity and ability. And hope that your previous outfit will not succeed in ruining your prospects forever. Still, your desire for a good reference – which cannot by law be forced out of your present employers – may encourage you, if possible, to leave on friendly terms.

What, then, is the best tactic, if you require a reference for a prospective employee? Write, if you wish. Send a questionnaire, if you prefer. But precisely because business people are afraid of putting defamatory words onto paper, I suggest that whenever possible you obtain the reference orally. It is just as defamatory to speak ill of someone by word of mouth – but it is far harder for them to prove that you did so. And the commercial world tends to be a great deal more frank in person or by telephone than with pen in hand.

Now a cautious word on wise 'disclaimers'. In the House of Lords case from which we have already extensively quoted, one bank gave another a reference concerning a customer's creditworthiness. It was incorrect – but it was headed with the following words: 'Confidential – for your private use and without responsibility on the part of the bank or its officials'.

The House of Lords unanimously decided that the reference giver was completely protected, even if those who suffered through relying upon the reference could prove negligence (as, indeed, they had done to the satisfaction of the original trial judge).

'The bank,' said Lord Reid, 'which gave the reference, by the words which they employed, effectively disclaimed any assumption of a duty of care. They stated that they only responded to the enquiry on the basis that their reply was without responsibility. If the enquirers chose to receive and act upon the reply, they cannot disregard the definite terms upon which it was given. They cannot accept a reply given with this stipulation and then reject the stipulation. ... The words employed were apt to exclude any liability for negligence.'

Lord Devlin put it this way: 'A man cannot be said voluntarily to be undertaking a responsibility if at the very moment when he is said to be accepting it, he declares that in fact he is not.'

So if you give a reference, you should take a substantial leaf from the book of every bank, by adding a disclaimer. 'Whilst every care is taken in the supplying of references,' you might say, 'no legal liability whatsoever is accepted in respect thereof by the company, its officers or staff.' Alternatively: 'We are pleased to provide information as a business courtesy, but it must clearly be understood that no responsibility is accepted in respect thereof.' Disclaim, loud and clear, and your words should bring no legal consequences in their train.

Of course, by disclaiming responsibility to the recipient, you do not cover yourself against a claim by the person named and defamed. But in the unlikely event of trouble arising, you should find 'qualifying privilege' coming to your rescue. And if the reference happens to be both favourable and inaccurate, at least there is no reasonable prospect of any resultant negligence action succeeding against you.

37 Redundancy Payments

Mass redundancy in the lower ranks of industry and commerce hits the headlines. Backed by their unions, such people can fight for their jobs or at least raise a public outcry if they are thrown out of work. Not so the executives and managers. They must fight their lone battles for their livelihood. And while the Employment Protection (Consolidation) Act

1978 provides a cushion for all who are 'dismissed for redundancy' its provisions are not well enough known in the ranks of executives.

For instance, just when are you regarded as 'redundant'? If the company is cutting back on its senior salaried staff, and you observe the way the wind is blowing, do you lose your right to redundancy pay if you move out before you are thrown out? How is redundancy pay assessed and what is the most you can get? Is redundancy pay taxable? If a dispute arises over redundancy money, who decides it? And what decisions have already been given on the meaning of the Act which you should know?

Here, then, are the legal rules as you are most likely to meet them – either on your own behalf or as an employer of others.

* * *

You can only claim redundancy pay if you are dismissed by reason of redundancy. You must be 'dismissed'; and you must be 'redundant'. These words are not as simple as they sound.

R. H. McCulloch Limited issued a notice addressed 'to all personnel in Sussex'. It informed them that after a certain date 'we shall have no further work in the Sussex area. But we can offer you continuation of your employment with similar conditions in other areas.' And it asked for an answer by return of post.

Mr J. W. Moore regarded himself as dismissed and took another job elsewhere. He claimed his redundancy money.

'The notice amounts to a dismissal,' said the Lord Chief Justice. An employee is 'taken to be dismissed by his employer if, but only if ... the contract under which he is employed by the employer is terminated by the employer, whether it is so terminated by notice or without notice ...', so says the Act. In this case, the notice given to Mr Moore and his colleagues 'amounted to a dismissal ... it was plainly saying: Your work in the Sussex area has come to an end, we cannot afford to employ you doing nothing, and accordingly our contract with you will be terminated on that date.' The fact that it then goes on to offer in effect a new contract of employment elsewhere in no way meant that Mr Moore was not dismissed as redundant.

On the other hand, a Mr Shaw lost his case against Morton Sundour Fabrics. They informed him that he would shortly be redundant. He found himself another job almost at once and gave in his notice. He claimed his redundancy pay, but the court held that for notice to terminate an employee's employment, there must be date of termination – or at least facts from which that date could be inferred. Simply to indicate that redundancy is on its way will not amount to a dismissal.

This point has been emphasized in *Doble* v. *Firestone Tyre and Rubber Co. Ltd*. The company decided to close its factory in Brentford and notified its employees that it intended to close on 15 February 1980 and dismissal notices expiring on that date could be expected in due course. The Employment Appeal Tribunal held that this did not amount to a notice of dismissal because the date of actual termination was not predictable – the date given was merely provisional, and the notice was not itself a notice of dismissal because it clearly contemplated that dismissal notices would follow later.

So be patient. If you see a merger or a take-over in the offing or redundancy coming over the horizon, do not jump the gun. If you have been continuously employed by the same concern for over two years, you will lose your redundancy pay. And that may be worth far more than your pay in lieu of notice. What is more, like the fabled golden handshake up to £25,000, it is tax free.

So you wait until you are dismissed. But are you 'redundant'?

'An employee who is dismissed shall be taken to be dismissed by reason of redundancy,' says the Act, 'if the dismissal is attributable wholly or mainly to:

a The fact that his employer has ceased, or intends to cease, to carry on the business for the purposes of which the employee was employed by him, or has ceased, or intends to cease, to carry on that business in the place where the employee was so employed; or

b The fact that the requirements of that business for employees to carry out work of a particular kind, or for employees to carry out work of a particular kind in the place where he was so employed, have ceased or diminished or are expected to cease or diminish.'

It follows that if you are sacked because your employers are not satisfied with your work ... because the company feels that you are not keeping up with developments in the industry ... because of any reason other than redundancy, as defined – you get no redundancy pay.

Not surprisingly, there are countless disputes over redundancy money. Initially, these go to industrial tribunals, whose procedure is comparatively swift and informal. But their decisions can be (and often are) challenged before an Appeal Court of three judges. Here are some cases in which the employee got no redundancy money:

A man was dismissed because of his employer's 'genuine suspicions of irregularities'; an employee declined to carry out work which was outside the scope of his normal duties but within the terms of his contract of employment; a workshop manager had extra responsibilities heaped on his shoulders, but his employers found that he was 'inefficient and incompetent' and appointed someone else to his position. None of these men got redundancy pay.

On the other hand, here are some decisions to the contrary:

At the time of a man's dismissal, there was insufficient work; a manager went on holiday and the company found that it could manage without his services, so he was dismissed on his return; employers engaged on secret government work failed to show that dismissal of an employee was 'necessary for security reasons'; an employee was replaced by his lower-paid female assistant. All these staff received redundancy pay.

Complications arise where there is an offer of alternative employment. Provided that the new contract would take effect on or before the date when the former contract came to an end and the terms and conditions of the new employment would not differ from the corresponding provisions of those in force immediately before dismissal, an employee who unreasonably refuses the offer will lose the right to redundancy pay. An employee must also not unreasonably refuse an offer of alternative employment which is different in its terms if that offer has been made in writing. In this case, the new employment can take effect immediately on the ending of the old job or after an interval of not more than four weeks. If the terms of the new contract differ from the previous contract there will be a minimum trial period of four weeks. An employee who, for whatever reason, decides during this period to terminate the contract will continue to be treated as having been dismissed for redundancy. The employer may also terminate the contract during the four-week period, but only for a reason connected with or arising out of the change to the new employment. Again, in such a case the employee will continue to be treated as dismissed for redundancy.

The mere fact that the company changes hands or the business comes into new ownership will not give you any claim to redundancy pay if the new employer re-engages you or you unreasonably turn down an offer of similar employment from new proprietors. Remember, too, that if control changes merely because shares change hands, in law you will still be employed by the same company. You leave them at your own financial risk.

If by any chance you are nearing retirement, bear in mind that once you are over 65 (or 60, if you are a woman), you get no redundancy pay. If you are to be dismissed for redundancy, try to encourage your employers to do so before your appropriate birthday. But note that the Act specifically allows employers to terminate contracts in case of misconduct. So no useful purpose is served by courting the sack through active discourtesy, disobedience or other breach of express or implied terms in your contract of employment.

Now suppose that redundancy money is payable. How much will you get?

Schedule 4 of the Act lays down the method of calculation of redundancy payments. In brief, taking into account only the period of employment over the age of 18, you should get:

1 One and a half weeks' pay for each year of employment in which you were aged 41 or over.
2 One week's pay for each year of employment when you were aged between 22 and 40 inclusive.
3 Half a week's pay for each year of employment when you were aged between 18 and 21 inclusive.

If in doubt as to whether you are entitled to redundancy pay, ask for it. If it is not received, consult your solicitor. And remember that the burden of proving that a dismissal was not due to redundancy lies firmly upon the employer.

Equally, if in doubt as to the amount of your redundancy pay, ask a solicitor (or your local office of the Department of Employment will help your calculations). The longer your service and the greater your age, the more redundancy pay you will get – provided that you do not exceed the upper age limit, even by one day, in which case, you would get nothing.

Those, then, are the basic rules as the manager needs to know them for his own purposes. Naturally, to discover the position for your employees, you simply apply those same rules in reverse. While staff at lower levels receive less remuneration and therefore less redundancy pay, the grounds for claiming redundancy money are precisely the same, whether you sit at the head of the boardroom table or at the foot of the filing cabinet. Either way, redundancy could mean disaster. But the law provides a cushion which you should know how to wield.

Section 84 of the Act provides that: 'if an employee's contract of employment is renewed, or he is re-engaged under a new contract of employment in pursuance of an offer (whether in writing or not) made by his employer before the ending of his employment under the previous contract, and the renewal or re-engagement takes effect either immediately on the ending of that employment or after an interval of not more than four weeks thereafter, then, [subject to the provisions in relation to trial periods] the employee shall not be regarded as having been dismissed by his employer by reason of the ending of his employment under the previous contract'.

Briefly, you may dismiss someone and then re-engage them and they do not become redundant. There may even be a four-week interval if you offer to take someone on before their present employment ends.

Section 85 adds a provision whereby an employee who anticipates the expiry of the employer's dismissal notice may still be taken to have been dismissed. Once notice is given the employee does not necessarily have to work it out or lose redundancy pay. But 'If, before the employee's notice is due to expire, the employer gives him notice in writing –

a requiring him to withdraw his notice terminating the contract of employment ... and to continue in the employment until the date on which the employer's notice expires, and

b stating that, unless he does so, the employer will contest any liability to pay him redundancy payment in respect of the termination of his contract of employment, but the employee does not comply with the requirements of that notice, the employee shall not be entitled to a redundancy payment ...'.

However, an industrial tribunal can, if the matter is referred to it, order the employer to pay all or part of the redundancy payment to which the employee would otherwise be entitled, if it is just and equitable to do so. Whether you are the employer or the employee, make sure that you serve the required notices.

If the business changes hands and employees are dismissed, we have the classic redundancy situation. They are entitled to their redundancy money. But if they are offered new employment by the successors to the business and in all the circumstances it would be unreasonable for them to refuse that offer, they get no redundancy money.

So if you see a take-over in the offing, take care before you leave – and conversely, if you are advising your company in connection with a sale – before redundancy pay is taken into account as one of the expenses of the change, ensure that the purchasers will not be willing to make the appropriate offers to your staff. Also bear in mind the possible impact of the Transfer of Undertakings Regulations and the duty to consult recognized trade unions.

In the old days, redundancy situations tended to be as uncomplicated as they were disastrous (for the employees, at least). Nowadays, their complication is matched by the benefits which can be acquired by the employees who know their rights. And employers who know their basic redundancy law can save themselves a good deal of money. Executives and professional people, who often have dual capacities, can serve themselves and their employers best by knowing the rules.

Until the Wages Act 1986, the employer could normally claim 35 per cent of all statutory redundancy payments back from the Redundancy Fund. This rebate is now only available to employers of nine or fewer employees.

38 Part Time Problems

Do you employ part timers? If so, then how safe are you in sacking them? Are they entitled to redundancy pay or compensation for unfair dismissal, in the same way as people who work full time?

* * *

Redundancy pay is designed as a cushion, to help people who are thrust out of work because their jobs have gone by the board. If you dismiss your assistant, manager or secretary because you move or close your business or works, your office, shop or studio, or because you no longer require a person to do that job, then you have created a redundancy.

To be entitled to redundancy pay, the employee must be under 65 (60 is the age for women) – and must have been continuously employed for at least two years at the date of dismissal. Continuous employment is computed in accordance with the rules set out in Schedule 13 to the Employment Protection (Consolidation) Act 1978. The basic principle is that any week in which the employee is employed for sixteen hours or more will count in computing a period of employment. If an employee's contract of employment usually involves employment for eight hours or more per week, but less than sixteen hours, he or she will only be regarded as being continuously employed once they have been employed under such a contract for five years. But, once employed for sixteen hours a week for six months, 8 hours per week thereafter is sufficient.

Assuming that a part timer's age is below the upper limit, then if they are made redundant they are entitled to redundancy pay, provided that they have worked the necessary number of hours.

What, then, of 'compensation' for 'unfair dismissal' under the Act?

If you fire a part timer, then he or she is 'dismissed', and while they cannot get 'damages' for 'wrongful dismissal' if they receive their proper notice, they may still be dismissed 'unfairly', even if they get far more notice than their minimum legal requirements.

The fact that your employee is a part timer gives you no right to sack him either 'wrongfully' or 'unfairly'. A person is dismissed 'wrongfully' if not given proper notice or pay in lieu. The same minimum conditions as to hours worked apply as for redundancy.

If you give your employee agreed notice or, in the absence of agreement, reasonable notice, or in any event not less than the statutory minimum – then you will not have dismissed 'wrongfully'. But give a full timer or a part timer less than their proper notice and you are in trouble – unless you can show that they have behaved so badly that they have 'repudiated' their own contract of employment. If they have destroyed the basis of their contract, then you may accept the repudiation and show them to the door.

So while part timers have the same rights to proper notice as full timers, they are just as bound to serve you faithfully, diligently, obediently, honestly and well.

Unfortunately for them, though, part timers are not protected by the Employment Protection (Consolidation) Act 1978 against 'unfair' dismissal unless they have been continuously employed for two years and work at least the hours specified on page 106.

Anyway, the business or professional person who takes on part timers for, say, twelve hours per week is fairly well protected – there is some leeway for overtime. But the person who does not know the law and employs people for sixteen hours per week or more might just as well have full timers on the books in so far as redundancy pay and compensation for unfair dismissal are concerned. Once employees work the magical sixteen hours per week for the required period, they have the same protection as those who labour for forty hours or more per week. The line may be arbitrary, but it must be drawn somewhere. For protection against unfair dismissal too, retirement age provides the upper limit.

Finally, these rules apply, of course, only to your actual employees. Many business and professional people use freelance help – they get assistance from self-employed men and women who are not protected against redundancy or 'unfair dismissal'. After all, if you make yourself redundant or put yourself out of a job, you have only yourself to blame.

So you can employ your freelance helpers for one hour, sixteen hours or for their full working day and they bear their own risks upon their own heads. The law is designed to protect the employees of others, and not those who see fit to employ themselves.

Part Three
Industrial Relations, Employment Protection and Unfair Dismissal

Introduction

In the old days, people used to talk about 'their job' – but in fact it belonged to the boss – to give or to take away, as he or she saw fit.

Then came the rules on 'wrongful dismissal', which at least ensured that a person was entitled to proper notice or pay in lieu. And increasing minimum periods of notice were introduced by various recent statutes.

Next: In its only uncontroversial Part, the Industrial Relations Act provided that an employee who was dismissed 'unfairly' had a claim for compensation, even if notice or pay in lieu was received.

Now: The Employment Protection Act 1975, the Employment Protection (Consolidation) Act 1978 and the Employment Act 1982 provide a series of rights and remedies designed to buttress employees in their jobs. And women are not to be treated less well than men in like occupations – so rules the Equal Pay Act 1970 as strengthened and amended by the Sex Discrimination Acts.

This Part of the book explains the main rules on dismissals, new and old; the protection now enjoyed by most employees, thanks in the main to the new legislation; the new status of women workers; the rules on race and ethnic discrimination; and sex and ethnic 'monitoring' and 'positive action'.

39 Dismissal

In the old days, however short the notice, however unfair the dismissal, employees could only claim damages if they did not get what they contracted for.

Today, a dismissal remains 'wrongful' if the employee does not receive the agreed notice (for details, see the contract or the written particulars supplied under the Employment Protection (Consolidation) Act 1978); in the absence of agreement, 'reasonable' notice – depending upon all the circumstances of the case; and in any event not less than the statutory minimum (see Section 49 of the Employment Protection (Consolidation) Act 1978). In addition an employee who is 'unfairly' dismissed can claim reinstatement, re-engagement or compensation under the 1978 Act.

For employees to obtain damages for wrongful *dismissal*, compensation for unfair *dismissal*, or redundancy pay – receivable if they were *dismissed* as redundant – they must prove that they were 'dismissed'. If they left voluntarily, or before they received their notice, they were not 'dismissed' (even if they were warned that a dismissal was on the way).

Dismissal may be *actual* – with or without notice; the employer may 'repudiate' the contract – smash it – by not paying salary, wage or commission due or (more likely) by a reduction in status or pay; or it may be 'constructive' – where the employee is forced out of the job through bad treatment by the employers.

An employee who resigns will still be 'dismissed' if it can be shown that the employer made it impossible for the employee to stay on at the job or otherwise smashed the contractual agreement.

The 1978 Act defines 'dismissal' as including a case where 'the employee terminates the contract of service with or without notice, in circumstances as such that he is entitled to terminate it without notice by reason of the employer's conduct'.

Janner's law: 'Never resign – unless you have a better job to go to' – or you will not be 'dismissed'. Today, the Tribunal will look at all the facts to see whether the employee was entitled to resign without notice. Had the employer treated the employee so badly as to show that he did not intend to be bound by the arrangement? Was the employee, in effect, sacked by implication ... 'constructively' ... without just cause ... ? If so, then the employee is 'dismissed' quite as effectively as he or she would have been, had the employer specifically sacked them.

Conversely: if you can prove that there was no 'dismissal', your employee remains entitled to every penny earned up to the date when the employment came to an end – but to nothing more.

Note: the law of unfair dismissal also applies if you don't renew a 'fixed-term' contract when it runs out – unless the employee has agreed in writing to waive their legal rights.

If you 'dismiss', the next question is: Did the employee get the proper notice or pay in lieu? If so, then they cannot get damages for 'wrongful dismissal' – the only possible claim will be to an Industrial Tribunal for compensation for 'unfair dismissal'.

You may decide to dismiss an employee without the normal notice or pay in lieu. You will be justified in doing so only if they have 'repudiated' the contract. They may smash it by one really serious act – like the assistant who smokes near inflammable goods or the manageress who steals; or as a result of habitual or persistent minor acts – disobedience, discourtesy, lateness or absenteeism, for instance. If you wish to show that the employee has repudiated, the burden of doing so will be on you. Summary dismissal is seldom warranted – and employees should be given their notice or pay in lieu and the benefit of the doubt.

If you are afraid that the giving of notice or pay in lieu may provide a weapon in the employee's hands in a claim for compensation for unfair dismissal and you say that you regarded the conduct as serious, then send a letter along with the money: say: 'This payment is made without prejudice to the company's right to dismiss summarily'; add, if you wish, that you appreciate the employee's previous service ... that you do not want to cause hardship ... whatever other reason is correct.

Exceptions: Employees are not covered if:

1 They do not have two years' continuous employment.
2 They are part timers – normally working less than 16 hours a week, or 8 hours after 5 years' continuous service.
3 The dismissal was in connection with a lock-out, strike or other industrial action (see Section 62 of the 1978 Act).
4 They ordinarily worked outside Britain (test for 'long distance commuters': where is the base for their work?).
5 They are over the normal (unisex) retirement age or, if there isn't one, over 65.

If employees claim compensation for unfair dismissal and can show that they were 'dismissed', unless they come within one of the above exceptions, you will have to show the reason for the dismissal and that you acted reasonably in treating that reason as sufficient to warrant depriving them of their livelihood.

Reasons given by the Act include: lack of capability, skill, technical or academic qualifications; conduct; redundancy; illegality, eg where a foreign employee's work permit has expired. A person may be 'incapable' of doing the job because of ill health or old age.

Once you have shown the reason for the dismissal, the determination of the question whether the dismissal was fair or unfair having regard to the reason shown 'shall depend on whether in the circumstances (including the size and administrative resources of the employer's undertaking) the employer acted reasonably or unreasonably in treating it as a sufficient reason for dismissing the employee; and that question shall be determined in accordance with equity and the substantial merits of the case.'

Therefore:

1 Never dismiss in anger.
2 Always get a second opinion before dismissing an employee (not covered by above exceptions). And
3 Always follow any dismissal procedure required by the employee's contract of employment or agreements with unions, incorporated into it. In any event ensure that the procedure which you do adopt is no less favourable to the employee than current ACAS Codes require.

Briefly: ACAS advises that employees should be warned in all but very serious cases of misconduct and that you should carefully investigate alleged wrongdoing and give the employee a chance to answer the allegation before reaching your decision. Whenever possible, there should be a right of appeal.

And remember – you will have to spend a lot of time and money replacing a dismissed employee, so it is good sense to be sure whether or not you need to take such a drastic step before you act.

The cost of an unfair dismissal claim may be high; the statutory maximum for a dismissal on or after 1 April 1987 is £13,240 (excluding the additional award). If in doubt as to the likely result of a claim or as to probable amount of compensation, consult your solicitor.

In fixing compensation, the tribunal will take into account the extent to which the employee contributed towards their own dismissal; and they must do what they can to 'mitigate their loss', ie to keep it to a minimum by finding other employment as soon as reasonably possible.

The 1978 Act also provides that the employee will still be taken to have been dismissed where, after the employer has given notice, the employee in turn gives notice to the employer which would expire before the employer's notice.

40 Information and Collective Bargaining

Before the demise of the Industrial Relations Act, one of our top trade union leaders was asked: 'What do you want in its place?'

He answered with one word: 'Information'.

Curiously, the requirement to give information was originally contained in the Industrial Relations Act; in the course of collective bargaining (although not in annual statements by companies); it was repeated in almost identical terms in the Employment Protection Act 1975, and in the long term it is likely to have far more impact than most of the sections of that Act which have received most of the publicity.

There are, of course, some companies that already provide substantial information to trade unions. On the other hand, there are some trade unions which simply do not want to know. 'How you cope with the company's problems is your affair', they say. 'Our job is to look after our members. ...' The industrial world is full of strange problems.

Again, trade union members often work in the accounts department; in every plant there is a grapevine; and sometimes the unions know far more than the management realize. Still, the information provided through hearsay often becomes rumour and the management may be well advised to translate that rumour into fact.

Consider, then, the 'general duty of employers to provide information'.

'For the purposes of all the stages of ... collective bargaining between an employer and representatives of an independent trade union ... it shall be the duty of the employer ... to disclose to those representatives on request all such information relating to his undertaking as is in his possession, or that of any associated employer, and is both

- *a* information without which the trade union representatives would be to a material extent impeded in carrying on within such collective bargaining, and,
- *b* information which it would be in accordance with good industrial relations practice that he should disclose to them for the purposes of collective bargaining.'

Note:

1 Only 'independent' trade unions benefit. A union is not 'independent' if it is controlled or financed by the employer. TUC unions are in; 'tame' staff associations and the like are out.
2 The trade union must also be recognized by the employer for the purpose of negotiating on behalf of the particular workers in respect of whom the relevant information is sought.
3 Information need only be provided 'on request'. If the union does not want it, it need not have it.
4 Only 'collective bargaining' – as opposed to bargaining over individual contracts – is affected.
5 The information to be provided is that which concerns the employer's 'undertaking' – which means, his entire business and not merely that part of it where the particular employees work. And the employer may have to provide information not merely regarding his own circumstances but also that of any associated company or 'employer'.

Now take the ordinary bargaining situation. The trade union representatives will no doubt want to know the state of the order book; whether the company as a whole or the unit in particular is making (and expects to make) a profit or a loss – and to be supplied with details; and if (as is almost inevitable) the employer declines to accept the wage claim in full, saying that he could not afford to do so, then the trade union would demand what lawyers call 'further and better particulars' of that allegation.

All that information is likely to come under (*a*) and (*b*) above. Surely the trade union representatives must be 'to a material extent impeded' in carrying on the collective bargaining if they do not know all the facts? And surely it must be 'in accordance with good industrial relations practice' that the employer should make full disclosure?

However, the Act provides some very important exceptions. Here they are:

'No employer shall ... be required to disclose –
a any information the disclosure of which would be against the interests of *national security*, or,
b any information which it could not disclose without contravening a prohibition imposed by or under an *enactment*, or,
c any information which has been communicated to the employer *in confidence*, or which the employer has otherwise obtained in consequence of the confidence reposed in him by another person, or,

d any information relating specifically to an *individual*, unless he has consented to its being disclosed, or,
e any information the disclosure of which would cause substantial injury to the employer's undertaking for reasons other than its effect on collective bargaining, or,
f any information obtained by the employer for the purpose of bringing, prosecuting or defending any legal proceedings.'

Sub-paragraph (*e*) is very important. Almost any employer can avoid giving almost any information by alleging that it would be liable to cause substantial injury to the undertaking if disclosed. Competitors must not know the state of the order book nor creditors that of the bank account.... If times are bad and the word gets out, the very jobs which the workers are trying to protect will be at risk because, as everyone knows, 'to him that hath shall be lent ... from him who has not shall be taken away'....

How, then, can these two apparently conflicting sections be reconciled in daily industrial practice? That was the question asked of the Commission on Industrial Relations in connection with the same provisions in the Industrial Relations Act. The Commission's answer was contained in a substantial document which may be summed up in a sentence: 'We don't understand it either ... but the courts will have to interpret the clauses, in the light of experience.' Some guidance is given by the ACAS Code of Practice on Disclosure of Information to Trade Unions for Collective Bargaining Purposes. The Code gives some examples of information which if disclosed in particular circumstances might cause substantial injury. These are:

a cost information on individual products;
b detailed analysis of proposed investment;
c marketing or pricing policies;
d price quotas or the make up of tender prices.

Information which has to be made available publicly, for example under the Companies Act, would not fall into this category.

Substantial injury may occur if, for example, certain customers would be lost to competitors, or suppliers would refuse to supply necessary materials, or the ability to raise funds to finance the company would be seriously impaired as a result of disclosing certain information. The burden of establishing a claim that disclosure would cause substantial injury lies with the employer.

There is a complex enforcement procedure where an employer fails to disclose information in accordance with the Act. An independent trade union may present a claim to the Central Arbitration Committee (CAC). The CAC will then refer the matter to ACAS for conciliation. If it is not settled the CAC must make a declaration as to whether or not the claim is good. If an employer fails to comply with a CAC declaration requiring disclosure, a further complaint can be made to the CAC. If the further complaint is held to be well-founded the CAC has power to make a determination of the terms and conditions of employees specified in the claim.

Since 1982 there has been a provision in relation to companies employing more than 250 employees requiring them to include in their annual reports a statement about employee involvement in the affairs of the company. This provision is now to be found in paragraph II of Schedule 7 to the Companies Act 1985. The directors' report must contain: 'a statement describing the action that has been taken during the financial year to introduce, maintain or develop arrangements aimed at —

a providing employees systematically with information on matters of concern to them as employees,
b consulting employees or their representatives on a regular basis so that the views of employees can be taken into account in making decisions which are likely to affect their interests,
c encouraging the involvement of employees in the company's performance through an employees' share scheme or by some other means,
d achieving a common awareness on the part of all employees of the financial and economic factors affecting the performance of the company.'

The duty, however, is not particularly onerous. There is no positive requirement to take any steps whatsoever to increase employee involvement. The company could satisfy the provision merely by stating that no action had been taken.

Information is an important issue that will not go away from the industrial scene — partly because our fellow members of the EEC tend to take the issue much more to heart than we have done. Watch out for possible developments in this area from EEC initiatives in the future.

41 Guarantee Payments

Too many companies and firms are forced into short time working or even laying off valued employees. In general, salaried staff continue to receive their pay as before. Unless they are made redundant, they continue to earn. They are not paid by the hour or (subject, of course, to possible bonuses and the like) on the basis of production achieved.

Hourly paid workers, on the other hand, must put in their hours or they will take out no pay. Thanks to the Employment Protection (Consolidation) Act 1978 most have a reasonable cushion against dismissal in the form of redundancy payments or the right to receive proper notice or pay in lieu. But while still employed, they have no guarantee of the opportunity to earn their pay. This causes particular anxiety in times of economic recession and depression. To meet this problem a right to a guarantee payment in certain circumstances has been introduced.

Who, then, qualifies for the protection, and how is it secured?

'Where an employee throughout a day during any part of which he would normally be required to work in accordance with his contract of employment is not provided with work by his employer by reason of –

- *a* a diminution in the requirements of the employer's business for work of the kind which the employee is employed to do, or
- *b* any other occurrence affecting the normal working of the employer's business in relation to work of the kind which the employee is employed to do,

he shall [subject to certain other provisions] be entitled to be paid ... a guarantee payment in respect of that day.'

Exceptions: there will be no entitlement to a guarantee payment in respect of a 'workless day':

- '*a* if the employee has not been continuously employed for at least one month. Where he is employed under a fixed term contract for three months or less or under a contract to perform a particular task which is not expected to last for more than three months, this qualifying period is extended to three months' continuous employment;
- *b* if the failure to provide work occurs in consequence of a trade dispute involving any employee of his employer or of an associated employer;
- *c* if his employer has offered to provide alternative work for that day

which is suitable in all the circumstances whether or not work which the employee is under his contract employed to perform, and the employee has unreasonably refused the offer, or he does not comply with reasonable requirements imposed by his employer.'

Next: how much and for how long?

In general, employees will be entitled to the guaranteed minimum remuneration which they would have received had they been normally employed – but subject to a maximum of £10.90 (effective 1 April 1987, but revised annually) in respect of any day. An employee will not be entitled to guarantee payments in respect of more than the specified number of days – normally five – in any of the 'relevant periods'. The 'relevant periods' are periods of three months.

Those are the broad outlines of the guarantee payments provisions. However, if you are unfortunate enough to need them, consult your local office of the Department of Employment, and do so before you run into disputes. If a dispute arises, an employee who considers that the employer has failed to pay the whole or any part of a guarantee payment can refer the matter to an industrial tribunal.

Note: an entitlement to a guarantee payment ranks as a preferential debt if the employer goes into liquidation before it is paid. And if there is not even enough money to pay the preferential debtors, the guarantee payments will be met from the Redundancy Fund.

Many employers in industries such as engineering are covered by negotiated 'guaranteed week' agreements. These are often more generous than the statutory scheme. If you are liable under such an agreement, so that the employees are entitled to be paid under their contracts, you can offset these payments against your guarantee pay liability – and vice versa.

42 Equal Pay, Sex Discrimination and Maternity Rights

On 29 December 1975 the Equal Pay Act came into full force. It became unlawful to pay less to a woman than you would to a man in the same or like employment or whose job is rated on an equivalent basis. There are, of course, disputes as to whether or not the particular job is equivalent to that done by men – and any disputes are sorted out by industrial tribunals.

There remained, however, a number of curious anomalies. Chief among these is the difference in qualifying ages for pensions. A woman qualifies at 60, but a man must wait until he is 65. This was highlighted by the European Court in Luxembourg in a case concerning a 62-year-old lady dietician who had been employed by the Southampton and South-West Hampshire Area Health Authority (Teaching). The Authority had waived its general policy by employing her for a further two years after she had reached the age of sixty. The court held that the dismissal of a woman solely because she had attained the qualifying age for a state pension, where that age was different for men and for women, constituted discrimination on the ground of sex contrary to European Community Law.

The Sex Discrimination Act 1986 brings our law into line with that of the other EEC countries. Section 2 of the Act brings within the scope of the Sex Discrimination Act 1975 any provision made by an employer in relation to retirement concerning dismissal, demotion, promotion, transfer or training. Discriminatory retirement ages in state undertakings are already unlawful under European law which is directly effective in the UK. When Section 2 comes into force (7 November 1987) private sector employers will also no longer be able to have policies which fix different compulsory retirement ages for men and women in comparable positions.

Section 3 of the 1986 Act (again, from 7 November 1987) amends the unfair dismissal provisions of the Employment Protection (Consolidation) Act to ensure that men and women in the same position will have the right to complain to an industrial tribunal of unfair dismissal up to the same age (65, unless there is a common 'normal retirement age' for both sexes which is lower – or higher).

The Sex Discrimination Act 1975 introduced powerful amendments to the Equal Pay Act. Not surprisingly, the Act made it unlawful for anyone to discriminate against those who seek to exercise their rights under the Equal Pay Act. No one must be discriminated against 'on the ground of her sex' – or victimized because she seeks to exercise her rights.

Again, married people of either sex are not to be discriminated against in the employment field. And (theoretically at least) the new protection also applies to downtrodden males. Men are (for instance) now entitled to equal treatment as 'midwives'.

Until recently there have been important exceptions – the most important, that undertakings with five or less employees are, in general, not included. And it is only unlawful for a firm which consists of six or more partners to discriminate against a woman in either the membership of that partnership or in the terms offered to members. Both of these categories have now been brought within the law by changes in the Sex Discrimination Act 1986.

All other businesses must not discriminate against females in connection with their hiring, firing, training or promotion. And the same rules protect 'contract workers' – people not employed by you but supplied by others for your business purposes.

The second exception – not affected by the 1986 Act – is charmingly described. It applies 'where sex is a genuine occupational qualification' – a term which only a Parliamentary draughtsman could have produced with a straight face. 'Being a man is a genuine occupational qualification for a job', we are told, 'only where the essential nature of the job calls for authentic male characteristics, so that it would be wholly different if carried on by a woman' or where 'the job needs to be held by a man to preserve decency or privacy because it is likely to involve physical contact with men in circumstances where they might reasonably object to its being carried on by a woman'. Also, where 'the holder of the job is likely to do his work in circumstances where men might reasonably object to the presence of a woman because they are in a state of undress or are using sanitary facilities', then discrimination is permitted.

Happily, there will be no need to employ male bunny girls – or female Catholic priests (further exception, of course, is made for religious employment). And the right not to make schools co-educational is specifically preserved.

Equal pay ... equal rights at work ... no discrimination or victimization because of sex ... so there are no financial incentives to employ women. The question: 'Whom shall I take on to fill a vacancy?' or 'Whom shall I promote?' will be answered (hopes the law) in accordance with merit and not on grounds of sex.

However: the Employment Protection Act provides special privileges that – at least in the case of women of childbearing age – may make it considerably more burdensome and expensive to employ a woman than a man in the same or in an equivalent job. Breach of the Sex Discrimination Act may lead to a claim in the Industrial Tribunal which may award very substantial compensation. Also, a woman who is dismissed because she is pregnant is given a tremendous advantage in bringing a claim for unfair dismissal. If the reason or the principal reason for her dismissal is that she is pregnant or the reason is connected with her pregnancy, she is treated as unfairly dismissed unless the employer can show one of the following:

a that at the effective date of termination of her contract she is or will have become, because of her pregnancy, incapable of adequately doing the work which she is employed to do;

b that, because of her pregnancy, she cannot or will not be able to continue after that date to do that work without contravention of a duty or restriction imposed by or under any enactment.

However: if there is a 'suitable available vacancy', then the woman must be offered that vacancy before or on the effective date of termination. And the new contract must take effect immediately on the termination of the previous one; the work to be done under that contract must be 'of a kind which is both suitable in relation to the employee and appropriate for her to do in the circumstances'; and the terms and conditions of that employment must not be 'substantially less favourable to her than the corresponding provisions of the previous contract'.

So you decide not to dismiss an employee (married or unmarried – that is a question of morality or preference, not of law). Watch out. If she is absent from work wholly or partly because of pregnancy or confinement she probably has a right to be paid statutory maternity pay (see below) and a right subsequently to return to work. The requirements for the right to return to work are that she must have been employed until immediately before the beginning of the eleventh week before the expected week of confinement. At that time she must have been continuously employed for at least two years, and she must have informed her employer of her forthcoming absence at least twenty-one days in advance or as soon as reasonably practicable. She must also inform her employer at least twenty-one days before her absence begins or as soon as reasonably practicable that she will be or is absent wholly or partly because of pregnancy or confinement, that she intends to return to work and of the expected week of confinement or, if the confinement has occurred, the date of confinement. You are also entitled, not less than 7 weeks after confinement was due, to ask the woman to confirm again, in writing, her intention to return.

A mother who qualifies under the Act is entitled to have her job back at any time within 29 weeks of the date of her confinement – with a possible extension of four weeks if she is still unfit at the end of the 29-week period.

As an employer, you should, as a matter of practice, require that all notices given by pregnant staff are to be in writing. If the employee states that she does not intend to return then you are free to employ a replacement. If she states that she does intend to return you must be careful in employing a replacement. Although the chances are that a replacement will not have the opportunity to acquire the right not to be unfairly dismissed because of the short period involved, you should ensure that you make it quite plain to him or her that the position is temporary only by reason of absence through pregnancy.

The Sex Discrimination Act, of course, makes it an offence to discriminate against a woman on the ground of her sex – in connection with appointment, transfer, training, promotion or any other benefits in the employment field. Unfortunately, the stringency of the rules puts the employer on the legal spot. Comparatively few mothers do come back after childbirth – but most who know their rights now state an intention to return. After all, if they change their minds and decide not to come back, they lose nothing; but if they burn their boats by stating an intention not to return, they lose their statutory rights, however good the reason for their alteration of intent. It remains a woman's privilege to change her mind, even though the cost for the employer may be extremely high.

Since April 1987 there has also been a new scheme of Statutory Maternity Pay. It is based on the Statutory Sick Pay scheme: the idea is that employers pay their pregnant employees and the government reimburses the cost (plus 7 per cent towards national insurance).

The rules, unfortunately, are complicated and somewhat different from the rules for the right to return. All depends on the position 14 weeks before the expected week of confinement. If the woman then has two years' service with you, she can get the higher rate (only payable for 6 weeks) which is 9/10 of her normal pay, then the lower rate for the next 12 weeks. Less fortunate souls just get the lower rate for 18 weeks (currently £32.45 a week). If she has not worked for you for 6 months at the relevant date she is entitled to nothing from you, but can make a claim (based on past employment record) to the DHSS.

The conditions are otherwise the same as for the right to return, except (confusingly) that she need not say she intends to return. Benefits are payable as soon as she stops work, but only if she has reached the start of the 11th week before her expected week of confinement – otherwise she must wait till then. Payment continues for 18 weeks or until she returns to work (if sooner).

To get your money back: simply give the required details with your monthly National Insurance Return, and deduct the amount you have paid, plus 7 per cent. *Note:* the pay you give is like any other salary – liable to tax; and you must deal with it under PAYE accordingly.

* * *

The Sex Discrimination Act has not made very much headway in getting rid of discrimination, often rooted in masculine prejudices –

largely because of problems of proving unfair treatment. The Equal Opportunities Commission has therefore been pressing a different approach, of getting firms to think positively about Equal Opportunities. For much the same reasons the Commission for Racial Equality has taken the same approach. Both have issued Codes of Practice – not law, but ignored at your risk. Both recommend:

1. an equal opportunities policy setting out what your organization intends to achieve and how you will go about it;
2. training, reviewing the dustier corners of past practices, and looking particularly at recruitment and promotion procedures;
3. record-keeping – 'sex and ethnic monitoring' – to enable you to establish where you stand and how you are improving your sex and racial 'mix'.

These are major issues and the best advice we can give here is – read the Codes of Practice, and if you feel you need to take action, get advice (either of the Commissions can help you here).

43 Equal Pay – Cammell Laird and After

When an industrial tribunal ruled that Ms Julie Hayward, a canteen assistant employed by Cammell Laird Shipbuilders Ltd, was entitled to equal pay with male tradesmen, it sparked off a round of new and careful calculation among informed employers and those who keep their books and accounts. The case has become a long-running *cause célèbre*; the appeal process is still running, but other cases are now following thick and fast. So here is your reminder and guide to the Equal Pay Act 1970, as altered by the Equal Pay (Amendment) Regulations 1983.

The Act came into force on 29 December 1975. Its purpose: To eliminate discrimination between men and women in basic rates of pay and other terms of their contracts of employment, including overtime pay, bonus and piece work, as well as other conditions of work such as holiday and sick pay entitlement and working hours. Only terms 'related to death or retirement' are excluded and then only in terms of cash benefit, not retirement ages (since the Sex Discrimination Act 1986). The general provisions of the Act do not apply to the Armed Forces. Special treatment is conceded to women in regard to pregnancy or childbirth. And the Act does not require men and women to be treated equally in respect of those terms of employment which are affected by compliance with laws (such as Part VI of the Factories' Act, 1961) which regulate the employment of women.

Unlike the unfair dismissal rules, which exclude part timers (people who normally work less than 16 hours a week or 8 hours after 5 years' continuous service), pensioners and others, the Act applies to all, of every age and category. And while statutory unfair dismissal and redundancy protection has always been subject to a minimum qualifying period, there is no minimum period before an employee gets the right to equal pay.

Please note, though: The Act only operates for the potential benefit of women and of employees paid at different rates on grounds of sex. There *were* rights (broadly) for employees doing similar work to claim comparable pay, under the Fair Wages Resolution and Schedule 11 of the Employment Protection Act, 1975 – but all such rights have now been repealed. The Act, and the Regulations which amend it, apply only so as to give equal rights to men and to women.

There is also a relationship between the Equal Pay Act 1970 and the Sex Discrimination Act 1975. Where a complaint relates to access to a benefit or to certain contractual issues to which the Equal Pay Act does not apply, an employee may bring a claim under the Sex Discrimination Act.

Under the Equal Pay Act, an employee could claim equal pay with a member of the opposite sex in one of two ways:

1 Where the employee was doing the same or similar work to a member of the opposite sex who was paid more. In general: This meant that a woman could claim what is still described as 'like pay for like work'.
2 If an employee's job had been given an equal value under a non-discriminatory job evaluation scheme, the employee could claim equal pay – even if the work was different from that done by a member of the opposite sex.

However: Other than under the job evaluation scheme exercise, like could not be compared with unlike. This, held the European Court of Justice, was contrary to the Treaty of Rome. Hence the new Regulations – which (as we shall see) may or may not bring the UK into line with its EEC obligations.

Anyway: The Regulations produced one crucial effect. A woman may claim that her work is 'of equal value' to that of a man in the same employment. 'Equal value' is assessed in terms of the demands made on her and her colleagues – for instance, under such headings as effort, skill and decision.

The previous categories – like pay for like work and work valued as equal under a proper job evaluation scheme – still apply. The novelty is the right to compare work of an entirely different nature.

Ms Julie Hayward first worked for Cammell Laird in 1975 as an apprentice cook. She held a City and Guilds qualification as well as certificates from the Royal Institute of Public Health and Hygiene. During her apprenticeship she was paid the same basic rate as other apprentices, regardless of the skills for which they were training.

At the age of 20, Julie became a qualified cook/chef. She was then paid at the rate for a canteen assistant. She claimed that since qualification she had worked as a canteen cook and carried out the work of a chef for a substantial period. Male apprentices in other trades who qualified at the same time as she did were put on higher post-qualification rates of pay and had remained on higher pay since. The reason, she maintained: sex. She and colleagues in the canteen and kitchen were mainly women; the tradesmen were (as their titles generally indicated) male; so she and her mates were not getting 'equal pay for work of equal value'.

That, of course, begged the question: Was the work done by the two categories of employee really 'of equal value'? The tribunal set in motion the procedure created under the Regulations.

ACAS has set up a panel of experts to prepare reports on questions of equal value. ACAS approves, but does not train, organize, or (still less) supervise or regulate the experts in their work. One of them now prepared a report on Julie Hayward's case.

The expert considered the jobs in question under five headings:

1 Physical demands
2 Environmental demands
3 Planning and decision making
4 Skill and knowledge required
5 Responsibility

He concluded that the working conditions, dangers and responsibilities of the tradesmen were balanced by the responsibilities of the catering assistants. There would be 'potentially disastrous consequences' for the workforce if Julie made mistakes with hygiene or cooking procedures. His conclusion – that the jobs were 'of equal value'. So those performing the jobs should receive equal pay.

The expert presented his report as evidence to the tribunal, which accepted his findings. It held that the canteen assistant's work was of equal value with that of skilled tradesmen – painters, joiners, thermal insulation engineers and the rest. Cammell Laird were therefore in breach of their obligation under the Act, as amended by the Regulations.

Cammell Laird did not dispute this finding: they argued instead that other 'fringe' benefits made up for the loss of pay. This point is still being argued through the courts*, and may yet end up in the European Court. But in the meantime, wise employers are taking the case to heart and re-examining all aspects of their wage and salary structures, anxious to avoid the same sort of litigation misery.

Meanwhile: Into the pipeline go claims for equal pay for work of equal value by (for instance) women office workers, clerks, VDU operators, cashiers and people doing traditionally female and less well paid industrial jobs – comparing their money and conditions with (for example) male sales staff, drivers, maintenance and other engineers and people doing traditionally male and better paid jobs in industry.

Each case must, of course, be decided on its own facts. So job evaluation experts are enjoying a boom. Just as no specific method of job evaluation is required by ACAS, so none is laid down in the Act or in the Regulations. Comparisons may be odious, but in this area of law they are inevitable. The relative value of different jobs is assessed within the organization in general by one of two methods:

1. the analytical method, involving measuring of value of jobs under various headings or demands, eg skill, effort, decision making, responsibilities and working conditions; or

2. the non-analytical method, which considers each whole job against other whole jobs, ranking them on the table of jobs, drawn up in order of importance, but without evaluating the demands made by the jobs under such headings as those above.

In equal value cases, the individual components of jobs – 'for instance, under such headings as effort, skill and decision' – must be evaluated. What matters is the demands made on employees by their work, rather than the value of the work to their employer.

The procedure in these new equal pay for work of equal value cases is lengthy, expensive, complex and contained in Regulations which are largely inexplicable. If your firm or your clients move into this morass, you will need expert help in the art of extrication. Better to know the rules and to keep out.

What, then, are the exceptions? When is work not 'the same' or 'broadly similar' and when is unequal pay justified?

In a 'like work' application, the claimant must show that her work is

---

* The Court of Appeal has now decided that when comparing the pay of men and women, account must be taken not merely of pay but also of all other benefits, ie of the entire contractual package.

the same or broadly similar to that of her male comparator. This is a question of fact, of common sense and of judgement. The tribunal must then decide whether any difference between the two jobs are of practical importance. If they are not, then the employer may wriggle off the hook by showing that there is a 'material difference' between the job holders to justify the gap in pay or other conditions. A tribunal will look at the reality, rather than at the names or job titles or descriptions.

In a recent case men and women bank cashiers at the same counter were held to be doing work of the same nature, as were men and women serving meals in the same restaurant. Men and women shop assistants in different sections of the same department store had 'broadly similar' work. So did a woman cook who prepared luncheons for the directors, and men chefs who cooked meals and snacks for employees in the canteen. But where a man and a woman both dealt with production schedules, the man was found to be dealing with more important items and as his job entailed greater responsibility it was in order to rate him higher than the woman. Their work was not 'broadly similar'.

So tribunals and courts must give consideration to the type of work involved and the skill and knowledge required to do them, rather than undertaking a complete examination of the detail of difference between the two jobs. What matters about the difference is their number, nature, extent and frequency.

What, then, is a difference of 'practical importance' between the two jobs? Again: That is a question of fact.

If there is no difference of practical importance, then is there any 'material difference'? This means essentially a difference other than one based on sex discrimination between what courts have called the 'personal equation' of the woman and the man – the things which they personally bring to a job, like degrees or diplomas or relevant experience. If that is the reason for the inequality, then it is 'material' and justified.

In equal value cases, differences are justified if there is a 'material factor' – a term which has not been defined but which in the view of many, including myself, means that we are still out of step with EEC requirements. If, for instance, a 'material factor' defence would allow the employer to take into account market availability, the track back to the European Court of Justice is clear.

Suppose that you advertise a particular job in your office which was done by two women, one of whom has left. In order to fill the job, you appoint a man who is only prepared to come for a higher rate of pay than you are giving to the woman doing that job. The state of the market is not a 'material difference' – but it is a 'material factor' which would justify the apparent discrimination of paying a man more than a woman for doing the same job, so it may be lawful under our Regulations, but it is contrary to the Treaty of Rome. One day soon we shall see. There will be a test case. May it not be yours!

Propelled by the decision in Julie Hayward's case and encouraged by the lack of precedent, equal pay claims will soon multiply – in tribunals and courts, but more often settled outside them. If you run into actual or potential trouble for yourselves or for your clients, take expert advice – at best and at its least expensive from the Equal Opportunities Commission, Overseas House, Quay Street, Manchester M3 3HN (tel: 061–833 9244). With good luck and with good advice, you and yours may avoid trouble in this new and crucial area of equal opportunity law and practice.

44 Time off – including time off for Trade Union and Public Duties

Adlai Stevenson once remarked: 'The worst sort of thief is the man who steals my time – I can never get it back.' You can never get back the time which your employee spends on public or trade union duties – but the Employment Protection (Consolidation) Act recognizes that, where reasonably practicable, the employee should not have to steal that time in order to serve the interests of good industrial or public relations. Whether you like it or not – and many employers already accept the inevitable, with excellent grace – employees may often be entitled to time off in working hours.

First, public duties.

'An employer shall permit an employee of his who is a Justice of the Peace, a member of the local authority, a member of a statutory tribunal, a member of (in England and Wales) a regional health authority or area health authority (or, in Scotland, health board)', or a manager of a local education authority, educational establishment (or, in Scotland, a school or college council or the governing body of the central institution or a college of education), or a member of a water authority or river purification board – to take time off during the employee's working hours. The object of the time off? 'The performance of any of the duties of his office or, as the case may be, his duties as such a member.'

The duties referred to are:

'a Attendance at a meeting of the body or any of its committees or sub-committees; or
b The doing of any other thing approved by the body, or anything of a class so approved, for the purpose of the discharge of the functions of the body or for any of its committees or sub-committees.'

How much time must an employee be permitted to take off and on what occasions and subject to what conditions?

The answer depends in each case upon what is 'reasonable in all the circumstances'. Special regard, says the Act, must be had to the following:

'a How much time off is required for the performance of the duties of the office or as a member of the body in question, and how much time off is required for the performance of the particular duty;
b How much time off has the employee already been permitted, either for public duties or for trade union work (see later); and
c The circumstances of the employer's business and the effect of the employee's absence on the running of that business.'

For the larger firm with many employees, the absence of one man or woman for an occasional public duty will go almost unnoticed. Remove the same employee for the same time from a small outfit and it may grind to a temporary halt. Again, the employee must not submit unreasonable demands for time off, while the employer must be reasonable in acceding to sensible requests.

Of course, the list of public duties is limited, and the Employment Secretary may add to it. And although jury duty is not included, it does not need to be – you cannot refuse to permit your employees to sit on juries. They may, though, ask for their jury duty to be postponed if it would create difficulties for the business for them to be away, and courts do try to oblige in cases of that sort.

Next, if any of your employees are officials of independent trade unions recognized by the company or firm for the purposes of collective bargaining, they are entitled to time off – during working hours – for two purposes:

1 To carry out official duties 'concerned with industrial relations between the employer and any associated employer and their employees' or
2 To undergo 'training in aspects of industrial relations relevant to the carrying out of those duties.'

Again, the amount of time off which must be allowed will be that which is reasonable in all the circumstances – and in considering reasonableness, regard will be had to any current Code of Practice issued by the Advisory, Conciliation and Arbitration Service.

Safety representatives appointed by a recognized trade union also have rights to paid time off to carry out their duties or undergo appropriate training.

How much time off? ACAS and the Health and Safety Commission have both published Codes of Practice on this. Their main advice: negotiate arrangements and procedures with the union *in advance*.

A trade union official given time off for industrial relations purposes (as opposed, for example, to engaging in general organization for the union) will be entitled to the normal remuneration. But the law will not require you to pay employees who take time off for public duties.

In addition all members of recognized trade unions are entitled to be given time off – but not pay – to take part in trade union activities, such as going to conferences.

Next: 'An employee who is given notice of dimissal by reason of redundancy shall ... be entitled before the expiration of his notice to be allowed by his employer reasonable time off during his working hours in order to look for new employment or to make arrangements for training for future employment.'

Once more, the employee is only entitled to time off as and when it is 'reasonable' to take it.

What happens, then, if employees do not get the time off to which they consider that they are reasonably entitled – for trade union or public duties or to replace the job which is about to disappear? As usual nowadays, they may complain to an industrial tribunal. Where reasonably practicable, the employee (again, as usual) has three months from the date when the complaint arose within which to bring it to the notice of the tribunal.

In the case of time off for public or trade union duties, the tribunal may award a successful claimant such compensation as it considers 'just and equitable in all the circumstances, having regard to the employer's default in failing to permit time off to be taken by the employee and to any loss sustained by the employee which is attributable to the matters complained of'. In addition, if the employer had failed to pay the employee the whole or part of any amount required to be paid as remuneration, if he or she properly took time off for trade union duties, then the tribunal may order the employer to pay the employee the amount which is due.

A redundant employee who is not given time off to hunt or make arrangements for training for other work may be awarded up to two-fifths of a normal week's pay.

Finally: pregnant employees must be given reasonable (paid) time off for ante-natal care.

If yours is a company or firm which already gives reasonable time off to employees for public or trade union duties or to search for other work when made redundant, these rules will not affect you. But if you are an outfit which is mean in any or all of these respects, you should note carefully the requirements set out above.

45 Employees' Rights in an Insolvency

Until the Employment Protection Act anyone employed by a business which went bust was in deep trouble. They would receive their redundancy pay – all of it – from public funds. If there was a little money in the kitty, then they had certain, pathetic, preferential rights. But if the cupboard was bare, they would get no crumbs. The Employment Protection Act changed this intolerable position by increasing preferential rights to such monies as are available and by enabling any balance unpaid to come from the (suitably buttressed) Redundancy Fund. Buttressed, of course, by additional payments made by solvent employers.

Preferential treatment in the winding up of a company or firm is now given to guarantee payments; remuneration on suspension on medical grounds – due to the employer's failure to comply with the rules; maternity pay; payments for time off for trade union or public duties; or remuneration under a protective award (where there is no sufficient warning of or consultation about proposed redundancy).

All those amounts are recoverable by the employee from the Redundancy Fund, if the Secretary of State for Employment is satisfied not only that the employer is insolvent but that the money is not available. In addition, the following debts will also be payable from the Redundancy Fund:

1. Arrears of pay for up to eight weeks.*
2. Pay in lieu of notice.*
3. Holiday pay for up to six weeks.*
4. Basic award of compensation for unfair dismissal (but not any compensatory or additional award).* And

---

* Up to a maximum of £158 per week (from April 1987).

5 Reasonable reimbursement for the whole or any part of a fee or premium paid by an apprentice or articled clerk.

In general, then, all preferential debts may (if necessary) be recovered from the Redundancy Fund; but not all money recoverable from that fund, eg pay in lieu, holiday pay or basic award of compensation for unfair dismissal, is preferential debts.

46 Redundancy Rights

The Redundancy Payments Act 1965 took some of the sting out of being industrially unwanted. But no one with less than two years service had (or has) any right to redundancy pay; that pay is itself on a sliding scale and only the long service employees get big money (maximum today: £4,740 and until the Employment Protection Act no employer was bound to give any prior warning of redundancy to any employee. To this latter inequity the Employment Protection Act turned its attention.

In a well-known Leicester factory the management discussed a rise in pay with workers' representatives on the Thursday. They called in the Receiver on the Friday. Eighteen hundred men were put out of work with no warning.

The directors of a northern works knew that they would shortly have to close down an entire department. Hoping, perhaps, that something would turn up, they said nothing to anyone. Three hundred men were left stranded, without notice – and, of course, with no opportunity to find alternative work.

To meet these regrettably typical cases, the Act provides that in all large-scale redundancies where there are no 'special circumstances' the employers must inform the Secretary of State and (where appropriate) trade union representatives. Failure to do so will lead to the making of a very expensive 'protective award'. The redundant employees will be entitled (in broad terms) to be paid by the employers the same money that they would have received for the required period of warning – in addition, of course, to their redundancy pay.

An employer who proposes to dismiss as redundant an employee who belongs to a 'recognized trade union' – or even a non-unionist who works in the group for which the union is recognized – is bound under the Act to consult representatives of that union about the dismissal. The trade union representatives are officials or other persons 'authorized to carry on collective bargaining with the employer in question by their trade union'.

So where the union is both independent and recognized for bargaining purposes, a representative must be 'consulted' – not merely to give its members the opportunity to look for other work but (hopefully) so that the consultations may provide suggestions from the workers' side which may help to keep the jobs alive.

Employers must consult 'at the earliest opportunity'. In any event, the Act lays down minimum consultation as follows:

1 Where the employer is proposing to dismiss as redundant a hundred or more employees at one establishment, within a period of 90 days or less, then at least 90 days before the first of those dismissals takes effect. Or
2 Where the employer is proposing to dismiss as redundant ten or more employees at one establishment, within a period of 30 days or less, then at least 30 days before the first of those dismissals takes effect.

There is no minimum period for fewer than ten redundancies but the general rule still applies even if only *one* person is expected to have to go.

The 'consultation' required involves disclosure in writing to the trade union representatives concerned of the following:

1 The reasons for the employer's proposals.
2 The numbers and descriptions of employees whom it is proposed to dismiss as redundant.
3 The total number of employees of any such description employed by the employer at the establishment in question.
4 The proposed method of selecting the employees who may be dismissed.
5 The proposed method of carrying out the dismissals, with due regard to any agreed procedure, including the period over which the dismissals are to take effect.

Delivery of the information must be by post to the address notified by the trade union to the employer or else to the head or main office of the union.

If there are 'special circumstances which render it not reasonably practicable for the employer to comply' with any of the above requirements, then the employer shall 'take all such steps towards compliance with that requirement as are reasonably practicable in those circumstances'.

A similar duty is imposed on all employers intending to dismiss the same number of employees at any one establishment to give the same period of notice, in writing, to the Secretary of State. And where there is a recognized, independent trade union representing the workers then the employer must also give a copy of the notice to representatives of that union.

A trade union that does not receive proper notice may complain to an industrial tribunal. If the employer's defence is that there were 'special circumstances' which rendered it 'not reasonably practicable for him to comply' with the rules, then the burden of proving that he comes within the exemption rests on him. And he must also prove positively that 'he took all such steps towards compliance with the requirement as were reasonably practicable in the circumstances'.

If a tribunal finds a union's complaint to have been well founded, then it will make a declaration to that effect and 'may also make a protective award'. A protective award, in effect, is an order that the employer shall pay remuneration to the employees in respect of whom notice should have been given, for a 'protected period'. This is a period beginning with the date on which the first of the dismissals to which the complaint relates takes effect or the date of the award, whichever is the earlier – and ending on such date 'as the tribunal shall determine to be just and equitable in all the circumstances, having regard to the seriousness of the employer's default'.

Maximum protective awards: where 90 days' notice should have been given – 90 days' pay; where 30 days' notice should have been given – 30 days; and in any other case – 28 days.

Note the last period. Consultation is required not only in the case of large scale dismissals but in every case 'at the earliest opportunity'. The specified periods apply 'in any event' – and they are also minimum and not maximum periods. Where it is possible to give more notice, then the unfortunate employee must have longer notice of the industrial Sword of Damocles.

The rate of remuneration payable to any employee under a 'protective award' will be 'a week's pay for each week of the protected period' – or proportionately for periods of less than a week. Employees will get the same normal pay as they would have received during that period. If employees consider that they have not received proper payment under the protective award, then they may complain to an industrial tribunal which may order the employer to pay the appropriate sum.

It follows that redundancies must be planned and notified as far in advance as possible. Failure to do so where there is no recognized trade union and which results in failure to notify the Secretary of State may lead to a comparatively small fine (up to £400), and/or the loss of up to ¹/₁₀th of the redundancy rebate (now only relevant if you employed fewer than 10 employees to start with – for all other employers redundancy rebates were abolished by the Wages Act 1986). Failure to notify the appropriate union may cost a small fortune – the employer will have to produce not merely the redundancy payment. He may also have to pay employees their normal remuneration – with no upper limit – and up to a maximum in some cases of 90 days.

Naturally, if the employer is insolvent, the various penalties will become irrelevant. It is businesses that stay alive which will suffer. Protective awards join the category of 'preferential debts', where the employer is insolvent; if there is insufficient cash in the (extinct) employer's kitty to pay the award even though it has been given preference, the entire award will be produced by the Redundancy Payments Fund.

So if redundancies are in the offing, you should anticipate them as far ahead as reasonably possible – and give notice accordingly. Undue delay may now prove more painful for you than for your dismissed employees.

Part Four
Health, Safety and Pollution

47   Duties to Employees

Every year over 400 lives are lost and hundreds of thousands of people are injured in industrial accidents. The object of the Health and Safety at Work Act is to combat this carnage. The industrial hazards that will (everyone hopes) be avoided by employees are matched by the hideous consequences that may flow from the Act for employers – including board members – who either do not know or who ignore the law.

Section 37 'Where an offence ... committed by a body corporate is proved to have been committed with the *consent* or *connivance* of, or to have been attributable to any *neglect* on the part of, any *director, manager, secretary* or other similar officer ... or a person who is purporting to act in any such capacity, he as well as the body corporate shall be guilty of that offence and shall be liable to be proceeded against and punished accordingly.'

So the company may be prosecuted – and if convicted on indictment (by a jury) may be fined an unlimited sum. The guilty executive may not only be fined an unlimited sum but also (in some cases) imprisoned for up to two years.

The main effect of the Act is to transfer the civil law on industrial injuries into the realm of crime. You can insure against your civil liability to injured employees, but no insurer will stand in your place in the dock, or vegetate on your behalf in your prison cell.

Section 2 creates the main general duties. Every employer must 'ensure, as far as is reasonably practicable, the health, safety and welfare at work of all his employees'. At civil law, the employer must not submit employees to unnecessary risk. In criminal law, he or she may be prosecuted if they do not take 'all reasonably practicable steps' to look after their employees at work.

To make sure that there is no doubt as to the breadth of the employer's duty, the Act spells it out. Among the matters to which the duty extends are:

> 'The provision and maintenance of *plant* and *systems of work* that are, so far as is reasonably practicable, safe and without risk to health ... Arrangements for ensuring, so far as is reasonably practicable,

safety and absence of risks to health in connection with the *use, handling, storage* and *transport* of articles and substances ...

The provision of such *instruction, training* and *supervision* as is necessary to ensure so far as is reasonably practicable, the health and safety at work of his employees ...

The maintenance of any *place of work* in a condition which is safe and without risk to health ...

The provision and maintenance of a *working environment* that is not only so far as is reasonably practicable, safe and without risk to health, but also 'adequate as regards facilities and arrangements for their *welfare* at work.'

Note that last phrase. If you do not take reasonable steps to provide adequate facilities for your employees' welfare at work, you may be convicted of a criminal offence, and (in theory at least) severely punished.

Nor must you keep your duty secret. You must prepare and, when necessary, revise 'a written statement of your general policy with regard to the health and safety at work of your employees and the organization and arrangements for the time being in force for the carrying out of that policy' – and you must bring that statement and any revision to the notice of all your employees.

Regulations have been made to provide for the appointment of representatives by 'recognized trade unions' to represent employees in consultations with employers. It is now every employer's duty to consult such representatives 'with a view to the making and maintenance of arrangements which will enable him and his employees to cooperate effectively in promoting and developing measures to ensure the health and safety at work of the employees and in checking the effectiveness of such measures'.

The protection of the Act goes beyond employees. 'It shall be the duty of every employer', says Section 3, 'to conduct his undertaking in such a way as to ensure, so far as is reasonably practicable, that *persons not in his employment* who may be affected thereby are not thereby exposed to risks to their health or safety'.

Suppose that you create noise, vibration, smoke or dust from your factory. Your neighbours are affected? There is a risk to their health? Then you are liable to be prosecuted – along with your company. (For duties to visitors, see Chapter 49.)

Non-domestic premises are covered. Where you have a place of work used by people not employed by you or used as a place where people not in your employment 'may use any plant or substance provided for their use there', then you must take all due care for their health and safety.

Launderettes are covered. So (for example) are car parks, social and sporting clubs, sites and other premises which you provide but others use. You are required by law to keep your visitors to your premises safe, on pain of potential prison.

Now for real trouble: 'It shall be the duty of any person who *designs, manufactures, imports* or *supplies*' any article or substance 'for use at work' to take all reasonably practicable steps to ensure that the article or substance is safe. You must carry out any necessary testing, research or examination. If you do not 'eliminate or minimize' risks, so far as you can, you may be prosecuted.

A manufacturer, designer or importer owes a duty of care at common law not to cause injury, loss or damage to 'the ultimate consumer' of the product. But that is a duty enforceable only by bringing a claim for damages in a civil court. These duties may also be banged home by the criminal courts under the Health and Safety at Work Act.

One way of discharging the duty is for the designer, manufacturer, importer or supplier of an article (as opposed to a substance) to obtain a written undertaking from the immediate supplier that the supplier has taken steps sufficient to ensure that the article will be safe. This part of the Act has been considerably strengthened by the Consumer Protection Act, 1987 (see Chapter 50).

Happily, others must still take care for themselves and for the safety of others. Every employee must avoid negligent acts liable to harm the health or safety of him or herself or of others. And they must 'cooperate ... so far as is necessary' to see that the new rules are complied with.

You may be entitled to dismiss an employee who refuses to use safety clothing or equipment. If one is injured, you may prove contributory negligence – alleging that the employee's own stupidity was the whole or partial cause of their own misfortune. If you have used sufficient 'publicity, propaganda and persuasion' to induce employees to make use of the clothing or equipment provided, then you should be in the clear.

Those are some of the main rules laid down by the Act. Other hideous possibilities lie lurking in the powers given by the Act to the government of the day. These come into two categories: regulations and Codes of Practice.

The power to make health and safety regulations is almost unlimited. These may cover almost any area of industrial or commercial life where there are any worries about the health and welfare of workers. Without Parliament having the chance to amend these rules, they will create new crimes with major penalties.

When an Act goes through Parliament, it may be amended – and usually is. MPs may accept one part and reject another. The public has reasonable protection against parliamentary mistakes.

Not so with regulations. Delegated legislation is a potential menace of the first order. Parliament may consider the regulations; it may have the opportunity to reject them; but it will have no power to amend. Instead, Parliament has created a 'comprehensive and integrated system of law', with new powers of delegated legislation attached to it.

A 'Health and Safety Commission' and 'Executive' have been created. The job of the Commission includes the duty to 'assist and encourage' ... to make 'such arrangements as it considers appropriate' for the carrying out of research and for the provision of training and information ... to institute enquiries into accidents ... and to keep all interested parties properly informed as to the law – and, above all, to submit to the government of the day 'such proposals as it considers appropriate for the making ... of regulations.'

You may be prosecuted, fined or imprisoned even if no accident takes place. But if your business is afflicted by a disaster, you may expect the new Commission to descend upon you and to carry out enquiries. The powers of prosecution, though, rest with the new Executive, through the factory inspectors and, generally, via legal authorities.

The Commission issues 'Codes of Practice'. Like the Highway Code and the Code of Industrial Practice, the Health and Safety Codes have powerful persuasive force. You cannot be either prosecuted or sued for breach of the Highway Code – but any breach may be quoted in evidence against you in a civil or criminal action. In a criminal action, however, failure to comply with a provision of a Code of Practice raises a presumption that the relevant safety requirement has been contravened. Such a presumption can only be displaced by proof that the safety requirement has been met in some other way.

It is the duty of the Executive to make 'adequate arrangements for enforcement'. Normally, the local authorities have the delegated delight of keeping you in line with the new regulations. Intention? To establish an integrated inspectorate. In the past, a machine or system may have been approved as safe in one part of the country and proscribed in another. Now there should be one standard for all.

Happily, it is unlikely that the offender will be clobbered by the law without due warning. An inspector comes onto your premises and decides that some arrangement is unsafe or some facility inadequate? Then he will probably serve an 'Improvement Notice', requiring you to put matters right within the period specified.

Alternatively, if the inspector considers that the activity concerned involves a 'risk of serious personal injury', he may serve a 'Prohibition

Notice', requiring the activity to be discontinued forthwith. Only if one of these notices is flouted will the offender be likely to find himself – personally and/or his company – literally as well as metaphorically in the dock.

General rules apply, then, to all employers – as well as to manufacturers, designers, importers, suppliers – and those who erect or who install machinery or equipment. But the Act also extends the scope and coverage of building regulations. If construction comes within the activities of your company, you should take special advice on its arrangements. Equally, if you provide materials for building, prepare for controls under the Act.

Where you can show that an offence is 'due to the act or default of some other person', you may wriggle off the legal hook and leave that 'other person' dangling. Thanks to a peculiarly unfortunate House of Lords decision in the case of *Tesco* v. *Nattrass*, an 'other person' may be a member of your own staff. In other words, if you can show that you set up a proper system but someone whom you employ failed to carry that system into full effect, then they may take the blame and you and your company will escape. Details in Chapter 52.

The present statutory rules remain in force. The Factories Act and the Offices, Shops and Railway Premises Act – and the regulations made under them – have lost none of their force. But under the 1974 Act they are supplemented by a mighty edifice of almost unlimited extent. And while it is splendid to be provided with defences, so that you may be acquitted once you are charged, it is infinitely better not to be charged at all.

The Act specifically stated that it was not intended to change the civil law. Whatever its intentions, the changes are mighty. If one of your employees is injured due to a breach of your duties under (say) the Factories Act, he or she will claim damages for breach of statutory duty. Although the general statutory duties imposed by the Health and Safety at Work Act do not themselves give rise to a claim for damages if they are breached, an action for damages does lie in respect of a breach of health and safety regulations. Where under the terms of any regulations a defence such as due diligence is available in a criminal prosecution for breach of regulations, it does not afford a defence in civil proceedings unless this is expressly provided by the regulations.

48 Your Duty to Non-employees

The case of *Regina* v. *Swan Hunter Shipbuilders Ltd*, decided by the Court of Appeal, is the most important in the world of health and safety for many a year. In brief, it established finally and with clarity that employers may be successfully prosecuted under both Sections 2 and 3 of the 1974 Act if they do not give the same necessary instructions and training to other people's affected employees as they do to their own.

Section 2 of the Act requires employers to take such steps as are reasonably practicable to protect their own employees. Section 2 (2)(a) of the Act requires an employer to provide such information and instruction as is necessary 'to ensure, so far as is reasonably practicable, the health and safety of employees'. By Section 2 (2)(b), their duty includes 'the provision and maintenance of plant and systems of work that are, so far as is reasonably practicable, safe and without risk to health'; and by Section 2 (2)(c) 'the provision of such information, instruction, training and supervision as is necessary to ensure, so far as is reasonably practicable, the health and safety at work of his employees'.

Section 3 of the Act is aimed at other people's employees. An employer must take such steps as are reasonably practicable to ensure so far as is reasonably practicable 'that persons not in his employment who may be affected thereby are not thereby exposed to risks to their health or safety'. That section covers contractors, subcontractors, visitors, neighbours and the general public.

Swan Hunter were building HMS *Glasgow* in their yard. A fire broke out, so intense that 8 men were killed. The vessel was badly ventilated and had become oxygen-enriched; oxygen had escaped from the hose left on the deck by an employee of the firm of subcontractors; but it was Swan Hunter's men who died. Swan Hunter were prosecuted.

Swan Hunter had compiled practical rules for the safety of users of oxygen equipment and had published them in a booklet distributed to their own employees. Unhappily, the subcontractor's employees were only given the book on request. Were Swan Hunter in breach of their statutory duties in not supplying to the subcontractor's employees the same instruction as they did to their own, so as to ensure the safety of all workers on the vessel?

Unanimously the Court of Appeal held that Section 2 of the Act requires an employer to provide a safe system of work for the benefit of his own employees. If that involves the provision of information and instruction as to potential dangers to people other than his own employees, then he is indeed under a duty to provide such information and instruction. His protection lies in the words 'so far as is reasonably practicable' which appear in all the relevant provisions.

Swan Hunter had failed to provide 'information and instruction' to the subcontractor's employees which would have avoided the catastrophe. So they were at fault and in breach of the law.

Nor do these rules (said the court) in any way diminish the duty under Section 3. The words of that section 'are wide enough to include the giving of information and instruction to employees other than one's own employees'. So the shipbuilders were doubly guilty.

What, then, are the practical results of this decision?

If you are the employer of people who work outside your own premises, then you owe a duty to them under Section 2 – and, of course, to other people's employees under Section 3. The further your employees are from your supervision, the better the instruction and training which you should give them. The Swan Hunter decision has in no way reduced your responsibilities. But it has increased the protection of your employees.

Now suppose that you have other people's employees on your premises. It is no longer enough (if it ever was) to check them in at the gates and perhaps to hand them a scrappy piece of paper outlining general areas of danger. If there are specific problems which affect their safety when on your premises – or which could make their work a particular hazard to your employees as well as to themselves – then it is a criminal offence not to instruct and to train them accordingly.

Indeed, if you do give special instruction and training to your employees regarding specific dangers, you are now bound to provide precisely the same to the employees of contractors or subcontractors on your premises. The fact that you do give specific instruction or training to your people and do not do so to other people's employees who could be harmed or cause harm as a result will make it almost impossible for you to avoid a conviction under the 1974 Act.

The prosecution in Swan Hunter's case, of course, was brought after disaster. But the Inspector is likely to pounce if he can in advance of trouble. He may serve an Improvement or a Prohibition Notice on you – or prosecute. So why wait? Now is the time to overhaul your system and to see that your safety instruction and training are directed not only to your own employees but also to those of your contractors and subcontractors.

49 Visitors – and Trespassers

Section 2 of the Health and Safety at Work Act imposes responsibilities on *employers* for the health and safety of their *employees* at work. Whether those employees are at work in your plant, office or workshop; travelling in their cars or yours, but about your business; or working for you on someone else's premises – you must take such steps as are 'reasonably practicable' to keep them safe and well.

Employees on what lawyers charmingly call 'an independent frolic' are unprotected. They are not then 'at work' – even if they happen to be on your premises.

Conversely, the Act defines premises with remarkable width. The word includes not only your buildings and your site but also (*inter alia*) your vehicles. Provided that your employee is doing your work (even in an improper, unauthorized or forbidden way), you must do what is 'reasonably practicable' to look after him or her.

Naturally, the further your employees wander from your supervision, the less 'reasonably practicable' it is likely to be for you to look after them. In general, though, the less the supervision the greater the training; the greater the responsibility shouldered by the employees the more careful the employer must be in selecting them for the work.

Section 3 is brief. Its major clause reads: 'It shall be the duty of every employer to conduct his undertaking in such a way as to ensure, so far as is reasonably practicable, that persons not in his employment who may be affected thereby are not thereby exposed to risks to the health or safety'. Your undertaking is your business – whether you are an industrialist, a trader or a professional advisor. You are now required by the criminal law to take such steps as are 'reasonably practicable' to protect not merely those who you employ but others who are affected by your business or profession.

Take, first, those who visit your premises in what the Occupiers' Liability Act describes as 'the exercise of their calling'. The contractor and the subcontractor; the insulator and the window cleaner; the erector and the installer ... the architect, surveyor or doctor ... the representative coming to sell or the buyer to purchase. All visit in the course of their jobs.

The civil law has long required that you comply with a 'common duty of care' to all of them. You must take such care as is reasonable in all the circumstances for their safety. And the civil law expects that these experts will take reasonable steps to guard themselves and their employees against risks 'ordinarily incidental to their calling'.

The fact, then, that someone is on your premises to do their job does not free you from your responsibility to take such care as is reasonable for their safety and that of those whom they employ. But they have duties (in civil law, to avoid negligence, and in criminal law to comply with Section 2 of the new Act) to do what they reasonably can for their safety. The master owes a duty to his servants – and the occupier to his visitors.

What about children? The Occupiers' Liability Act 1957 says that you must expect them to take less care of themselves than would adults in similar circumstances. And recent court rulings have made it plain that visitors in general and children in particular may be regarded as lawful guests even when you would consider them to be trespassing. You owe both a legal and a moral duty to those whom you ought reasonably to expect will be on your premises.

In criminal law, now, that duty becomes more pronounced and far more dangerous to flout. You must take care for the safety of all your visitors on pain of potential penalties.

What about trespassers? The Occupiers Liability Act 1984 provides that an occupier of premises owes a duty to a person who is not his visitor to take such care as is reasonable in all the circumstances of the case to see that that person does not suffer injury on the premises. However, that duty is only owed where there is a risk of that person suffering injury on the premises by reason of any danger due to the state of the premises or to things done or omitted to be done on them and:

a the occupier is aware of the danger or has reasonable grounds to believe that it exists;
b the occupier knows or has reasonable grounds to believe that the other is in the vicinity of the danger concerned or that he may come into the vicinity of the danger; and
c the risk is one against which, in all the circumstances of the case, the occupier may reasonably be expected to offer that person some protection.

It can be seen therefore that an occupier owes only a very limited duty to trespassers.

How, then, should you cope in practice with the contractor or sub-contractor who erects an unsafe scaffold, leaves wiring, tools or boxes lying around or behaves in some other way which you regard as a danger – either to themselves or to your employees?

No longer can you afford to turn a blind eye and hope for the best. If you observe the danger and do nothing about it, then you may be 'consenting' to its continuation. Any active participation in the misdeed is 'connivance'. Any failure to take proper steps is 'neglect' – and any director, manager, company secretary – or, indeed, any individual – who consents to, connives at or neglects to cope with a hazard is liable not only to the same indeterminate fine as the company which employs them – but (as an individual, however mighty) to a maximum of two years' imprisonment.

So complain about the hazard to the visitors; remonstrate with the boss; and if special tact is required, then telephone and speak to someone at the top of the visiting outfit. Refer to the duties under the Act; whisper a warning that the factory inspector is expected at any moment – and you are almost certain to get both results and thanks, speedily and in a way which should remove the hazard to the benefit of all at risk.

Today, then, each of us is his brother's keeper – at least in the eyes of the criminal law on health and safety at work.

50 Duties to Customers and Clients

Section 6 of the Health and Safety at Work Act 1974 imposes a criminal liability on 'designers, manufacturers, importers and suppliers' (broadly) where they have failed to take such steps as are reasonably practicable to ensure the safety of articles or substances supplied for use at work.

In practice, the Section has proved unenforcable. Clause 36 Schedule 3 of the Consumer Protection Act is designed to put that matter right. The object: To ensure that designers, manufacturers, importers and suppliers 'exercise reasonable foresight in product design and construction'.

The Act extends the range of activities to which the duty applies. And other amendments include power to prohibit immediately the supply of products likely to cause serious personal injury.

Remembering that the Health and Safety at Work etc. Act is a criminal statute, industry must take note. The duty to comply extends to all 'directors, managers and company secretaries' with whose 'consent or connivance' or as a result of whose 'neglect' the hazard or breach occurred.

Section 6 is amended by the Consumer Protection Act to read: 'It shall be the duty of any person who designs, manufactures, imports or supplies any article for use at work ... to ensure, so far as is reasonably practicable, that the article is so designed and constructed that it will be safe and without risk to health at all times when it is being set, used, cleaned or maintained by a person at work.'

Note first that you are only required to do that which is 'reasonably practicable'. There is no absolute duty.

The prosecution must prove the breach. But if you claim that you did whatever was 'reasonably practicable' in the circumstances, then the burden of proof would shift to you. In effect, at that stage you will have to prove your innocence.

Second: The section now refers specifically to machinery or equipment which is being 'set, used, cleaned or maintained'. The equipment – including that used in the manufacture, repair or maintenance of machinery – is as likely to cause death and destruction while being 'set, cleaned or maintained' as it is when in normal use.

Third: Like the rest of the 1974 Act, this Part deals with people 'at work'. Unlike the remainder of the Act, which is primarily designed for the protection of 'consumers', this Part is aimed to increase the health and safety of people 'at work'.

Next: designers, manufacturers, importers and suppliers will have a duty 'to carry out or arrange for the carrying out of such testing and examination as may be necessary for the performance of the duties imposed on them by the preceeding paragraph'. So test and examine – and be prepared to prove if necessary that you have done both.

Next: Those affected must 'take such steps as are necessary to secure that persons supplied' by them 'with the article are provided with adequate *information* about the use for which the article is designed or has been tested, and about any conditions necessary to ensure that it will be safe and without risks to health and at all such times as mentioned ... above' – when it is being 'set, used, cleaned or maintained by a person at work' – and also 'when it is being dismantled or disposed of'.

Information is crucial. And always remember that this duty to instruct and to warn so far as is reasonably practicable may extend beyond your own employees to those of contractors, subcontractors or others working for you or (especially) on your site.

Finally: Those affected must revise information provided, so far as is reasonably practicable, if they later discover that 'anything gives rise to serious risk to health or safety'. Once will not necessarily be enough.

'Manufacturers, importers or suppliers' of any substance – as opposed to an article – have other duties. They must do what is reasonably practicable to see that the substance is safe when being 'used, handled, processed, stored or transported ...'; once again, they must ensure adequate 'testing and examination' during the course of such activities; and they must provide appropriate information, with necessary revisions.

The above used to apply only to 'substances for use at work' – but now the words 'for use at work' are removed. And so even if the substances are (for instance) only for use at home, the rules will still apply.

In the past, then, Section 6 of the Health and Safety at Work etc. Act has proved almost impossible to enforce. The duty was too light and the burden of proving its breach too heavy. But now all that is required is that 'designers, manufacturers, importers and suppliers' did not exercise 'reasonable foresight in product design and construction' and those affected will be in legal trouble.

What is 'reasonable' or 'reasonably practicable' will – in this case as in all others – depend upon all the circumstances. In practice, you will still not have to repeat research or testing done by others; if you can prove that customers have agreed to take on the task of testing for you, you will avoid the need to do so yourself. And if your documentation is in immaculate order, all should be well. Otherwise beware!

51 Your Personal Liabilities

The object of the Health and Safety at Work etc. Act? To save lives and limbs ... to cut down the rate of industrial injuries, physical and mental, caused by over a quarter of a million accidents at work each year.

No one enjoys imposing fines on business enterprises or on their executives or, still less, sending company directors or secretaries, managers or executives, shop stewards or workers to prison. Punishment is a last resort – but if making an example of a few will save the lives of many, then watch out. The Act puts everyone in peril, from the bottom of the industrial or commercial heap to the peak of achievement.

The company itself may be fined but it can scarcely languish behind the wrong sort of bars. That privilege is reserved for those by whom it acts.

Section 37: 'Where an offence committed ... by a body corporate' – that is, a company, statutory or local authority or anyone other than an individual or a firm – 'is proved to have been committed with the consent or connivance of, or to have been attributable to any neglect on the part of' the individuals named, they will be guilty of the offence.

'Consent' ... 'connivance' ... 'neglect' – those are the key words. The individuals? 'Any director, manager, secretary or other similar officer of the body corporate or a person who was purporting to act in any such capacity.' Any executive, then, or anyone who is acting in an executive role.

The company may still be convicted, but the individual will be guilty and 'liable to be proceeded against and punished accordingly'.

'Where the affairs of the body corporate are managed by its members, the preceding ... shall apply in relation to the acts and defaults of a member in connection with his functions of management as if he were a director of the body corporate.' Members of boards, of corporations and of other 'bodies' must watch out.

Naturally, the mere fact that you are a servant or agent, an executive or officer of a company will not of itself make you criminally liable – under this Act or any other – for its wrong doings. You must have played some personal part in the affair.

A company which operated gaming establishments failed to obtain appropriate licences and the chairman was prosecuted and convicted.

The conviction was set aside on appeal. The chairman was non-executive; she had no knowledge of the offence; she had played no part in it – and on the wording of the statute concerned, she was not to be held personally liable merely because she held office.

Under the Act, the prosecution must prove 'consent', 'connivance' or 'neglect'.

To 'consent' means to agree to the commission of the offence. To 'connive' at its commission imports not merely a positive approval but some sort of active role – perhaps a deliberate closing of both eyes.

It is the word 'neglect', though, which provides wider scope. You 'neglect' your duties if you are guilty of some act of omission which has led, directly or indirectly, to the commission of the offence.

If you are a mere non-executive director, then 'neglect' may not bother you. But if the Act is flouted and you should have done something to ensure that it was complied with – either through training, supervision ... personally or by delegation ... then you are one of those at whom the Act points an accusing finger. You may find yourself literally in the dock.

52 Passing the Buck

With maximum penalties as hideous as two years' imprisonment and an unlimited fine, the Health and Safety at Work Act places a new and shining premium on passing the legal buck. 'It weren't me what done it' made a quick (but not unique) shift from classroom to court.

The famous case of *Tesco Supermarkets Limited* v. *Nattrass* pointed the way to the successful blaming of managers for the faults of the company. Potential defences open to those charged with 'applying false trade descriptions' to goods or services are much the same as those provided for people who fail to take reasonably practicable steps to protect the health, safety or welfare of employees at work or of others affected by that work.

Washing powder was displayed at a Tesco supermarket at a reduced price. A pensioner tried to find a packet at the special offer rate but was told that there were none in stock. She bought one at the higher price and reported the company to the Weights and Measures Authorities, who prosecuted under Section 11 of the Trade Descriptions Act, which makes it an offence to offer to supply goods after giving 'by whatever means, any indication likely to be taken as an indication that goods are being offered at a price less than that at which they are in fact being offered'.

There was no dispute on the facts, but Tesco's relied on a special defence. They claimed 'that the commission of the offence was due to a mistake or to reliance on information supplied to them or to the act or default of another person, an accident or some other cause beyond their control' – and maintained that they 'took all reasonable precautions and exercised all due diligence to avoid the commission of such an offence by themselves or any person under their control'.

They proved that they had set up an excellent system and that the offence resulted from the failure of their manager properly to operate that system. He (they said) was 'another person'.

The magistrates held that the manager was not 'another person' but was acting as servant or agent of the company and that therefore the company could not rely on his failure to do his job. The prosecution appealed and the Divisional Court held that the manager was 'another person' but that as a person 'acting in a managerial or supervisory capacity' had failed to exercise due diligence, the company must take the legal responsibility. Tesco's appealed to the House of Lords.

'I find it almost impossible to suppose', said Lord Reid, 'that Parliament or any reasonable body of men would as a matter of policy think it right to make employers criminally liable for the acts of some of their servants but not for those of others. I find it incredible that a draftsman, aware of that intention, would fail to insert any words to express it. . . . I think that it was plainly intended to make a just and reasonable distinction between the employer who is wholly blameless and ought to be acquitted and the employer who is in some way at fault, leaving it to the employer to prove that he is in no way to blame.

What good purpose would be served by making an employer criminally responsible for the misdeeds of some of his servants but not for those of others? A board of directors can delegate part of their functions of management so as to make their delegate an embodiment of the company in the sphere of the delegation. But here the board never delegated any part of their functions. They set up a chain of command through ... supervisors, but they remained in control. The shop managers had to obey their general directions and also to take orders from their supervisors. The acts or omissions of shop managers were not acts of the company itself.'

This remarkable view – that the acts of managers, supervisors or other executives are not in the circumstances 'acts of the company itself' – was supported by all the other law lords. Lord Dilhorne, for instance, said that managers in a large business 'cannot properly be regarded as part of the company's directing mind and will and so can come within the reference to "another person".'

'To treat the duty of an employer to exercise due diligence as unperformed unless due diligence is also exercised by all his servants to whom he has reasonably given proper instructions and on whom he could reasonably rely to carry them out', said Lord Diplock, 'would destroy the power of the defence provided and thwart the clear intention of Parliament.'

There are those who maintain that it could not have been 'the clear intention of Parliament' that managers should be prosecuted in place of their staff. But while there is considerable variation of approach and system as between enforcement authorities in various parts of the country, managers – sometimes together with their companies, sometimes on their own – are feeling the full force of the old law. They must now beware of further miseries.

Section 36 of the Act provides that where 'the commission by any person of an offence under any of the relevant statutory provisions is due to the act or default of some other person, that other person shall be guilty of the offence, and a person may be charged with and convicted of the offence by virtue of this sub-section whether or not proceedings are taken against the first mentioned person'.

Whether or not the company is prosecuted, the executive is at risk. The company which wishes either to preserve its high reputation for looking after the health, safety and welfare of its employees – or which is merely mean and nasty and ready and willing to cast off the blame on individuals, when it can – may certainly rely upon this section which, in combination with the decision in Tesco's case, will provide it with a let out – provided, of course, that the company – like Tesco – had set up a first-class system and that it was the manager who was himself at fault.

So while the company may elbow its way out of trouble by legal buck-passing, the executive may himself be in the front rank of the accused.

53 Inducing Employees to Obey the Safety Rules

It is not enough for business and professional people to supply employees with all necessary plant, materials and appliances, including safety equipment. They must also do their best to ensure that their employees make use of that which they provide.

If employees fail to take the precautions specified by you, then you may still be held liable (in whole or in part) if they are injured as a result. Courts have held that in addition to providing safety guards and equipment, the employer must 'use all reasonable persuasion and propaganda' to induce employees to use that equipment.

Under the Health and Safety at Work Act the employer's civil liability for the safety of employees is turned into a criminal responsibility. Fail to take all steps that are reasonably practicable to ensure that your employees are safe in and about their work and your company or firm may be fined an unlimited sum and/or you and any other director, manager or other officer may be fined and imprisoned for up to two years. It is therefore vital not to be legally guilty of any 'consent, connivance or neglect'.

It follows that – for the safety and welfare both of your company, its employees and yourself – you must 'persuade and propagandize' your employees, whether in shop or works, to take proper care for themselves. They may prefer not to use guards or equipment because these slow down their work and reduce their piece work earnings; because they find the equipment uncomfortable, guards clumsy; or out of laziness. Whatever the reason, here is a suggested procedure, designed to put the maximum, fair pressure on employees to look after their own safety, and so to avoid civil or (eventually) criminal liability which may otherwise fall on the company and/or on you.

1 Check that the system of working and the equipment concerned are really adequate and satisfactory.
2 Train, instruct and supervise the employees in the use of the system and/or equipment.

3 Consult any workers' organization or committee, so that they fully understand the arrangements and approve of them – and seek their help in the enforcement of the rules.
4 Speak personally to employees who are not complying with the rules; emphasize the importance of doing so; and warn them of the consequences of failure.
5 Refer employees to Sections 7 and 8 of the Act which required employees to take proper care of their own safety and not to interfere with safety equipment and the like – and which (theoretically, at least) render them liable to the same penalties for breach as the employing company or managers.
6 If the oral request to reform fails, deliver a written one, preferably by hand. If possible, obtain a signed receipt acknowledging the warning.
7 If danger (actual or potential) is being caused to fellow employees, emphasize the unfairness of the conduct to others.
8 If dangerous behaviour persists, consider dismissal. Factors to be taken into account include:
   a the nature and extent of the danger – to the employee concerned and to others;
   b the effect of dismissal on good industrial relations;
   c the employee's length of service, degree of responsibility and general conduct; and,
   d all the other circumstances of the case which might make the dismissal 'unfair', so as to give the employee a right to compensation.
9 Collate documentation – including records of efforts to persuade employees to take care and discussions with safety representatives, trade unions and/or fellow workers.
10 Deliver a second written warning, stating:
   a if applicable, that further non-compliance will leave you with no alternative other than to dismiss; and in any event,
   b drawing attention to previous warnings and to Health and Safety at Work Act rules; and stating that no responsibility can in any event be accepted by the company in the event of the risk giving rise to injury, loss or damage to employee. (*But note*: This disclaimer may be of help in a civil action but it will not necessarily free the employers from liability.)
11 Consider whether equipment or system of work requires redesigning, either to remove employees' objections or so as to make it impossible for the machine or equipment to be used in the dangerous manner complained of.

You will not necessarily wish to use the above steps in the order given. Adapt them, as best suited to your business and circumstances. But follow the rules and it can hardly be said that you did not take 'reasonable steps' to influence your employee.

In the event of an accident, you would probably avoid liability – the employee's responsibility would be 100 per cent. The employee knew of the dangers; you could prove your case; and the responsibility would be that of the employee.

Equally, if you are prosecuted either under the Factories Act, the Offices, Shops and Railways Premises Act, or under the 1974 Act, your defences would be well prepared.

54 Procedures for Coping with the Health and Safety at Work Act

With the possibility of huge penalties under the Health and Safety at Work Act, all business people must ensure that their procedures are designed to avoid legal battles. The main problems can be broken down into 11 areas of concern. Here is a checklist. Cover each point and – with luck – you should be safe.

1 Contracts of employment

What changes should you make in your employees' contracts of employment or service, so as to take the Act into account? Consider especially whether to include the following:

1. A term that employees shall submit to medical examinations at the request of the management. A refusal to accept this term will cast inevitable suspicion on the person's health.
2. A requirement that the employee shall wear protective clothing and/or make full use of all guards or other equipment provided for personal safety.
3. A requirement that the employee shall co-operate in all safety procedures.

Your contracts may provide that failure to comply with these rules may result in dismissal. Your employees will then at least know where they stand and be unable to allege that you have sprung a legal surprise upon them.

2 Medical examinations

Do you arrange medical examinations (1) for existing employees; or (2) for prospective employees? If so, are you satisfied that these are sufficient? Have you made adequate arrangements for resident or consultant doctors — with job specifications for them to include the requirement that they supervise your compliance with your duties under the Act? They should equip themselves with the rules and make any necessary inspections within your premises or concerning your processes. The Act does not specifically require medical examinations, but the power which the Act gives to make regulations in this regard has already been used to require medical examinations and surveillance of employees working with lead or asbestos. However, even if there are no such regulations covering your line of business, you ought to consider whether by not providing medical testing you are taking all reasonably practicable steps to protect your employees.

3 First aid

Regulations prescribe that an employer shall provide or ensure that there are provided such equipment and facilities as are adequate and appropriate in the circumstances for enabling first aid to be rendered to employees if they are injured or become ill at work. The employer must also provide or ensure that there are provided such number of suitable persons as is adequate and appropriate in the circumstances for rendering first aid to employees. Only a person who has undergone such training or has such qualifications as the Executive may require is 'suitable'.

What if your 'suitable' person is off sick? The regulations provide that for periods of absence which are temporary and are in exceptional circumstances, it is sufficient to appoint someone to take charge of the situation relating to an employee requiring first aid. The employer must inform employees of arrangements made in connection with the provision of first aid, including the location of equipment, facilities and personnel.

4 Employers and safety measures

Do you operate a sufficiently firm and safe procedure to deal with employees who fail or refuse to make use of safety clothing, equipment or procedures? You must plan methods; establish procedures; insist that these be followed with as much firmness as those established in accordance with the Code of Industrial Relations for dismissal purposes; and you must decide whether and when to dismiss employees who refuse to take sufficient care for the safety of themselves and for that of their colleagues.

5 Bomb warnings

The industrial concern which does not suffer from 'bomb scares' is extremely fortunate. You will already have (and should keep well oiled) procedures to deal with fires or fire alarms. Similar procedures are essential for bomb scares.

Consult your local police; if co-operation from authorities is inadequate, either in connection with advice or search, then consider seeking pressures from your trade association or chamber of commerce. Also: Are you satisfied that your security arrangements are sufficient to deter would-be bombers? And have you arranged for your mail to be scanned when letter bomb outrages are in vogue?

6 Notification of accidents

The Reporting of Injuries, Diseases and Dangerous Occurrences Regulations 1985 lay down stringent requirements for the reporting of accidents. The Regulations require the reporting of a wide range of injuries which are specifically defined in the Regulations, but broadly cover most injuries from a simple broken wrist to death of an employee. There is also a catch-all provision that requires the reporting of any injury which results in a person being admitted immediately into hospital for more than 24 hours. Injuries must be reported to the enforcing authority forthwith by the quickest practicable means *and* within 7 days a report must be sent to the enforcing authority on an approved form. Also certain specified diseases arising from specified activities and certain specified dangerous occurrences such as the collapse of buildings, explosions, fires and the failure or overturning of lifting machines must likewise be reported. Further, a record must be kept of any event which is required to be reported.

7 Insurance

Most insurance policies contain exclusion clauses. Check your policies with care to ensure that you will remain insured in spite of the Act. If there are exclusions in respect, for example, of breaches of the Act or damage etc. caused by bombs, then you may have to pay an additional premium in order to exclude the exclusions. If in doubt, consult your insurance brokers or your insurers.

8 Written statements

The Act requires all employers to prepare and, where necessary, to revise written statements of the policy, organization and arrangements they made for the safety and health of their employees. The statements must be brought to the notice of all employees.

Do you provide a statement to all employees separately or as part of your works or organizational rules? If so, then you may be left with the problem of providing detailed instructions for each process or job. Guidance from the Health & Safety Commission requires you to identify the main hazards affecting each job and to state how these hazards may be avoided. Details in Chapter 55.

9 Documentation

Breaches of the Act may prove extremely serious. It is therefore vital for you to prepare your defences in advance. This may best be done by a careful system of documentation.

The object of the documents: to show that your safety, health and welfare arrangements are in accordance with the Act and any default is that of 'some other person' and is not your fault.

Management at every level must be prepared to prove that they prepared and passed on adequate instructions to the next level down. Where sufficiently important, not only should documents be provided but signed copies should be obtained and filed.

Alternatively, documents may go up the line. For instance, you may consider that certain procedures require improvement; that machinery should be adapted or changed; or that more employees are needed for a particular operation, in the interests of safety. If you wish to be able to prove that you passed on this advice to higher authority, then put that advice in writing and keep a copy.

10 Warning the board

Are the company's top executives aware of the legal risks to them personally? Directors, secretaries, managers – all are equally in peril. So everyone from the chairman down should be warned of their responsibility under the Act.

Conversely: has adequate training – including instructions and warnings arising from the Act – reached down to foremen, shop stewards and operatives? Do your procedures for establishing or maintaining communication between various levels of management of safety, health and welfare matters require overhaul?

11 Training

The Act specifically requires adequate training, in the interests of safety and health. Are your current training methods adequate at every level and are you giving sufficient authority to your training, personnel or safety officers or managers?

12 Consultations and committees

Responsibility on safety matters is spread over every level. Consultation should be aimed at ensuring that better and not worse relations are created due to the inevitable shared responsibility.

Regulations have been made, requiring consultation with workers through their 'recognized trade unions'. Have you established sufficient 'consultation'? Are your 'safety watchdogs' properly trained?

Safety committees should be set up. If you already operate a safety committee, are you satisfied that it meets sufficiently often; that there is sufficient involvement of both management and workers in its efforts; and that it has sufficient backing from the board?

13 Supplying information

The Act recognizes that those fully informed on safety and health matters are least likely to suffer injury. Specific information is required under four heads. Do you supply it?

1 Employers are required by Section 2 to provide all necessary information to employees; this will be set out in the written statements and also in instructions concerning specific machinery or equipment.
2 Section 3 requires occupiers to provide adequate information to visitors, neighbours and the general public. Take special care to ensure that visiting children and those who have charge of them (including cleaners and lorry drivers) are fully and carefully warned of any special dangers to children in their care.
3 Section 4 requires occupiers and those in control of non-domestic premises to provide adequate information to those who use equipment provided by them on such premises – which includes not only

launderettes and car parks but also social and sporting clubs provided or operated as part of the employer's undertaking.
4 Section 6 requires many factories, designers, importers and suppliers of plant, components and substances designed or intended for use at work to provide all necessary information to users.

The information should be supplied, wherever necessary, in writing. Is your documentation sufficient?

14 Problems for buyers

Section 6(6) provides that there is no need to repeat testing or examination carried out by others; and buyers supplied with a written undertaking from the seller, are freed from their responsibility. Therefore all buyers and purchasing departments should reconsider their procedures to ensure that they require details of testing and examination carried out by their suppliers; and, further, to require the provision of written undertakings by all suppliers.

Conversely, sellers must be prepared to provide details of testing and of examination, plus written undertakings. Are these available for your customers?

* * *

Most industrial and commercial concerns already operate excellent procedures in some of the above respects. Thanks to the new Act, all these procedures must be complied with by those who wish to avoid the risk of infringing the rules and suffering heavy penalties. As always, Parliament hopes that the existence of the penalties will avoid the necessity for their use. So check the above list with care and get your procedures and documentation into first-class order.

55 Written Statements of Policy, Organization and Arrangements

Commenting in the House of Commons on the Flixborough disaster, Harold Walker MP (the then responsible Minister) said that, had the Act been in force at that time, there would have been no hesitation in bringing prosecutions before Crown Courts ('on indictment') – maximum penalties: 2 years' imprisonment and/or unlimited fines. He also emphasized the responsibility of every level of employer, from boardroom downwards, for ensuring compliance with the rules.

One of the first requirements which every business or professional person should have complied with? The issuing of a written statement of their health and safety policy, organization and arrangements – on their own behalf and, where appropriate, on behalf of their company or firm. The Inspectorate allowed latitude to those who took time so as to produce a statement properly. But the Act provides no time limit – and the sooner your statement is prepared and 'made available' to all your employees, the better. Here, then, are the rules, together with guidance (from the Health and Safety Commission and from experience) on how to apply them.

* * *

Section 2(3) of the Act reads: 'Except in such cases as may be prescribed, it shall be the duty of every employer to prepare – and as often as may be appropriate, to revise – a written statement of his general policy with respect to the health and safety at work of his employees and the organisation and arrangements for the time being in force for carrying out that policy, and to bring the statement and any revision of it to the notice of all his employees'.

Exceptions: undertakings with less than five employees. If you employ four or fewer people in your entire company, firm or undertaking, then you are excluded. The fact that each office may have a small staff is irrelevant. The law looks at the totality.

So you must prepare as soon as possible – and, where necessary, revise – a written statement of your general policy on health and safety.

So far, no difficulty. 'Our company gives paramount importance to the health and safety at work of employees ....' 'The Health and Safety at Work Act enables us to restate our company's policy: that every level of management is expected to give top priority to the health and safety at work of all employees... .' 'The health and safety at work of employees is a major concern of your board.... Our policy is to take all reasonably practicable steps for the protection not only of employees but all others affected by our undertaking....'

In business, as in government, it is far easier to state a policy than to carry it out. The subsection therefore requires the written statement to include details of 'the organisation ... for the time being in force for carrying out that policy'.

What is your safety organization? Do you have one? Is there a safety officer in your outfit – and if so, then is he or she properly trained?

To whom should your employees turn if they consider that a particular practice is unsafe? If yours is a larger outfit, do you have a safety committee? What steps do you take to enable your employees to make their views felt on safety and health matters?

The Health and Safety Commission has issued regulations requiring you to consult with appointed representatives of recognized trade unions. If you deal with trade unions for the purpose of collective bargaining, you must consult them as part of your safety 'organization'. As a result of the Employment Protection Act, you are not forced by law to consult with elected representatives of non-unionized employees.

Every business or professional person who employs five or more people must arrange such 'organization' as best suits their business and as is most likely to produce results. Once your organization is worked out, you can then put it onto paper.

Finally, the subsection requires the written statement to specify the 'arrangements for the time being in force' for carrying out the health and safety policy. This means that the notice must set out the main risks which any particular employer faces and how to deal with them.

The Health and Safety Commission has produced guidance for employers. It says: 'The main hazards should be identified and reference made in a statement to additional rules and regulations which must be observed'.

So set out your safety 'arrangements', briefly and clearly. And refer employees to additional rules – such as 'the dangers of untidy working areas or, of the failure to use guards or to wear protective clothing, the introduction of new machinery or substances; maintenance work, etc.... Procedures should be laid down for accident reporting and for the results of accident analysis to be made available to all management levels and to the Safety Committee.'

It is up to each business or professional person, then, to prepare their own statement – or to get together with colleagues in the same trade or business with similar set-ups and to share ideas. The inspector's first question, on next visiting your outfit, is likely to be: 'Have you prepared your written statement?' If you have not, then you will need a good reason for your failure. You are, after all, breaking the law.

Once your statement is prepared, you must 'make it available' to each individual employee. At best, give every employee a copy. Or maybe each employee will get a copy of the main statement on policy and organization, while details of 'arrangements' are put on a notice board in a prominent position. How you make statements available is a matter for you. That you must do so as a matter of urgency is a specific and extremely important requirement of this vital statute.

56 The Control of Pollution

Parliament steps in where voluntary effort and the civil law have failed to achieve acceptable minimum standards. In the field of pollution, neither public realization of the perils to our environment nor civil remedies sometimes available to those whose environment is threatened or destroyed (nuisance actions, in particular) have been sufficient to induce industrialists to conform.

So there has been a burst of statutory effort designed to clout the polluter into reasonable submission – often on pain of mighty penalties from the criminal law.

Section 5 of the Health and Safety at Work etc. Act 1974 came into force on 1 April 1975. It deals solely with emissions into the atmosphere and, like the rest of the Act, is in addition to and not in substitution for existing legislation. It immensely strengthens the hand of the public health authorities, and is enforceable through the use of 'prohibition notices' (appeal to the Industrial Tribunal by all means – but meanwhile, comply – the appeal does not suspend the operation of the notice) and by 'improvement notice' (appeal carries suspension, pending withdrawal or decision).

Above all: Section 5 may be enforced through the imposition of the usual penalties available under the Act. Any director, manager or company secretary (for instance) through whose neglect or with whose consent or connivance the offence has been committed may receive up to two years' imprisonment and unlimited fine for their efforts – with an unlimited fine available for their employers.

Section 5: 'It shall be the duty of the person having control of any premises of a class prescribed ... to use the best practicable means for preventing the emission into the atmosphere from the premises of noxious or offensive substances and for rendering harmless and inoffensive such substances as may be so emitted.' The prescribed classes of premises are listed in the Health and Safety (Emissions into the Atmosphere) Regulations 1983.

Note, first, that there is no absolute prohibition against polluting the atmosphere. All that is asked is the use of the 'best practicable means'. If it is reasonably practicable to avoid any pollution at all, then pollution must be avoided.

If pollution there must be, then (once again) 'the best practicable means' must be used to 'render harmless and inoffensive' those substances which are so emitted. The Act does not define the words 'reasonable' or 'reasonably practicable'. But Section 40 provides that if there is a contravention of the Act and the accused maintains that he or she did in fact use 'the best practicable means' to avoid that contravention – or that they did what was 'reasonably practicable' to comply – then it shall be for the accused to prove innocence.

The shifting of the burden of proof onto the accused is comparatively rare in criminal law – and should be causing grave concern to the polluters of the air*. Suppose, for instance, that it would be possible greatly to reduce the harmful or offensive effects of the pollution if enough money were available to install machinery or devices – or to alter systems – but that 'in the current economic climate' the 'body corporate' concerned may feel that the cash should not be laid out for the venture.

Is it, then, in those (sadly common) circumstances 'reasonable' not to take means which are available because cash is tight? Could it be said that it is 'practicable' to use 'means' to avoid or cut down pollution, when you do not have the financial means to make any necessary purchase or changes?

The Inspector will decide on whether or not to serve a notice and, if that notice is breached, then to prosecute – or, indeed, whether to institute proceedings at once. And if a prosecution is launched, then it will be for the appropriate court (Magistrates' Court, where trial is to be 'summary' – otherwise a Crown Court) to consider the question of 'reasonableness' along common sense lines. The greater the pollution and/or the smaller the cost of the remedy, the greater the burden on the accused. Conversely: the less harm that is actual or imminent or prospective and the greater the cost of its remedy, the more reasonable it will become not to take otherwise available means.

Note: Section 5(2): 'The reference in sub-section (1) above to the means to be used for the purpose there mentioned includes a reference to the manner in which the plant provided for those purposes is used and to the supervision of any operation involving the emission of the substances to which that sub-section applies.' 'Operation of plant', then, and 'supervision' are specifically covered.

'(3) Any substance or a substance of any description prescribed for the purposes of sub-section (1) above as noxious or offensive shall be a noxious or ... offensive substance for those purposes, whether or not it would be so apart from this sub-section.'

A number of substances have been prescribed as noxious or offensive. These are listed in the Health and Safety (Emissions into the Atmosphere) Regulations.

---

* This rule applies throughout the 1974 Act. He who relies on his having done what was 'reasonable' must prove it.

Finally: '(4) Any reference in this section to a person having control of any premises is a reference to a person having control of the premises in connection with the carrying on by him of a trade, business or other undertaking (whether for profit or not) and any duty imposed on any such person by this section shall extend only to matters within his control.'

Matters under the control of others come outside the section. And so do all domestic premises.

What of other law on pollution?

A large part of the Control of Pollution Act 1974 is now in force. However, there are still some important provisions of this Act which are on the statute book but have not been brought into effect, primarily because of the expense which would be caused to the relevant local authorities upon whom the duty of carrying them into effect would fall.

The Act deals with four principal areas: waste on land; pollution of water; noise; and pollution of the atmosphere.

1 Waste on land

Under the Act unlicensed disposal of controlled waste is prohibited. 'Controlled' waste is defined as household, industrial or commercial waste. Controlled waste must not be deposited on any land unless the land is occupied by a person licensed by the local authority in respect of such deposits on that land. Unlicensed depositing of controlled waste is a criminal offence punishable by six months' imprisonment. It is, however, a defence to a charge under these provisions that the person took care to inform themselves from persons in a position to provide information as to whether the deposit would be illegal and they had no reason to know or suppose that the information was false or misleading and that the deposit would be illegal.

Are your employees guilty of the offence if they deposit the waste illegally on your instructions? No, so long as they neither knew nor had reason to suppose that the deposit was illegal. Employers will only avoid liability if they took all such steps as were reasonably open to them to ensure that the Act was complied with.

What if I have to dump some controlled waste in an emergency? In such a case there will be a defence where it can be shown that the deposit was made in order to avoid danger to the public and you also give particulars of the deposit to the relevant local authority as soon as reasonably practicable.

If controlled waste is deposited illegally, the authority may serve a notice requiring the occupier of the land to remove and/or eliminate or reduce the consequences of the deposit. There is a right of appeal to a magistrates' court against such a notice and the court will quash it if it is satisfied that the occupier neither deposited nor caused nor knowingly permitted the deposit of the waste. Failure to comply with such a notice is an offence and gives the authority the right to do what was required under the notice and charge you for the cost of doing so. In an emergency, where it is necessary for the authority to take immediate action to prevent pollution of water or danger to public health the authority may also charge the cost of doing so to the occupier. In any case the costs incurred by the authority can be recovered from the person responsible for the deposit.

The Secretary of State has power to make regulations for the disposal of deposited waste which is other than controlled waste or for the disposal of controlled waste which is so dangerous or difficult to dispose of that it requires special provisions.

2 The pollution of water

The Act provides that a person commits an offence who causes or knowingly permits –

- *a* any poisonous, noxious or polluting matter to enter any relevant waters; or
- *b* any matter to enter a stream so as to tend to impede the proper flow of the stream in a manner leading or likely to lead to a substantial aggravation of pollution; or
- *c* any solid waste matter to enter a stream or certain restricted waters.

There are a number of exceptions to these provisions, including the situation where a person is licensed or authorized under any enactment to do any of the proscribed acts; or the entry is attributable to an act or omission in accordance with good agricultural practice unless that practice has been specifically prohibited by a notice under the Act; or the act or omission complained of was done in an emergency and particulars were given to the relevant water authority as soon as reasonably practicable.

The punishment of an offence under these provisions is subject to a maximum of two years' imprisonment and/or a fine. Where the offence is a continuing one it is punishable on summary conviction by a fine of up to £50 per day.

The Secretary of State has power to make regulations to prohibit or restrict activities in a particular area if he considers that the activities are likely to result in pollution. He may also make contravention of such regulations a criminal offence.

Where it appears to a water authority that any poisonous, noxious or polluting matter or any solid waste matter is likely to enter or is or was present in any relevant water within its area, the authority may carry out such operations as it considers appropriate to prevent entry or remove or dispose or remedy or mitigate any pollution and may restore the flora and fauna affected by it. The cost of such action necessarily incurred may be recovered from those responsible for the pollution or the risk of it.

In order to prevent pollution to waters within its area, a water authority has power to make bye-laws excluding vessels from its waters unless they are registered with the authority.

3 Noise

Where a local authority is satisfied that noise amounting to a nuisance exists or is likely to occur or recur it must serve a notice:

a requiring abatement of the nuisance or prohibiting or restricting its occurrence or recurrence;

b requiring the execution of works or other steps as may be necessary for the purpose of the notice.

The notice must specify the time within which the requirements are to be complied with.

But your business will have a defence if you can show that the best practicable means have been used to prevent or counteract the effect of the noise. You will also be protected if you are covered by a notice issued by the local authority consenting to the making of the particular noise.

If, in the local authority's opinion, criminal proceedings in respect of the offence created by these provisions are inadequate, it may bring civil proceedings to abate, prohibit or restrict the nuisance, even if the authority has suffered no damage.

A local authority also has power to make regulations in respect of noise on construction sites or from plant or machinery. Another wide power which it has is to create noise abatement zones. Where an area is designated as a noise abatement zone, the local authority measures the level of noise emanating from premises of any class prescribed by the authority and keeps a register of the levels. It must then send a copy of the relevant entry in the register to the owner and the occupier of the premises.

If you receive one of these check it very carefully. You have a right of appeal against the record in the register, but you must act quickly. If no appeal is made within 28 days, the validity or accuracy of the entry in the register may not be questioned in any proceedings under this part of the Act.

Once the level has been recorded in the register, it may not be exceeded without the consent of the local authority. To exceed the level without consent is a criminal offence. A refusal of consent may be appealed to the Secretary of State.

The EEC Directive on Noise must be implemented in the UK by the beginning of 1990. Regulations will have to include provisions on worker protection and provision of information by manufacturers and suppliers of machinery.

4 Pollution of the atmosphere

The Secretary of State, after prescribed consultations, may make regulations for the purpose of limiting or reducing air pollution. Regulations may impose requirements as to the composition and contents of any fuel of a kind used in motor vehicles and may prevent or restrict the production, treatment, distribution, import, sale or use of any such fuel which is for use in the United Kingdom. Enforcement of such regulations is undertaken by the local weights and measures authority.

There is also a provision in the Act for regulations to be made in respect of the sulphur content of oil fuel for engines or furnaces.

You are obliged under the Act, when required to do so by a notice from the local authority, to furnish information concerning the emission of pollutants and other substances into the air from the premises.

Part Five
Contracts and Contractors

57 Have You Made a Contract? – a Checklist

Business and professional people are constantly making contracts. Every agreement to buy or sell anything – goods, equipment or services, including your own – creates a contract, once it becomes binding.

But the crucial question is: how binding is your agreement? Upon the answer depends your right to cancel the deal as opposed to the right of the other party to force you to go on with it. Conversely, you need to know when you can force the other party to comply with his side of the bargain.

The tougher the times, the more vital it becomes to know the answers to these questions. Here, then, is a contractual checklist.

* * *

1 Has anyone made a firm offer or are you still at the stage of 'ifs' and 'provided thats'? The goods on display in the shop window or trade exhibition, or advertised in the paper, are not 'offered'. Offers are invited. Equally, an offer which is conditional upon something or someone else approving is no offer at all – and may be 'accepted' without risk. The acceptance will itself constitute the 'offer'.
2 If there has been an offer, has it been unconditionally accepted? If you receive an offer and reply by sending the 'acceptance' subject to your terms, then if those terms differ substantially from any in the offer, yours is merely 'a counter-offer' and not an 'acceptance' at all. At that stage, you are still negotiating – even if the other party thinks that the deal is sewn up.
3 Has anyone accepted the 'counter-offer', either formally or, more likely, by delivery of the goods or provision of the services? If not, then at any time before action completes the deal, either party (if he knows it) may take advantage of the situation. The buyer may cancel or go elsewhere. The supplier may put up his prices or withdraw the goods or services from the market.
4 Have you agreed on all the main terms? If not, then the contract is

probably 'too vague to be enforceable'. Exception: if you have agreed on the way in which future agreement can be arrived at, thus: 'The price to be agreed or, in the absence of agreement, to be such price as is fixed by the Chairman of the Chamber of Commerce'. Only in the rarest cases will the court decide on major terms. Example: where contractors do 'extras' on your property, with no price agreed in advance. The law then implies a term into the contract that you will pay a 'reasonable price' – that the contractor will be paid on a so called *quantum meruit* basis. The implication of a reasonable charge for services provided has now been placed on a statutory basis by the Supply of Goods and Services Act 1982.

5 Is the contract one which needs to be made in or evidenced by writing, if it is to be effective? These exceptional deals include: Contracts for transfer of interest in land, for insurance or HP or for the transfer of shares; and contracts of guarantee. If it comes within these exceptions then no writing means no deal. Otherwise, the fact that you made your arrangement orally is legally irrelevant.

6 Could you prove that the above main essentials of a contract are all present? Writing, of course, is a great help – most contested cases are eventually decided largely on the documents. But the absence of writing (in all cases other than the above exceptions) does not turn a legally binding contract into a mere 'gentleman's agreement'. In law, if you only have a 'gentleman's agreement' – then you or the other party may break it with impunity.

7 Is there any element of illegality in your deal? Conspiracies (for example) to contravene the tax laws or the Customs and Excise Authorities – for gaming transactions – are void.

8 Have both parties 'capacity to contract'? Minors (aged under 18) can avoid any contracts which are not for 'necessaries' – goods reasonably necessary for them at the time when the deal is done – and that includes all business contracts and contracts of loan. But note: Contracts which are *ultra vires* a company – that is, which go beyond the powers contained in the objects clause in the company's memorandum or articles of association – are enforceable against it if the transaction is one which has been 'decided on by the directors' (see Section 35 of the Companies Act 1985).

9 Can you identify the other contracting party with certainty? Take particular care to avoid dealing with or, later, billing a small or rocky company instead of the (hopefully) completely solvent parent company or outfit with which you believed that you were

doing business. Watch out especially for changes in name or notepaper.
10 Are there any 'post-contractual documents' – like receipts or delivery notes – which seek to add terms or conditions which were not contained in the original arrangement? Initially, these have no effect and can be ignored – they come after the contract. But if either party knows from previous experience that the other side invariably does business only on those terms, then they may become incorporated into future arrangements.
11 If you find that you have a binding contract on your hands and it contains exclusion clauses, you may find that they are ineffective by reason of the Unfair Contract Terms Act 1977. That Act renders void any term which purports to exclude or limit liability for death or personal injury resulting from negligence. It also renders void a wide range of terms limiting or excluding liability arising from the sale or supply of goods to persons dealing as consumers and subjects the same terms to a requirement of reasonableness when dealing with others (in particular persons dealing in the course of trade).
12 If you are liable under the contract, can you pass the buck back to anyone else? Have you retained a 'right over' against your supplier, so as to obtain an indemnity from him?
13 Have you obtained any necessary insurance – to cover you, perhaps, if you must bear the loss if the goods disappear or are damaged in transit?

IF YOU CANNOT ANSWER ANY OF THESE QUESTIONS, THEN THE TIME HAS PROBABLY COME TO SEE YOUR SOLICITOR.

If the answers are not obvious, then they may be extremely complicated. To save the solicitor's time (and hence your money) remember to bring with you all letters, order forms, acceptances or other relevant documents when you see the solicitor and also, if you can, a typed statement, clearly setting out the facts as you remember them – and, preferably, as you would be prepared to prove them.

58 Buyers' Rights – a Checklist

Every business person who buys materials or equipment for their office, shop or factory needs to know how the effect of the old rule *caveat emptor* has been whittled down. It is vital to understand the modern protection provided by a combination of the Sale of Goods Act 1979, the Trade Descriptions Act 1968, the Misrepresentation Act 1967, the Fair Trading Act 1973, the Unfair Contract Terms Act 1977 and the Supply of Goods and Services Act 1982.

1 The Sale of Goods Act 1979

Section 14 of the Sale of Goods Act – which applies to both business and private buyers – requires (in general) that goods supplied shall be (a) of merchantable quality, i.e. as fit for the purpose or purposes for which goods of that kind are commonly bought as it is reasonable to expect having regard to any description applied to them, the price (if relevant) and all other relevant circumstances, and (b) reasonably fit for the purpose supplied.

2 The Unfair Contract Terms Act – excluding the exclusions

A person cannot by reference to any contract term or notice exclude or restrict their liability for death or personal injury caused by negligence. In respect of loss or damage caused by negligence, liability cannot be excluded or restricted except in so far as the term or notice satisfies the requirement of reasonableness.

The Act also gives wide-ranging protection to persons dealing as consumers. Where a consumer deals with a business person on that person's standard terms of business, the business person cannot by reference to any contract term:

- *a* when themselves in breach of contract, exclude or restrict any liability of their own in respect of the breach; or
- *b* claim to be entitled to perform the contract in a way which is substantially different from that expected or to render no performance at all,

except in so far as the contract term satisfies the requirement of reasonableness.

Nor can a consumer be bound by a contractual term to indemnify a person for their liability for negligence except in so far as the term satisfies the requirement of reasonableness.

A manufacturer or distributor of goods cannot exclude or restrict his or her liability for loss or damage caused by their negligence by reference to a guarantee of the goods where the goods are of a type ordinarily supplied for private use or consumption and the loss or damage arises from the goods proving defective while in consumer use. However, this provision does not apply as between the parties to a contract under or in pursuance of which possession or ownership of the goods passed.

Perhaps the most important provision of the Act so far as the business person who retails goods is concerned is Section 6, which prevents exclusion or restriction of liability to anyone in respect of the implied undertakings as to title in the Sale of Goods Act and the Supply of Goods (Implied Terms) Act. The same section also prevents exclusion or restriction of liability to a consumer for breach of the undertakings implied by the Sale of Goods Act as to conformity of goods with description or sample, or as to their quality or fitness for a particular purpose, and in the case of a person dealing otherwise than as a consumer subjects the purported exclusion or restriction to a requirement of reasonableness.

The 'requirement of reasonableness' referred to throughout the Act is that the term shall have been a 'fair and reasonable one to be included having regard to the circumstances which were, or ought reasonably to have been, known to or in the contemplation of the parties when the contract was made'. And a party 'deals as a consumer' if:

a he or she neither makes the contract in the course of business nor holds him or herself out as doing so; and
b the other party does make the contract in the course of business; and
c in the case of a contract for the sale of goods or of hire purchase the goods passing are of a type ordinarily supplied for private use or consumption.

3 Misrepresentations

Thanks to the Misrepresentation Act, anyone who enters into a contract after a false statement of fact has been made to them may avoid the deal and get their money back *or* regard the contract as subsisting and claim damages to compensate them for any loss suffered as a result of the misrepresentation. They need not prove fraud – that is, intention to deceive or 'recklessness'. But the buyer must still beware of 'mere commercial puffs' – statements of opinion which do not bind the maker.

4 The Fair Trading Act

The Director General of Fair Trading has remarkable powers under the Fair Trading Act, all designed to protect 'consumers' against actions on the part of sellers which are 'contrary to the economic interests of consumers in the UK'. An offender may be asked to give a written undertaking not to repeat the wrongful behaviour. If the undertaking is given and then broken, then the offender may be taken to the Restrictive Practices Court which may grant an injunction against him or her – breach of which is a contempt of court. If the undertaking is refused in the first place, the offender may be taken straight to the court.

The Director General also has the power to recommend the making of Statutory Instruments to curb economic practices which are unfair to consumer interests – business and professional people should watch out for action from the Director General – in co-operation with the Consumer Protection Advisory Committee and the government.

5 The Trade Descriptions Acts

The civil law is designed to provide remedies as between citizens – individually or in firms or companies or other bodies. The criminal law sets minimum standards by which all must comply for the benefit of society. The Trade Descriptions Act 1968 makes it a criminal offence to 'apply a false trade description' to goods or services. A description is 'false' if it is misleading. And the culprit may be both fined and ordered to pay compensation to the innocent victim.

The Trade Descriptions Act 1972 requires imported goods to be fully marked. Like its predecessor, it is administered by the Consumer Protection or Weights and Measures authorities.

6 The Supply of Goods and Services Act

This Act has the effect of introducing into the majority of contracts for the transfer or hire of goods which are not already covered by the Sale of Goods Act and the Supply of Goods (Implied Terms) Act the implied conditions of title, conformity with sample and correspondence with description and the implied warranties as to merchantable quality and fitness for a particular purpose. However, the Act does provide that where a right, duty or liability would arise under the contracts covered by the foregoing provisions it may be negatived or varied by express agreement or by the course of dealing between the parties, or by such usage as binds both parties. An express condition or warranty which is inconsistent with a term implied by the Act will also have the effect of negativing the implied term. However, any term purporting to negative or vary a term implied by this Act is made expressly subject to the Unfair Contract Terms Act 1977.

The Supply of Goods and Services Act 1982 also has a very important impact on contracts for the supply of services. Where the supplier is acting in the course of business, there is now a term implied that the service will be carried out with reasonable care and skill. Also, if the time for the service to be carried out or the charge to be made for the service is not fixed by the contract, left to be fixed in a manner agreed by the contract or determined by the course of dealing between the parties, there is an implied term that the service will be carried out in a reasonable time and that a reasonable charge will be made. These provisions may also be negatived or varied by express agreement, by the course of dealing between the parties or by such usage as binds both parties, and an inconsistent term will negative the implied term. Again any term purporting to negative or vary such an implied term would be subject to the 1977 Act.

* * *

So the business buyer must still beware of exclusion clauses. But the law is increasingly designed to protect the 'consumer' against the perils caused by inexperience. Business and professional people who make deals as part of their livelihood are also 'consumers' in their private capacity – and should know the rules for their personal protection, when they are buying for their home or family.

59 Trade-ins and Trade Descriptions

The Appeal Court decision in the case of *Fletcher* v. *Budgen* – in which it was held that the Trade Descriptions Act applies to buyers as it does to sellers – has turned the law on its learned head. Those who sell and at the same time buy in secondhand goods must take great care to tell the truth when they buy as they do when they sell.

First, the facts: Howard Budgen is a car dealer who inspected a vehicle offered to him on a trade in. He convinced the seller that there was no possibility of repairing it; that repairs would not make it safe; and that the only possible course of action was for the car to be written off and scrapped. As a gesture, he paid £2 to the owner.

Shortly afterwards, the owner was staggered to see the car advertised for sale at £136 – complete with MOT certificate. Mr Budgen had carried out repairs costing about £56 which had in fact made the vehicle safe and roadworthy.

Mr Budgen was prosecuted under Section 1(1)(a) of the Trade Descriptions Act, for applying a false trade description to the goods which he was buying.

York Justices found that Mr Budgen's statements about the car were to his knowledge untrue. But they held that there was no case to answer because (they said) the Act 'has no application when the descriptions are applied to goods in the course of their acquisition'. The prosecutor appealed – Mr Budgen neither appeared nor was represented at the hearing.

The Lord Chief Justice delivered the decision of the Appeal Court. He referred to the well known case of *Hall* v. *Wickens Motors (Gloucester) Limited*. There the Court considered the case of the seller who, some weeks after the vehicle had been bought, inspected it and honestly (but incorrectly) certified that the vehicle should not receive an MOT certificate because of a fault in a tyre. He was acquitted because he had not applied the Trade Description 'in a transaction associated with the sale or supply of the goods'.

Section 1(a) of the Act bans the application of any false trade description to goods 'in the course of a trade or business' and in connection 'with the sale or supply of the goods'. Reading the Act as it stands and 'looking at the language used in giving it its natural consequences', had Mr Budgen broken the law?

The Lord Chief Justice admitted that he had previously 'subconsciously thought that the Act only applied to false trade descriptions used by sellers'. He had 'never before been required to think about circumstances in which the public need to apply restrictions to a buyer was very much the same as the public need to apply them to the seller'.

Still, while the judge 'confessed to being surprised at the conclusion to which he had ultimately come', he ruled that the Justices were wrong; the case must be sent back to them with the direction to conclude the hearing; and unless and until Parliament overrules this decision (which is incredibly unlikely), dealers who buy in must not mislead the seller by falsely running down the state or value of the goods.

'Surely,' you say, 'this destroys the whole basis of bargaining?'

It undercuts the basis of dishonest bargaining – but it does not interfere with the honest haggle.

After all, dealers are experts who (as the Act requires) are engaging in transactions which come within the scope of their own business. 'The potential buyer', said the judge, 'was engaged in the trade or business of buying cars', and it is not 'in any sense illogical and is not likely to run counter to any intention that Parliament might have had' to extend the prohibition of falsehood to the buyer.

On the contrary. 'It is perfectly reasonable and logical that when the buyer is the expert and the seller might be the amateur, and the buyer makes an examination of the goods in his capacity as an expert and then proceeds to pronounce on the quality or otherwise, he should be as much liable to be restricted in his language as is a seller who, in the normal course of events, knows all about the goods and has to be restricted in any temptation to make false and misleading statements about them.'

After all, if you are selling in the course of your business, you must not falsely describe your goods or services – whether by word of mouth or otherwise. Equally, if you are buying when conducting your trade or business, why should you be allowed to tell lies? You negotiate a sale, without engaging in falsehood? Then you must do the same when you make a purchase.

This does not mean (as the Lord Chief Justice made clear) that every buyer runs a risk of committing a criminal offence merely because they deprecate or make 'somewhat derogatory remarks' about goods offered to them. 'It would be sad', said the judge, 'if such a situation arose.' But when you remember 'that it is only a buyer conducting a trade or business and therefore in most instances himself an expert who could fall foul of the Act', to hold that a buyer must tell the truth would be 'in accordance with the language of the Act ... and would also make very good sense, in view of the fact that its effect is to restrict those who carry on a trade or business'.

So you must be careful not only when you sell but also when you buy. The expression *caveat emptor* – let the buyer beware – has acquired a new and potentially perilous meaning for all purchasers.

60 Hiring and Leasing

If you hire or lease vehicles or equipment, how far will the law protect you against contractual terms set out in the supplier's documents? Hiring or leasing differs from hire purchase since there is no right to acquire ownership, so the protection which is given to purchasers under a hire purchase agreement does not apply. Further, companies are unable to seek protection from the provisions of the Consumer Credit Act 1974, which apply only to individuals.

However, if you are self-employed or are a partner in a business, you are entitled to protection under the Consumer Credit Act 1974 in respect of your regulated consumer hire agreements. This Act will provide you with a large measure of protection. For instance, the owner of the goods may only terminate the agreement for one of two reasons:

a a repudiatory breach, e.g. a failure (not mere delay) to make payments over such a period that it seems clear that the hirer is not going to keep the agreement;
b a breach stipulated in the agreement as giving the owner a right of termination, e.g. the hirer becoming more than 10 days late in making any payment.

Even when owners are entitled to terminate the agreement, they cannot do so, nor can they recover possession or enforce any security, until they have served a default notice which gives the hirer time to rectify the default and also allows the hirer to apply to the court for an extension of time.

The 1974 Act also gives an individual a right of termination of certain regulated consumer hire agreements. The agreement may not be terminated until it has run for eighteen months and a period of notice must be given which is the lesser of: (i) three months; and (ii) the shortest interval between the due dates of the hirer's payments under the agreement.

Thus if the agreement provides for monthly payments the hirer may terminate it after eighteen months upon the giving of one month's notice. However, certain regulated agreements are excluded from the application of this provision. They are:

a any agreement under which the hirer's payments are to exceed £900 per year;
b certain agreements for the hire of specialized goods required by the hirer for business purposes;

c any agreement where the hirer requires the goods so that they can in turn in the course of business be let out to someone else;
d agreements excluded by the Director General of Fair Trading from the application of this provision.

Where under a regulated consumer hire agreement the owner recovers possession of the goods by reason of the default of the hirer, the court may grant financial relief to the hirer. This relief can take either or both of two forms:

a an order that any payment still due from the hirer shall be reduced by an amount stated by the court;
b an order that the whole or any part of any sum already paid by the hirer shall be repaid.

The purpose of this provision is to enable the court to ensure that when the agreement is terminated, the hirer does not end up having to pay or having paid an amount which is far in excess of the rent which would have been payable for the period for which the agreement actually lasted.

If, however, your business is run through a body corporate and you are not entitled to protection under the Consumer Credit Act, the protection which the law offers to you is much more limited. There are two types of clause which call for particular attention.

The first is the clause, which is extremely common in hiring agreements, by which the owner seeks to protect himself from loss in the event that the agreement is terminated by reason of the hirer's default. This is done by seeking to impose a minimum payment in respect of the hire. However, unless great care has been taken in drafting the clause it may be struck down as a penalty clause. Unless the clause is a genuine pre-estimate of the owner's liquidated damages arising from breach of the agreement and does not operate *in terrorem* (i.e. does not operate so as to force compliance with the terms of the agreement through fear of the dire consequences of this term), then it is open to challenge as a penalty clause.

When a minimum payment clause is being drafted, it must be remembered that although at first sight the owner's loss is the amount of the rental which would have been received under the agreement, this must be reduced in order to take account of the fact that the owner will be receiving accelerated payment under the minimum payment clause.

The second type of clause which calls for specific consideration is that by which the owner seeks to be exempted from liability for defects in the subject-matter of the hire. Such a clause is now covered by the Supply of

Goods and Services Act 1982. Where under a contract for the hire of goods (not being a contract of hire purchase), the owner hires out the goods in the course of business, there is an implied condition that the goods are of merchantable quality and where the goods are hired out for a particular purpose there is also an implied condition that the goods will be reasonably fit for that purpose. Where the goods are hired by reference to a sample, there is an implied condition that the bulk will correspond with the sample in quality, that the hirer will have a reasonable opportunity of comparing the bulk with the sample and that the goods will be free from any defect rendering them unmerchantable which would not be apparent on reasonable examination of the sample.

Any attempt to exclude or restrict such implied conditions is subject to the Unfair Contract Terms Act 1977, so that if the hirer is a consumer the conditions cannot be excluded or restricted at all, but if the hirer deals otherwise than as a consumer they can be excluded if they satisfy the requirement of reasonableness imposed by the Act (see Chapter 58).

The Supply of Goods and Services Act also implies a condition that the owner has a right to transfer possession of the goods by way of hire in accordance with the agreement made between the parties.

Do not assume that you are necessarily bound to accept standard terms and conditions which are sought to be thrust upon you. Such terms and conditions may always be varied, provided that the owner's wish for your custom is sufficient to induce him or her to be reasonable.

For instance, if you are renting equipment and a minimum term is specified, you could always try your hand getting that term reduced, and you will probably succeed – often without even having to pay a higher charge.

On the other hand, if you have agreed to the clause, then, however unreasonable your agreement may be, you will be bound by it. If you have actually signed an agreement, it is absolutely hopeless to say that you did not understand or know of the existence of any particular term.

Finally, the Fair Trading Act. This gives the Director General of Fair Trading the power to curb any commercial practice which he regards as 'unfair to the economic interests of consumers in the UK' – but it bears no relation to contracts for hire, in the world of commerce.

Happily, many suppliers do not rely on their exclusion clauses. But those who hire equipment or vehicles should do so in the full knowledge that the owners are entitled to rely upon their rights, if and in so far as they see fit to do so.

61   Your Servants – Your Agents?

The law makes an important distinction between 'servants' and 'agents'. A servant is a person who works under a contract of service (see Part Two). An agent is one who acts for you and on your behalf, whether or not their name appears on your payroll. And to every employer, the vital question is: Are we entitled to avoid the consequences of the acts of the individual concerned?

Suppose, for instance, that a senior employee attends a trade fair and sees fit – probably in a burst of misguided enthusiasm – to place an order for machinery, equipment or supplies which the company does not require. Is it entitled to cancel the order or is it bound by the unwanted deal?

Or you give authority to your employee to do a particular job on your behalf. She sees fit to exceed that authority. What are the legal consequences?

How far, then, must you go in limiting your employees' authority, if that limitation is to affect others? Conversely, to what extent need you inform others of the limits you place on the authority of your staff? And how far can erring employees who overstep the limits of their responsibilities be made personally liable for the results? Could they be sacked? Could they be forced to pay the losses out of their own pocket?

Important – and everyday – problems, these, in the world of industry and commerce. So here are the legal answers.

*   *   *

However small the business, the boss will not be able to do it all. Indeed, if he or she happens to operate through a company, all business has to be done by 'servants or agents' on its behalf. Whether the employer is an individual, a firm or a company, he, she or it is almost always bound by deals made on behalf of the business – and it is irrelevant whether the person who actually makes the bargain happens to be on the payroll, and whether or not the deal is actually a 'bargain' at all.

Someone acting on your behalf may have your actual authority. If you come to regret the authority you have given to your employee or agent, that will be your misfortune.

Troubles usually come when the employee or agent oversteps the authority. Whether a buyer or representative, a seller or stand-in, it matters not. The power given is limited by the instructions; the agent ignores the orders and places the employers or 'principals' in difficulty. What then?

There are two angles to this one – that of the third party and that of the individual. From the viewpoint of the other party – the person who has relied upon statements made by the individual on the organization's behalf – it is irrelevant whether the authority displayed was actual or only apparent. If the person representing the business had the 'ostensible' authority to make the deal, then the business is bound by it.

It follows that you must take care not to 'hold out' your servants or agents as having more authority than they actually possess. If you 'clothe your servants with apparent authority', then even if their clothing is deceptive ... even, indeed, if you stripped them of authority which they held in the past ... those who deal with them are entitled to consider the appearances. If these are deceptive, then it will be the employers or principals who suffer, not those who are taken in.

Your assistant or stand-in, representative or agent places or accepts an order? An ordinary, sensible, reasonable person dealing with them and knowing the position that they hold with your outfit – or the position which they appear to hold, thanks to the apparent authority which you have given them – would take it that they are acting within their instructions? Then however unsatisfactory the deal, it cannot be avoided because of any lack of actual authority. The commercial sheep in wolf's clothing may eat into the profits of the business which employs him, whether as servant or agent or both.

If, then, you wish to place really effective limits on the authority of those whom you command, you should inform those with whom they deal. 'Mr Smith is entitled to place orders up to £X, on the company's behalf ...', 'You will appreciate that Mr Y's authority is limited to ...', 'We shall be obliged if you will assist Mr Z to buy/sell ... in connection with the above department only ...', 'I am pleased to introduce Miss A, who is our newly appointed ——, fully entitled to ...'. Provided that the limits are set out clearly, anyone who sees fit to assist your representative (in the widest sense of that word) to exceed those limits does so at their own risk.

Second, it is essential to emphasize to your representatives that they must not exceed their authority – and that if they do so, they are asking to be dismissed. There is, of course, an implied term in the contract of service of an employee and in the contract of agency of any other sort of representative that the authority given will not be exceeded. If that term is broken either in a major respect or persistently, then the person concerned may be sacked.

Finally, what if you attempt to repudiate a contract on the grounds that your employee had no authority to make it? The other party will doubtless rely upon the agent's 'apparent' or 'ostensible' authority. The agent may be brought into any legal action which results, as a 'second defendant'. Damages may be claimed against the agent for 'breach of warranty of authority'. The agent has warranted that he or she had the authority to make the deal? Then in the unlikely event of the action failing against the employer or principal, the agent may be made personally liable under the contract.

Conversely, if your employees or agents land the business in trouble through exceeding their authority, they have broken their contract and (in theory at least), they may be forced to indemnify the business for any resultant loss.

In practice, of course, erring servants and agents are seldom made to pay for their sins out of their own pocket. Their employers or principals (or their shareholders) are the sufferers. So the clearer the limits placed on the authority of servants or agents – and the more those limits are made known both to the individuals concerned and to others with whom they deal – the less that loss will be.

This advice has become doubly important since a company secretary landed his outfit in huge expense. He hired cars at his company's expense for his own use and was clearly guilty of a criminal offence. His company was held liable to pay every penny of the account submitted by the owners of the cars. They had 'held out' their secretary as having the power to order the cars. He had the 'ostensible' or 'apparent' authority to place the orders – and from the point of view of the innocent third parties, that was as good as actual authority.

Even if your employee is a criminal, you may be liable in a civil court for the results of his or her misdeeds. Happily, you will only be liable in criminal law for the crimes of your servant or agent if you were in some way at fault.

62 When You are Mistaken

Most notorious mistakes are, of course, made by other people.

Suppose that a customer notices an item marked with a £10 price tag. 'I'll have it,' she says. 'Terribly sorry, Madam,' you answer, 'but there's been a mistake. Someone left a nought off the ticket.'

'Your mistake,' she says, triumphantly. 'You put the goods up for sale at the marked price – and I'm entitled to buy at that price.'

'Wrong,' says the law. 'No one is entitled to buy goods on a display in a trade or industrial exhibition or in a shop window or showcase or on the counter. By putting the goods on display, the seller is not "offering" to sell them, in the legal sense of the word. He is simply issuing an "invitation to treat" – he is inviting you to make an offer for the goods. When you do so, he can either accept or refuse it, as he sees fit.'

It follows that the seller is not bound to dispose of goods to any particular customer or to anyone at all, either at the marked price or at any price. Unless and until there is an unconditional offer, unconditionally accepted, there is no deal.

Not long ago, an executive saw a magnificent office machine in a shop window, with a nought left off its price. He went inside and bought it at the price marked. He thought he was getting a great bargain – and he was right. The shop did not discover its mistake until after the deal was done. By that time, the error could not be undone. The customer had made his offer. The shop had accepted it. The price was agreed – and the fact that there was a 'unilateral mistake' on the part of the shop did not destroy the effect of the contract.

The essence of a binding agreement is that the parties are *ad idem* – that their minds are at one. By definition, no agreement means no contract. If one party makes an offer to the other which the other party accepts in quite a different sense from that intended by the offerer, there is probably no deal. Where the parties are at cross purposes, there tend to be bitter arguments as to whether or not there is any agreement at all.

There is seldom room for argument where a party has signed a deed or document. 'I didn't realize that there were conditions on the back,' says the startled purchaser. The front of the document read: 'For conditions, see reverse.' The fact that the signatory did not read the terms ... could not have understood them anyway ... was ignorant of their very existence – that is his misfortune.

In general, only if you did not know the nature of the document you are signing will you be able to avoid the transaction because you were mistaken as to its contents. A man who was told that he was signing a guarantee similar to that signed on a previous occasion but in fact put his signature on to a bill of exchange escaped from liability.

Where both parties are mistaken, the contract is normally *void ab initio* – stillborn. Although both parties are agreed (so there is *consensus ad idem*), the law will usually let both parties off the contractual hook. And there is a possibility of having contractual documents 'rectified', so as to express the intentions of the parties.

Now suppose that you get a bill for rent, light, heat, telephone – or anything else for that matter. You pay. A few weeks later, you receive a letter: 'We very much regret that, due to a clerical error, you were undercharged. We enclose a revised statement herewith and shall be pleased to receive the balance due at your earliest convenience.' 'The matter is concluded,' you reply. 'You have received the sum demanded in respect of the goods or services provided. You are entitled to no more.'

You are wrong. In consideration of your agreeing to pay the contractual price, the other party undertook to provide the goods or services. They carried out their side of the bargain. You will not be allowed to take advantage of the error in their accounts department.

The converse applies. Due to a mistake in your accounts department (or of the young lady who happens to be that department), a customer is undercharged. When the mistake is spotted, you write asking for the balance of your money. Your customer cannot rely on your mistake to avoid paying the money which is properly owed.

Again, suppose that you owe £500. By mistake, you send a cheque for £5,000. Clearly, you are entitled to the return of the excess and if you do not get it you would have a good claim for 'money received to your use'.

But note: while money paid under a mistake of a fact 'or through excusable forgetfulness of a fact' may normally be recovered back, the same does not apply to money paid under a mistake of law. Where the plaintiff paid money voluntarily and with full knowledge of the facts to satisfy a claim which he could successfully have resisted, it was held that his funds were gone for ever. In the eyes of the law, ignorance of the law is usually inexcusable. It is more tolerant of errors of fact.

The law on mistakes, then, is miserably complicated. And about the only errors which bring real joy are those perpetrated in print and discovered by the hawk-eyed reader.

63 Collecting the Money You are Owed – a Checklist

The more money you are owed the more vital the need to know how far and when the law can help you to recover your debts. 'To sue or not to sue?' That is the first question. Allied to it: 'If you obtain a judgment, how can you best enforce it?'

* * *

Steps before action

Litigation is a luxury and a last resort. Normal preliminaries are the following:

1 Submission of accounts; statements; polite reminder (oral, by all means – but confirmed in writing, especially if debtor's representative promises payment).
2 Stiff written demand; then threat to place matter in hands of lawyers or debt collecting agency.

Professional help

If your efforts to get in the money you are owed all fail then – unless the debt is very small – you should put it in the hands of your solicitor for collection. But it is essential for you to understand the basics of collection so as to provide the solicitor with the information required; to issue appropriate instructions so as to ensure that you are not simply throwing good money after bad; and so that you can assess tactics together.

The alternative – which requires at least equal knowledge – is to consult professional debt collectors. The basic principles which now follow remain the same. But unless you know of or are recommended to a thoroughly reliable debt collecting agency of excellent repute, or unless your solicitor recommends the use of such an agency having regard to the nature of the debt concerned, you are better off to leave the collection to your lawyer.

Legal preliminaries to action

Before starting proceedings, your lawyer will normally write a 'letter before action', informing the debtor that unless payment is made forthwith (or within such time as is stated), proceedings will be commenced.

If oral pressure is required – or especially if a debtor has indicated intention to defend proceedings and has himself appointed solicitors – direct approach (oral and/or writing) will be made to them.

To sue or not to sue?

Before suing, the following must be taken into account:

1 Amount of the debt. The smaller the sum, the greater the temptation to write it off.

2. Solvency of the debtor. Suing a man (or a company or firm) of straw is throwing good money after bad.
3. Availability of debtor. If they have 'done a midnight flit' or gone abroad, the cost of employing process servers, enquiry agents or others to serve the writ or summons is probably not worthwhile.
4. Nature and strength of defence. The more real the defence and the more likely the prospect of the debtor pursuing it, the greater the incentive to compromise or (at worst) to write off.

Defences

Likely lines of defence would probably have been disclosed in the pre-litigation discussions and/or correspondence. Unfortunately, a determined debtor (or one who is fending off the day of payment as best they can – probably because of their own poor cash flow position) has many possible answers. Common examples include:

1. No contract, i.e. denial of agreement to supply goods or services charged for.
2. Defective goods or services: (*i*) breach of express term, e.g. goods or services not in accordance with specification or quotation, and/or (*ii*) breach of implied term, e.g. that goods will be 'of merchantable quality' as services carried out 'in a workmanlike manner and with reasonably suitable material'.

The cost of proceeding

The vast majority of legal actions never reach trial. Either the defendant pays or there is a compromise. But the most unlikely defendants fight – and before proceedings start, you must either place a limit on the sum which you are prepared to spend in the hope of recovering the debt, or you must be prepared to go the whole way – or you must take a preliminary view. In any event, you must ask your solicitor to estimate the cost involved.

A business or professional person may (with allowances for contingencies) estimate with some degree of certainty the sum likely to be involved in a project. A solicitor can rarely give more than an interim and provisional estimate. The following items are seldom possible to assess precisely in advance:

1. The vigour with which the defence will be pursued and in particular, the number and nature of interim applications or summonses – and/or the appeals which it will be necessary to make – or to defend.

2 The extent of 'discovery' – that is, the cost of inspecting and, where necessary, copying relevant documents.
3 The experience and eminence of counsel who will be employed by the debtor – and which will of itself often dictate which counsel are engaged on your behalf. (For example, will the debtor employ leading counsel?)
4 The eventual length of the trial – which will depend not only on the complexity of the issues and the extent of the dispute between the parties, but also upon the number and nature of the witnesses and upon the personality and patience of the judge.

* * *

Into the scales go all the pros and cons – and whichever course you choose – to sue or to write off – you make your choice in full knowledge of all the facts and with your eyes wide open to the potential risks and results.

64 Fending Off Your Creditors – a Checklist

Obviously, the best way to get rid of your debts is to pay your creditors. And I am certainly not advising non-payment. But when times are rough and business and professional people cannot themselves get in the money they are owed, they may be forced to use the law so as to beat the great enemy – time.

Here is a summary of how the law can help you to preserve your cash flow – or that of your company or firm – together with the limits on that help.

* * *

1 Check that the sum claimed is indeed due. In a computerized age, bills, accounts, invoices and statements are frequently incorrect. Further: ensure that you have not already paid the sum concerned. Are you satisfied that your own accounting system, which may have been quite adequate when cash flowed readily, gives you sufficient control now?
2 If the claim is prima facie correct, i.e. the goods or services are accurately stated and the sum specified is the contract price, have

you a legal defence to the claim – and if so, then what is its strength? Typical defences include the following:

a That the goods, materials or equipment were not in accordance with contract. Check:
   (i) Was there a breach of an express term in the deal? Were the goods (or any of them) different to those ordered?
   (ii) Was there a breach of an implied term; were the goods defective (and hence not 'of merchantable quality' or not 'reasonably suitable for the purpose supplied') so that there was a breach of the Sale of Goods Act 1979?
   (iii) Were the services supplied in accordance with contract? Or was the work done in a manner or with materials other than those demanded?
   (iv) Was the work defective? Is the creditor in breach of an implied term in the contract: that the work will be done in a proper and workmanlike manner and with reasonably suitable materials?

b That the goods were delivered – or the work done – late. Check:
   (i) Was there an express term making time an essential of the deal?
   (ii) Was there some obvious implication which would show that the parties must have intended time to be 'of the essence' of the arrangement?

c That the contract itself was not completed – probably through the absence of some essential term. Check:
   (i) Was there an *unconditional offer*, as opposed to (1) a mere 'invitation to treat' – or (2) a 'conditional' offer perhaps dependent upon someone else's consent?
   (ii) Was there *unconditional acceptance* – as opposed to (1) acceptance subject to a condition or, more likely, to (2) 'a counter offer' – usually contained in a document which may be called an 'acceptance' but which in fact attempts to impose terms which contradict those contained in the offer?
   (iii) Was there 'consideration' – normally the price or some other *quid pro quo*?
   (iv) Was there sufficently clear agreement on all essentials – price, quantity, quality etc.? (Exception: Where services are carried out and the claimant is entitled to reasonable payment on a *quantum meruit* basis.)
   (v) Was delivery of the goods or the carrying out of the services accepted by the other party?

3 Next: double check all contractual documents; do they provide you with any other technical defence? If in doubt, consult your solicitor.
4 When taking legal advice, to save time and money bring with you all relevant contractual documents, including all correspondence; and also bring full statements as to circumstances, so as to prevent solicitors having to prepare those for you – in their time and at your expense.
5 By this stage, you should be able to assess your prospects of fending off a legal action by your creditors, and you can then decide on tactics. Considerations include the following:

  a Whatever the nature of strength of your defence, are your creditors likely to be fair, reasonable and helpful – bearing in mind their own cash flow difficulties and their assessment of the advantages or otherwise of pushing you? They will consider the value of (hopefully) past and (certainly) future business from you;
  b Whether suing you would or would not be likely to produce a speedy outcome. If you have no *prima-facie* defence then they might well obtain summary, i.e. swift and cheap, judgment. Conversely: if you have at least an arguable defence which is visible on the correspondence, suing may not be worthwhile. Also: if they push too hard, will they be likely to make you insolvent and hence produce exactly the opposite result to that which they require, i.e. payment of money due?
  c Correspondence: and how it will appear to a court – including your apparent defences. Note: 'without prejudice' letters will not normally be disclosable.

6 Lawyers can normally fend off the day of judgment – or the payment of a debt – for a considerable time. The length of that time depends upon the strength of the defence; the vigour and efficiency of the creditors or their lawyers; and whether or not they can rake together a counter-claim, for loss suffered e.g. as a result of defective materials or work or due to delay. But lawyers are entitled to their proper costs. So when assessing need for their help, consider the following:

  a Would a satisfactory compromise on the amount of the claim be more or less likely to be obtained with the lawyer's help?
  b In so far as there is no adequate defence or no defence which you would wish to argue, to what extent would your prospects of obtaining reasonable terms for payment be more likely to be

achieved with a lawyer's help – as opposed to a direct (and probably totally frank) approach by you to the appropriate creditor's representative?

c What delay do your lawyers believe that they would be able to obtain from you – and what would be the likely legal cost?

* * *

Interest rates are high; a premium is placed on non-payment; and one branch of the legal profession which is burgeoning is that concerned with the collection of debts – and the fending off of debtors. The law is not always a moral instrument. But business and professional people who wish to survive must know how best to use it.

65 Time

If you agree to carry out the terms of a contract, when must you do so? If you submit an estimate, how long will it remain open? And if goods are sent to you for a job to be done on them, how long may you allow before you submit an estimate?

* * *

An expensive appliance was handed in for repair at a branch of a nationalized undertaking at the beginning of December. The customer asked for an estimate of the cost. The appliance, according to the board, at the end of March, 'was returned to the manufacturers on 23 December ... and since then we have written to them on two occasions and also telephoned them requesting the estimate which was eventually received and duly forwarded ... on 3 March'. Nearly three months to provide an estimate for a small job. We 'must apologize on behalf of the manufacturers for the delay ...', said the board.

The 'manufacturers' took a different line. They wrote to the customer – after she had written to them three times inviting a reply – stating that 'it would appear that the delay in dealing with your appliance was due to the delays of the board'.

Well, we hold no particular brief for boards. But let us give credit where credit is due. The board did all it could – and the manufacturers took months to deal with the customer, and then tried to put the blame on the board. And, incidentally, when the estimate did arrive, it was so high that the customer decided not to accept it and to use the money to pay a substantial part of the cost of a new machine produced by rival manufacturers.

'But what were the legal rights on each side?'

When the customer asked for an estimate, she was simply inviting the firm to make an offer to repair the goods. When that offer – in the estimate – was given, she could either accept it or reject it. She rejected it.

What about the time taken in giving the estimate?

The manufacturer would be allowed 'a reasonable time'. In theory, if that were exceeded the customer could sue for damages, to compensate her for the time – or, at least, the unreasonable time – that the goods had been out of her hands. In practice, this is hopeless. If no financial loss is suffered, you might get a few pounds for the inconvenience caused – but court proceedings would hardly be worthwhile. The customer's remedy is to take their custom elsewhere.

'What if the estimate had been accepted – when should the job have been finished?'

If a time was specified in the acceptance and it was clearly a matter of importance to the customer that the job be finished within that time, then the date fixed would be the required date of completion. But if no date was specified, then once again the firm would have 'a reasonable time'.

The leading case on this branch of the law is *Charles Rickards Limited v. Oppenheim*. Rickards agreed to supply a car chassis to Mr Oppenheim and have a body built on to it within seven months. It was made quite clear that the work had to be finished on time – that 'time was of the essence of the contract'. But seven months passed and the car was not ready. Rickards themselves were not personally at fault. Their subcontractors had let them down. In any event, Mr Oppenheim was told that the car would be ready in two weeks and he gave a written notice to Rickards' subcontractors saying that unless he received the car within four weeks, he would refuse delivery. This notice was duly passed on to Rickards.

The car was not delivered within four weeks, and when eventually it did turn up Mr Oppenheim refused to accept it. The company brought an action against him, claiming the price of the body work. He counter-claimed for the chassis or its value.

The first question for the court? Whether or not time was 'of the essence of the contract'. It was. The customer had picked a date and made it clear that this was to be an essential term.

Next question: after that time had passed and the customer still said that he would give extra time, could he still rely on the set period? No, said the court, he could not. He had 'waived' the stipulation as to time. He was 'entitled to give reasonable notice', reintroducing time as 'of the essence of the matter, whether the contract was for the sale of goods or for work and labour. The reasonableness of the notice had to be judged at the time at which it was given ...'

There had been a waiver – but when Mr Oppenheim said, 'I'll give you four more weeks', he was attempting to reintroduce the period of time. Was this a successful attempt? That would depend on whether or not the new period was 'a reasonable one'. Was it? 'Yes', said the court. 'On the facts of the case it was reasonable ... and it was a good notice to the Plaintiffs, even though it was given by Mr Oppenheim only to the subcontractors.'

So if you are going to be late in delivery, do not think that you can get away with it simply by getting your customer to grant an extension of time. If that, too, were to pass, the customer would be entitled to refuse delivery and to claim damages from you – as Mr Oppenheim did from Charles Rickards.

You will have noticed that the same rule about waiver applies both in contracts for the sale of goods and those for work and services. In general, in this respect, the law does not make any difference between them. But the Sale of Goods Act 1970 does give us a little special help with regard to contracts for the sale of goods.

'Unless a different intention appears from the terms of the contract,' says Section 10, 'stipulations as to time of payment are not deemed to be of the essence of a contract of sale. Whether any other stipulation as to time is of the essence of the contract or not depends on the terms of the contract.' So unless you make it clear that if you are not paid by a certain date you are not going on, the time that you are to be paid is not regarded as an essential part of the contract.

Otherwise, the section is clearly of no assistance at all. All it says is that if you want to find out whether or not time is 'of the essence' in any particular case, you must look at the terms of the particular contract. Nevertheless, as one learned authority puts it, 'as regards stipulations other than those relating to the time of payment, time is usually of the essence of the contract, at any rate in mercantile transactions'.

If you are anxious to have something done on time, then say so. If you are doing the job, then try not to be tied down as to time. And remember that the fact that your lateness – like that of Charles Rickards – may be due to factors entirely beyond your control won't help you at all. This is one occasion where it may not be better to be late than never. Late and never may be synonymous.

Now another, but equally common, contractual problem involving time. There are a number of good firms that provide excellent equipment for businessmen, their factories and offices. And they do so on a rental basis. You hire the machinery, you pay a comparatively modest price, the owners do the servicing for you – but the contracts usually provide that the machinery shall remain something like fourteen years from the date of installation.

This is not an unreasonable stipulation in most cases. The machinery – telephone installations or what-have-you – must be manufactured and the owners will probably make a loss over the first few years. Their profits come later on. But please do not think that you will be able to opt out of your obligations in those few years, if you decide that you do not like the machinery ... if you want something new ... if you go out of business of change your line ... if you move into other offices, which are already equipped ... You will be bound by your agreement.

Still, if you do not like the period set – or any other clause in the proposed agreement – then do not agree to it.

'But that's no good,' you reply. 'They'll never agree to install them for less than fourteen years – or whatever the particular period is.'

Wrong. To avoid losing your business, the company may well relent on the time period. They do not wish to lose their profits. They will simply drive the best bargain they can. So read the agreement, discuss it with the representative, see if you can get the company to budge. If you can and are happy, then rent their equipment. If you cannot, then you must decide whether or not it is worth your while to accept their terms. But what you must not do is to make an agreement and then expect to get out of it.

66 Import/Export – and Foreign Accounts

It is all very well to be patriotic and to help the export drive by building up your foreign accounts. But what happens if the accounting parties fail to pay up? Equally, it is splendid for international goodwill that you should buy goods from abroad. But what happens if they are defective or you lose money because they do not arrive, as contracted for or at all? After all, if the deal involved UK firms, you could sue them soon enough. But what of foreign contractors?

* * *

If the overseas contractors come to England or maintain a registered office here, you can slap a writ on them and treat them like Englishmen.

All being well, you will get your judgment. If they have property over here, you will then be able to force your judgment against that property. You can levy execution upon it ... send in the bailiffs ... or if the deal was done through an English affiliate, you may be able to wind it up.

But even if you can serve the proceedings in this country and even if you get your judgment, that will not be the end of the matter if the foreigner has no property here which can be reached to satisfy the judgment. In that case, the judgment may not be worth the paper it is written on. If you want your money, you have to start all over again, suing in the court of the foreign country concerned.

There are exceptions. For instance, there are arrangements made under *the Administration of Justice Act 1920* under which countries in the Commonwealth mutually agree to enforce each other's judgments. And under *the Foreign Judgments (Reciprocal Enforcement) Act 1933*, similar arrangements have been made with certain non-Commonwealth countries – Austria, Belgium, France, the Federal Republic of Germany, the Isle of Man, Israel, Italy and Norway in particular. There are also important new provisions contained in the Civil Jurisdiction and Judgments Act 1982, which intended to enable judgments given in one EEC member country to be recognized and enforced in another both quickly and cheaply.

The Civil Jurisdiction and Judgments Act incorporates into United Kingdom law the provisions of the 1968 Convention on Jurisdiction and the Enforcement of Judgments in Civil and Commercial Matters and also the 1971 Protocol on Interpretation of the Convention by the European Court. Apart from recognition and enforcement of judgments in member countries the Act also introduces some important jurisdictional provisions. As a result of the Act, a person domiciled in an EEC member country will only be able to be sued in the courts of that country, unless a special or exclusive jurisdiction is spelled out. However, alternative jurisdiction will be available in a wide variety of cases – for instance, special provision is made in the Act for consumer matters.

However, it is crucial to note that although parts of the Act are already in force, much of it is not yet and it is only being brought into force in a piecemeal manner. Accordingly, if you are involved in a dispute which might be affected by any of these provisions you should check with your solicitors whether the relevant parts are in force.

Much of the foregoing presupposes that you can serve your writ on the proposed defendant within the jurisdiction of the English courts. But what happens if you cannot do so? The answer lies in Order II of the Rules of the Supreme Court. This sets out a number of cases in which leave will be given by the High Court to a plaintiff in this country to serve a writ outside the jurisdiction. Here are the cases:

'a If the whole subject matter of the action begun by the writ is land situate within the jurisdiction ... ' The English courts will exercise jurisdiction over anyone where there is a battle concerning English land.

'b If an act, deed, will, contract, obligation or liability affecting land situate within the jurisdiction is sought to be construed, rectified, set aside or enforced in the action begun by the writ.' Once again, it is the land within the court's jurisdiction which attracts the court's power to grant leave to serve outside it.

'c If in the action begun by the writ, relief is sought against a person domiciled or ordinarily resident within the jurisdiction.' This one is designed to catch the Channel hoppers, international travellers and others who do midnight flits over the water to avoid the process servers. If such persons usually live here or are domiciled here (this country being a permanent place of abode), then they can be reached, wherever they fly.

'd If the action begun by the writ is for the administration of the estate of a person who died domiciled within the jurisdiction or if the action begun by the writ is for any relief or remedy which might be obtained in any such action as aforesaid.' Someone dies here. Their property lies here. And the court will ensure that it can consider here matters arising out of the death.

'e If the action begun by the writ is for the execution, as to property situate within the jurisdiction, of the trusts of a written instrument, being trusts that ought to be executed according to English law and of which the person to be served with the writ is a trustee or if the action begun by the writ is for any relief or remedy which might be obtained in any such action as aforesaid.'

'f If the action begun by the writ is brought against a defendant not domiciled or ordinarily resident in Scotland to enforce, rescind, dissolve, annul, or otherwise affect a contract, or to recover damages or obtain other relief in respect of the breach of a contract, being (in either case) a contract which:
  (i) was made within the jurisdiction, or
  (ii) was made by or through an agent trading or residing within the jurisdiction on behalf of a principal trading or residing out of the jurisdiction, or
  (iii) is by its terms, or by implication, governed by English law.'

To sue a Scot (or a Scottish company) upon a contract made here or through an agent here or which is governed by English law, you must still go to Scotland. But otherwise you may serve abroad. It is this rule which is relied upon in most commercial cases in which leave to serve out of the jurisdiction is obtained. If the deal is made in England, you may enforce it in England. If the person who made it was an agent trading or residing here on behalf of a foreign individual or corporation, a foreign contractor may be served with a writ. And if, expressly or by implication, it is the law administered by our courts which will apply, our courts will give leave to serve the foreigner abroad.

'g If the action begun by the writ is brought against a defendant not domiciled or ordinarily resident in Scotland or Northern Ireland, in respect of a breach committed within the jurisdiction of a contract made within or out of the jurisdiction, and irrespective of the fact, if such be the case, that the breach was preceded or accompanied by a breach committed out of the jurisdiction that rendered impossible the performance of so much of the contract as ought to have been performed within the jurisdiction.'

Never mind, then, where the contract was made. If it was broken by some act committed in this country, leave will be given to serve the foreigner abroad.

'h If the action begun by the writ is founded on a tort committed within the jurisdiction.'

If a foreigner is guilty of negligence, nuisance, making a defamatory statement — and the civil wrong is committed in this country — then they may be followed abroad by the long arm of the law.

'i If in the action begun by the writ, an injunction is sought ordering the Defendant to do or refrain from doing anything within the jurisdiction (whether or not damages are also claimed in respect of the failure to do or the doing of that thing)'.

Foreigners, then, may have their behaviour within the jurisdiction controlled, even though they have gone outside it. They may, after all, return ...

'j If the action begun by the writ being properly brought against a person duly served within the jurisdiction, a person out of the jurisdiction is a necessary or proper party thereto.'

The foreigner may be joined as a party in the English proceedings. Even if they could not have been a sole defendant, they may be made a co-defendant.

'k If the action begun by the writ is either by a mortgagee of property situate within the jurisdiction (other than land) and seeks the sale of the property, the foreclosure for estate duty or capital transfer tax; of the mortgage or delivery by the mortgagor of possession of the property but not an order for payment of any moneys due under the mortgage or by a mortgagor of property so situate (other than land) and seeks redemption of the mortgage, reconveyance of the property or delivery by the mortgagee of possession of the property but not a personal judgment.

'l if the action begun by the writ is brought under the Carriage by Air Act 1961, the Carriage by Air (Supplementary Provisions) Act 1962, the Carriage of Goods by Road Act 1965, the Nuclear Installations Act 1965 or the Protection of Trading Interests Act 1980;

'm if the action is a probate action within the meaning of Order 76;

'n if the action begun by the writ is brought to enforce a claim in respect of a liability incurred under the Merchant Shipping (Oil Pollution) Act 1971;

'o if the action begun by writ is brought against a defendant not domiciled or ordinarily resident in Scotland or Northern Ireland in respect of a claim by the Commissioners of Inland Revenue for estate duty or capital transfer tax;

'p if the action begun by the writ is one in which a claim is made for a sum to which the Directive of the Council of the European Communities dated 15th March 1976 No. 76/308/EEC applies, and service is to be effected in a country which is a member of the European Economic Community.'

That, then, is the Rule. English courts have given themselves considerable powers in bringing foreign contractors within their grasp. Once leave to serve has been given, service can usually be effected through the British Consulate in the country concerned or in accordance with the law of the country where the service is to be effected. But in Commonwealth countries service may be effected without the intervention of the British representative. And there are detailed rules relating to certain other countries with which we have Conventions.

Note, however, that Order II will be substantially amended when the Civil Jurisdiction and Judgments Act comes into full force. Again, this is a matter which should be checked with your solicitors.

So, while suing in this country may be an expensive operation, suing abroad or suing those who are abroad is inevitably even more so. Happily, where the foreigners have a place of business in this country, they can be served at that place of business. But conversely, you may find yourself sued in a foreign court and the foreign judgment enforced in this country, if you are in the wrong. Equally, if you sue a foreign defendant in our courts, he may counter-claim here against you. And if you sue abroad, you may be faced with a counter-claim there.

All these are unhappy rules, dealing with deals which have gone sour. But then, it is not from the sweetness of satisfied customers that lawyers who deal in litigation make their living...

67 Common Market Law

What real affect does EEC law have on the business world? Specific Regulations apart – and you will, of course, check how these apply to you and yours – what is the overall picture, after all these years of community membership?

We have, of course, not been swamped by the Code Napoleon or any other foreign law. All essential features of UK law have remained the same, including our court systems, trial by jury, habeas corpus and the rest.

Nor have the rules on 'tort' been altered. For instance, the principles on negligence are unaltered. And so are those on contract. Whether you make your deals at home or abroad, ruling law is that which (expressly or by implication) affects the particular agreement. If you wish our courts to retain their jurisdiction, build the appropriate clause into your contract and it will bite.

Do not presume that you can serve a Common Market debtor, outside the UK, with your UK writ or summons. Indeed, under the Civil Jurisdiction and Judgments Act 1982 you may be obliged to pursue your remedy in the member country in which the prospective defendant is domiciled. Your lawyers should check on whether this Act is in full force when you need it.

Still, there have been many changes in our law since we entered the EEC, and as a result of its Directives. Most recent and in many ways commercially the most important is the introduction of 'product liability' under the Consumer Protection Act 1987 (see Chapter 74).

In brief, a UK manufacturer or 'own brander' or a business that imports products from outside the EEC will generally bear a 'strict liability' if those goods are defective and if the defect then causes loss or damage. Subject to the so-called 'state of the art' defence, 'no fault liability' will give the victims of defective goods a head start in any proceedings. Rules that previously applied in France, West Germany and (incidentally) in the USA will be grafted onto our law.

Employees have achieved new protection under EEC pressure. For instance:

1 Under the Transfer of Undertakings Regulations, employees' rights are (generally and broadly) transferred from the selling to the buying employer; and selected, recognized trade unions must be consulted.
2 Equal Pay Regulations have introduced 'equal pay for work of equal

value'. Women are not merely entitled, as in the past, to like pay for like work.
3 The Data Protection Act 1984 also had its origins in Europe. 'Subject access' – that is, the rights of individuals whose personal data has been automatically processed to have access to such computerized information about themselves – became effective in November 1987.

Again: there is now mobility of labour within the EEC. You and your employees may live and work in any Common Market country of your choice. Once there, you are free to enjoy all the benefits of that country's social security system. No permits are needed for employers to import EEC people to live, to work or to settle in the UK.

Under EEC law, there is also freedom of movement of capital within the Common Market. Details from your bank or from your accountant.

Each EEC country retains (in the main) its own tax system. Specific tax problems require precise and individual choice.

Each country retains its own company law, but some rules have been adapted. For instance, the *ultra vires* rules have been altered. Your company's powers are contained in the Objects clause of its Memorandum of Association. The company was previously entitled to operate only within the scope of its Objects. Any contract made outside those powers was *ultra vires* – beyond the company's powers, and hence a nullity. An *ultra vires* act was not even capable of subsequent ratification. It was dead and useless.

Where the other party acts in good faith and without knowing of the lack of power in Objects clause, that rule no longer applies. Those who deal with your company in good faith are entitled to presume that it is acting within the scope of its lawful powers. If the deal is made before the company actually has any powers at all – prior to its formation or registration – then the person making the contract is personally liable. So mind what deals *you* make on behalf of unborn corporations.

Once in business within the Community, a company or other business must avoid 'restrictive practices'. EEC law forbids the making of any arrangement 'the object or effect of which is to prevent, restrict or distort competition within the Common Market'.

If public tenders are a substantial part of your work, then check on the extent to which the EEC companies have harmonized their law on public tendering. Harmonization is a slow and painful process. It cannot be enforced directly by an EEC Directive. New legislation must be passed by our own Parliament, which must act and enact so as to accord with Common Market policy and decisions.

Naturally, if you live or do business in another EEC country, you must comply with its internal laws. Like the UK, it retains its sovereignty and its relations between individuals and businesses within its own jurisdiction, regulated by its own civil and criminal courts.

If you are launching into the Common Market and need legal advice here, you should consult a specialist lawyer. If you operate abroad, then you should seek legal help in the country concerned.

68 Some Principles on Interest

'It has been our custom for some years now to charge interest at 6 per cent per annum on accounts which are over three months overdue for payment, and this is clearly stated at the bottom of our invoices and statements. It has been suggested to us that we have, in fact, no legal right to charge this interest, and that there is no obligation on the part of the debtor to pay it, should he settle his account voluntarily or, alternatively, be sued for payment.

'Many of our customers are notoriously slow payers and use their supplier as a cheap way of getting the use of money. We have always felt that the 6 per cent charge was some recompense for the facility. What is the legal position?'

* * *

The essence of the question? If you are not paid when you should be, can you charge interest? The essence of the answer? Only if there is an agreement, express or implied, between you and your customer, which allows you to do so.

Express agreement is simple to make and to understand. If you want to charge interest on overdue accounts, then you should tell your customer that this is one of the terms upon which you trade. Just as you specify a price, a delivery date, a period within which payment must be made, so you may specify an interest charge if payment is late.

It is much too late to attempt to do this in an invoice or a statement. Terms printed on these documents are no part of the contractual agreement. That was concluded days, weeks or even months before these documents were drawn up or received. Business people have a peculiar idea that they can introduce new terms into an agreement by printing them on demands for payment, confirmation slips, delivery notes and the like. In law, this is not permitted.

On the other hand, if you have traded for a long time with a particular firm or individual and you have brought your interest charge on late payments to his notice, it may be that you will have his implied agreement to pay them. True, the first time he is late in payment and you bang on the 6 per cent he can refuse to pay the interest. But if he pays it and still carries on trading with you, a court might be prepared to accept that he knew of your system and had consented to it. In that case, the fact that he had not expressly agreed would not matter. An implication will do.

'Unless a different intention appears from the terms of the contract,' says Section 10 of The Sale of Goods Act 1979, 'stipulations as to time of payment are not deemed to be of the essence of the contract of sale.' So if a customer owes money for some goods which you have sold them, then even if you have stipulated a certain time for payment, this term will not be 'of the essence' of the agreement, unless you have expressly made it so.

It follows from this that in contracts of this kind you most certainly cannot charge interest if payment is late. It may be a breach of contract, but it is not normally an essential one. You may give your customers more time to pay, or agree to accept payments by instalments, if they will agree to pay you interest. Then a new agreement is created, and your customer is bound by it.

If the time comes that your patience is exhausted and you decide to sue for your money, the situation as to interest changes. A number of Acts of Parliament may come to your rescue.

Section 3 of the Law Reform (Miscellaneous Provisions) Act, 1934, says that: 'In any proceedings in any Court of Record for the recovery of any debt or damages, the Court may, if it thinks fit, order that there shall be included in the sum for which judgment is given interest at such rate as it thinks fit on the whole or part of the debt or damages for the whole or any part of the period between the date when the cause of action arose and the date of judgment.' However, in relation to the High Court and the County Court this provision has been superseded by Section 35A of the Supreme Court Act 1981 and Section 69 of the County Courts Act 1984. Under these two Acts rules of court have been made:

a allowing for interest to be included in any judgment;
b specifying both the rate of interest and the periods for which it is payable.

These two Acts also provide that interest may be allowed on any part of the debt or damages claimed which is paid before judgment is given and that, in a debt claim, interest may be allowed even if the whole debt is paid after commencement of action, thereby obviating the need for any judgment.

In an action on a cheque which has bounced, Section 57 of the Bills of Exchange Act 1882 provides that: 'The holder may recover from any party liable on the bill, and the drawer who has been held to pay the bill may recover from the acceptor, and an indorser who has been compelled to pay the bill may recover from the acceptor or from the drawer or from a prior indorser ... (a) the amount of the bill; (b) interest thereon from the time of presentment for payment if the bill is payable on demand, and from the maturity of the bill in any other case ...'

No rate of interest is specified by the Bills of Exchange Act and the Supreme Court Act and the County Courts Act expressly do not affect the recovery of damages in respect of a dishonoured bill of exchange. It is therefore open to the plaintiff to claim interest at a rate which he thinks is appropriate in the circumstances. The practice seems to be that an appropriate rate will be taken to be a rate which is at or slightly above bank base rate.

So if a customer's cheque is dishonoured, take heart. Here at least the law takes an interest in your problems and gives you interest on the money you're owed. Assuming, that is, that the customer concerned is worth suing, even for the principle.

69 The Cost of Contractors

Like all businesses, we employ contractors to maintain, convert, insulate or to do other work on our premises – or, for that matter, on our vehicles. We have far too many disputes with them over prices and quality of work. What are our rights, please?

Conversely, what are we entitled to charge when we carry out work for our customers? And what sort of standards are they entitled to demand from us?

* * *

First, consider the situation when you are the customer.

Contractors (by definition) are those whom you employ under contract. If the terms of that contract are agreed, both sides are bound.

Suppose that you book a builder and agree his price. You then discover some 'little man' who will do the job for you for much less money. Too bad. You have no right to avoid your bargain. If the contractor is prepared to let you off the legal hook, you are lucky.

Conversely, suppose that your contractor underestimates. He holds down his price to some uneconomic level so as to get your job. He is not entitled to say: 'I can't do it for the agreed price.' As with most other contracts not made by infants, they either bind both sides or neither.

'But what happens where no price has been agreed in advance? you say. 'Is the man entitled to demand whatever the market will bear?'

Certainly not. He may charge only on a so-called *quantum meruit* basis – what the job is worth ... a reasonable charge ... and what is 'reasonable' depends on all the circumstances of the case including the standard of the work, the time taken and by whom, the skill and cost of the labour used and the nature and cost of the materials.

In relation to the supply of services for which no charge has been agreed between the parties, Section 15 of the Supply of Goods and Services Act will imply a reasonable charge.

In practice, 'extras' usually cause the trouble. 'Let's have an extra shelf over there,' you say. 'While you're here, would you mind fixing our damaged floorboards, repainting the corridor ...?' You've accepted the contractor's firm estimate for the main job and you do not trouble to get estimates for the extras.

Maybe the contractor has discovered that he will be out of pocket on the estimated work. He knows that he cannot raise his agreed price. So having undercharged on the contract, he overcharges on the extras. Alternatively, you simply do not realize how the extras are mounting up so when you receive the bill you retire to bed with a migraine and a tranquillizer. Your magnificent afterthoughts and changes of mind (or, of course, those of your managerial staff) are costing you a fortune.

If this happens to you, don't panic. Take stock, if necessary with the help of a surveyor, of the work done and the prices charged. If they are reasonable, you will just have to pay. But if the prices are unreasonable, refuse to pay them. Offer a reasonable price and no more.

The obvious way to avoid this sort of trouble is to tie down every contractor to precise figures on every item of work done, including all the extras. Reputable contractors would rather be at work than in court and realize that prior agreement on prices (preferably confirmed in writing) would help both sides to keep clear of lawyers. So they provide written estimates on request. Conversely, if a contractor refuses to give an estimate for an extra, this (in most cases, at least) is a pretty clear hint to you to take your work elsewhere.

If, then, you obtain your estimate and the asking price is too high, bargain. If haggling proves hopeless, then you can either order the work with both your eyes and your pocketbook wide open – or refuse to accept the estimate.

But what if the job is defective? Suppose that the pipes leak ... the paintwork blisters ... the building subsides ... the roofing falls ...?

Every contractor impliedly promises to do your work in a proper and workmanlike way and with reasonably suitable materials. This duty is also now laid down by the Supply of Goods and Services Act.

If either the work or the materials are defective, the contract has been broken. You are entitled to claim damages, to compensate you for your loss. In practice, this means that you are entitled to deduct from the bill the reasonable cost of putting the work into proper order.

Note that you are not bound to allow the contractor a second try. You can drive them forth from the site and call in someone else to put things right. But in general, wisdom demands patience because experience tells that impatience leads to litigation, and any sort of court action involving the work of contractors should be regarded as a luxury to be indulged in only where there is no reasonable alternative.

When a contractor's case does get to court, the proceedings tend to be lengthy and costly. Usually, a schedule is drawn up showing all the work alleged to be defective, all the prices charged and in dispute, the comments of both sides and the bare bones of the argument. By the time that experts have given evidence on both sides, counsel have examined and cross-examined the witnesses and addressed the judge, wrangling and haggling has proceeded in the corridors and all the documents have been copied, produced, read out ... the odds are that the legal costs exceed the amount in dispute between the parties and whoever wins the case, both sides lose.

The best way to avoid litigation is to pick the right contractor at the start and to agree all prices in advance. Impossible? Then if you see a dispute in the offing, try to head it off with any sort of reasonable compromise. If that fails, then call in your lawyer and your surveyor at the earliest possible stage. They may achieve a compromise where you have failed. But if the worst comes to the worst, then at least you will know that your case will be properly prepared and your chances of winning it greatly improved. Most losing litigants have destroyed their own cases long before trial. And then the true meaning of the word 'trial' becomes all too expensively obvious.

In your capacity as a contractor for others, apply the above rules in reverse. You may charge the agreed price or else a reasonable sum. And you must do the job in a proper and workmanlike way and with reasonably suitable materials.

70 What Can Repairers Charge?

Vehicles, adding machines, computers, typewriters and all the rest of the modern allegedly labour-saving devices dominate the world of the efficient business or professional person. The trouble is, of course, that machines are like people – they break down, for good reason or none. They must then be repaired.

So consider: What is a repairer entitled to charge? If they take your car or computer into their premises, are they entitled to keep it until you have paid their bill – however exorbitant that bill may be? And what are your rights if the job is bungled?

* * *

Whenever you arrange for your machinery to be fixed, you enter into a contract with the repairer. In return for their undertaking to do the job required, you agree to pay their proper price. The rules are almost exactly the same as they would be if you arranged for your premises to be repaired or maintained and as explained in the previous chapter, the contractor is entitled to the agreed price or, in the absence of agreement, to a reasonable price. The danger of not fixing a price in advance? That the contractor will tend to underestimate on the main job, so as to have the price accepted – and then try to make up the money by overcharging for the extras. If you give the contractor extra work, then my advice is: Get a price for that, too, before you give the go ahead.

Still, the one advantage you have when contractors are working on your premises is that (literally) they cannot take them away. If there is a dispute, they cannot (for instance) remove parts of your building or items of your machinery, until they receive their money – even if their claim is fully justified. But when you put your car or equipment into their hands, the law gives them a special advantage. They have what is known as a 'lien' – the right to hold the property upon which they have done work until you pay them their proper charges.

'But what if we say that their charges are not proper?' you ask, with justification.

What, indeed? They say: 'Our charges are reasonable and right. Until you pay them, we shall not release your property.'

You probably need your vehicle or equipment very urgently. If you want it back, then you will either have to pay – or to sue. As suing will take a very long time indeed, the chances are that you will give way to the financial blackmail and pay up. You may then have to sue for the overcharge – which is probably not worth doing.

What, then, if the work is defective?

There is an implied term in every contract under which services are performed in the course of a business that the supplier of the service will carry it out with reasonable care and skill. This is implied by statute in the Supply of Goods and Services Act 1982. The common law, however, implies a further duty that, in the absence of agreement to the contrary, the job will be done in a proper and workmanlike manner and with reasonably suitable materials.

If the vehicle or equipment does not work when the repair job is completed, the odds are that the repairer has not earned the money. You have then suffered damage and are legally entitled to damages – these being designed to put you in the same financial position as you would have been in had the work been carried out in accordance with contract. Normally, you may deduct from the repairer's bill the reasonable cost of putting the work into proper order.

In theory, you are not even bound to allow the repairer a second chance. In practice, it is normally wise to give contractors the chance to fix their own work, if only because otherwise you are not taking reasonable steps to 'mitigate your loss' – you must do what you can to keep your loss to a minimum, and if you rush off to some other repairer, it may be said that you are incurring unnecessary charges. Still, by that time you will have your equipment (or vehicle) back in your possession, and at least you will not have to battle against a repairer's lien – not, that is, until the second repairer takes over where the first left off. And I hope that they will do a better job!

71 Rights of the Unpaid*

If you remain unpaid, you may sue for your money. Conversely, the moment that you owe a debt, your creditor may issue legal proceedings. Whether or not legal battle is worthwhile is a problem that was considered in Chapter 63. Now, consider the other rights of the unpaid seller.

A contractor installed a heating plant in business premises. It never worked properly, so the proprietors declined to pay the bill. They received a letter in the following terms:

'We would refer to our accounts rendered. Unless these are paid in

---

* See also Chapter 101, Legal Aspects of Billing.

full within seven days hereof, we shall return to the premises, dismantle the plant, hold you responsible for the cost of dismantling, and claim such damages for breach of contract as we may be advised.'

Not every unpaid contractor puts his demands quite so blatantly, nor his threats in such extravagant form. Still, this sort of arm twisting by the unpaid seller of services is remarkably common. But how far are such threats enforceable at law? What are the rights of those who sell their time and skill, either as such or in combination with the supply of materials?

A contractor who has carried out the job properly is entitled to the money. If you fail or refuse to pay the money when it falls due, you are in breach of contract. You may be sued for damages – but the only damage suffered will be the amount due but unpaid under the contract. If there was some express term that interest would be chargeable if the debt was overdue, then this could be added on to the unpaid capital. If legal proceedings are actually commenced, then interest may be claimed. That is all.

It follows that contractors have no right to claim the return of 'their' materials. Once they have affixed them to your premises, the material undoubtedly become yours. Parts used to fix the boiler ... radiators installed as part of a new central heating plant ... insulation materials, nailed to the roof or walls – these 'adhere to the freehold'. They become part of your property. The contractors have no right whatsoever to their return. If they were to sue for them, they would fail. It follows that they have no conceivable right to snatch them back. That which they cannot obtain through legal action would be doubly unobtainable by the use of 'self help.'

In any event, ownership in goods passes when the parties intend it to pass; in the absence of express agreement to the contrary, the rules as to intention are laid down by the Sale of Goods Act. In the broadest terms, ownership generally passes when goods are set aside by the seller for the buyer, even if they have not yet been paid for or delivered. By the time the contractors have used their spare parts or their appliances for your needs, ownership has passed – and the contractors cannot possibly recover the items. They are no longer theirs.

Anyway, even had the contractors the right to the goods (which, I repeat, they most emphatically have not), if they were to enter your premises without your consent in the hunt for their own property, they would be trespassers. Even if you were wrongfully detaining their goods, that would give them no right to invade your territory. The moment they did so, you could ask them to go and if they refused you would be entitled to use reasonable force to eject them. Many business people are ignorant of the law and trespass upon the land of others. They are liable to find themselves in very deep trouble (details in Chapter 84).

It follows that the person who sells services and is unpaid for them should put lawyers on the trail. Like a pea in a biscuit tin, an empty threat may rattle loud but strikes no fear into the soul of the knowledgeable.

The rights of the unpaid seller of goods are specifically laid down in Part 5 of the Sale of Goods Act 1979. The seller of goods is deemed to be 'an unpaid seller', for the purposes of the Act –

'*a* When the whole of the price has not been paid or tendered:
b When a bill of exchange or other negotiable instrument has been received as conditional payment, and the conditon on which it was received has not been fulfilled by reason of the dishonour of the instrument or otherwise.'

So tender of only part of the price – or payment of only a proportion – will not prevent the seller from being 'unpaid', and hence entitled to exercise their Sale of Goods Act rights. What are they?

First, Section 39: In general, even if ownership of the goods has passed to the buyer, the unpaid seller has 'by implication of law –

'*a* A lien on the goods or right to retain them for the price while he is in possession of them;
b In case of the insolvency of the buyer, a right of stopping the goods in transit after he has parted with possession of them;
c A right to resale as limited by this Act.'

If you are a manufacturer, wholesaler or retailer and goods have been set aside for the buyer, ownership in the goods may have been transferred. But this does not mean that you will be forced to deliver if you are unpaid. You are free to say: 'Until I am paid the price, I will not disgorge the materials – however much you may need them.'

Conversely, if a supplier says: 'Not having done business with you on any previous occasion, we regret that we must insist upon payment prior to delivery', he is fully entitled to do so. By statute, he may demand payment before he releases his lien on the goods. 'While he is in possession of them' he has a 'right to retain them for the price'.

Naturally, if there were some agreement to the contrary, the situation would be different. Maybe you arrange that a supplier will give you credit?

You are to pay at the end of the month following delivery perhaps? Then the Act (as always) in no way interferes with the contractual bed in which you have seen fit to lie. But otherwise, I repeat, the unpaid seller's first right is to exercise a lien on the goods, if they remain in his possession.

Now suppose that you sell goods and the buyer becomes insolvent before acquiring possession of the property. Even if the property has left you ... even if it is in the hands of a carrier, perhaps, on its way to its destination ... you may stop it in transit.

What, then, of the right of resale? Section 48:

'Subject to the provisions of this Section, a contract of sale is not rescinded by the mere exercise by an unpaid seller of his right of lien or retention or stoppage in transit. Where an unpaid seller who has exercised his right of lien or retention or stoppage in transit resells the goods, the buyer acquires a good title thereto as against the original buyer. Where the goods are of a perishable nature, or where the unpaid seller gives notice to the buyer of his intention to resell, if the buyer does not within a reasonable time pay or tender the price, the unpaid seller may resell the goods and recover from the original buyer damages for any loss occasioned by his breach of contract.'

So if unpaid sellers exercise their lien or stop goods which have left their possession and are in transit to the buyer, the contract of sale remains alive.

Unpaid sellers are not entitled in all circumstances to resell property. But if it is perishable or if they give notice of their intention to resell, then unless they are repaid within a reasonable time, they may consign the goods to another buyer, who will acquire a good title to them. The law expects sellers to be reasonably patient where the goods will not perish as a result. Again, where the buyer is not informed of the intention to resell, to resell is to break the contract, unless the goods are perishables. So sensible sellers who are unpaid will give notice of intention to resell. They will discuss with their lawyers how long a time would be 'reasonable' – and when that time has passed, if they have not received their money they will mitigate their loss by finding some other buyer who is more likely to produce the money.

Even where a lien is exercised or goods are stopped in transit, the contract remains alive. Even where the original buyer does not pay when he should, and the goods are sold elsewhere, damages may still be claimed from the man who should have paid them. As usual, these will be designed to compensate the seller for any loss suffered as a result of the breach of contract. They will be the difference between the price which the original buyer was to have paid and that which the seller eventually managed to get from the people who did pay for the property. The original buyer's best hope? That maybe the seller will break even or even make a profit on the deal, second time round – in which case the buyer will pay no damages whatsoever.

'Where the seller expressly reserves a right of resale in case the buyer should make default, and on the buyer making default resells the goods, the original contract of sale is rescinded – but without prejudice to any claim the seller may have for damages.' Some sellers specifically state in their contracts that if the buyer does not pay on a specified date, he shall be entitled to resell the goods. If that happens, the contract of sale dies – but the seller may still have a claim for damages.

Section 46 lays down how stoppage in transit is effected. The seller may exercise his right of stoppage in transit 'either by taking actual possession of the goods, or by giving notice of his claim to the carrier or other bailee or custodier in whose possession the goods are. Such notice may be given either to the person in actual possession of the goods or to his principal. In the latter case the notice, to be effectual, must be given at such time and under such circumstances that the principal, by the exercise of reasonable diligence, may communicate it to his servant or agent in time to prevent a delivery to the buyer.'

Very sensibly, the law says that you have a choice: You may inform the head office of the carrier or the boss of the firm which has the goods in its care, or the actual person who holds the goods at the particular time. Telephone the head office of the carriers, if you wish – or inform the driver of the vehicle with your goods on board. Either will do.

'When notice of stoppage in transit is given by the seller to the carrier, or other bailee or custodier in possession of the goods, he must redeliver the goods to, or according to the directions of, the seller. The expenses of such redelivery must be borne by the seller.' So the carrier must do as you ask. He must comply with the notice you give to him. You will have to bear the expense of the redelivery – but, of course, this will be added on to your claim for damages against the buyer.

'Goods are deemed to be in course of transit,' says Section 45, 'from the time when they are delivered to a carrier ... or other bailee or other custodier for the purpose of transmission to the buyer, until the buyer, or his agent in that behalf, takes delivery of them from such carrier or other bailee or custodier.' The transit is at an end 'if the buyer or his agent ... obtains delivery of the goods before their arrival at the appointed destination'.

From the time that you deliver goods to a carrier or other bailee until the buyer obtains delivery or possession, you may stop them if you are unpaid and the buyer becomes insolvent. You do not have to allow your goods to be amongst the assets to be used to pay off the buyer's creditors, whom you will then join.

In practice, what matters is to move swiftly. If you are not only unpaid but suspect the buyer's solvency, you can still jump the queue if you retain the goods in your possession (and hence can exercise a lien) or if they have not yet reached the hands of the buyer (in which case they may be stopped in transit). But please note: These rights are only exercisable where the buyer is insolvent – and not, for instance, because you find that you can obtain a higher price elsewhere.

When understood, the rights of the unpaid seller are comparatively simple. But fail to understand them and exercise rights which you do not have and you are asking for problems. And that is precisely what the contractor discovered when he attempted to recover parts of the central heating installation which he had put in. His clients had been to their lawyers; and the police awaited the contractor at the door of the premises.

Another useful device which has been developed in order to protect unpaid sellers is a retention of title clause. Such a clause, often called a Romalpa clause after the case in which its use was first approved, provides that the property in the goods is not to pass to the buyer until the goods are fully paid for. It will also usually provide that if the buyer sells the goods before they are paid for, the buyer will hold the proceeds of sale on trust for the seller, which has the effect of giving priority to the seller. In addition, the seller will usually require the goods to be kept by the buyer in such manner that the seller's goods can be distinguished and will reserve to himself the right to require the return of the goods and will insist that the buyer grants him a licence to enter the buyer's premises without notice to recover the goods.

Romalpa clauses are now a very common feature of a seller's standard terms and conditions of trading, but if you are wondering whether you need one you should go to see your solicitor, who can advise you and if necessary draft a clause appropriate to your needs.

72 Unsolicited and Uncollected Goods

It is a rare business or professional person who does not from time to time receive unsolicited goods.

The Unsolicited Goods and Services Act 1971, was designed to deal with these problems. So consider: What does this important statute really say? What are you entitled to do with goods which arrive in your hands, uninvited and unwanted? And can the sender be prosecuted?

* * *

In general, the recipient of any goods is their 'bailee'. Whether you ask for them or not ... whether you are paid to look after them or receive them gratuitously or as a favour ... you are bound to take reasonable care of the goods placed in your charge.

The Disposal of Uncollected Goods Act attempted to give repairers the right to sell goods which were not picked up. But in practice the Act required so many formalities from the trader that it was almost useless. So in 1977 the Act was repealed and replaced by the Torts (Interference with Goods) Act. This Act is much more straightforward. Where a bailee of goods has possession or control of the goods and the bailor is in breach of an obligation to take delivery of them, or the bailee is unable to trace or communicate with the bailor in circumstances in which he could impose such an obligation by giving notice to him or in which he could reasonably be expected to be relieved of any duty to safeguard the goods on giving notice to him, then a power of sale may arise. However, where the bailee is able to trace or communicate with the bailor then he must serve a notice upon him requiring him to comply with his obligations and giving notice of his intention to sell the goods before a right to sell will arise. In any case there will be no right in the bailee to sell unless he is reasonably satisfied that the bailor owns the goods.

Although a sale under the 1977 Act gives good title as against the bailor, it will not give good title as against the owner. You will also not be entitled as bailee to keep the proceeds of sale of uncollected goods. You will have to account to the bailor for the proceeds – although you are of course entitled to deduct the costs of the sale. Bailees can also protect themselves by obtaining an order from the court that they are entitled to sell the goods.

As for the receivers of unsolicited goods, they were, until 1971, bound to take reasonable care of the unwanted property. However, the Unsolicited Goods and Services Act 1971 removed that troublesome burden.

A person who now receives unsolicited goods 'with a view to his acquiring them' may, in many cases, 'use, deal with or dispose of them as if they were an unconditional gift to him, and any right of the sender to the goods shall be extinguished'.

Note, first, that the law is in no way altered if you asked for the goods to be supplied to you on sale or return or on approval. The Act deals with goods sent 'on spec'.

Second, the recipient must have 'no reasonable cause to believe that the goods were sent with a view to their being acquired for the purposes of a trade or business'. So this section is not designed to protect traders. It is there for the benefit of the public at large.

If, then, you receive unsolicited goods which are intended for you to sell, I suggest the following:

1. Write to the suppliers forthwith, describing the goods, setting out the date when you received them, and requiring them to be collected forthwith.
2. If that does not do the trick, send a further letter, saying that you will charge for storage;
3. If you have space available, put the stuff out of reach – and try to return it to a representative of the suppliers, when next he or she calls – remembering, of course, to get a receipt;
4. Alternatively, see whether you can ship the goods back, letting the recipient meet the bill; and if this is impossible, then
5. Write to your Member of Parliament; – who may take the matter up with the suppliers, perhaps hinting that they will try to have the Act extended to traders – in which case the senders may see sense.

Now assume that the goods were sent to you at your home and you 'have neither agreed to acquire nor agreed to return them'. When can you 'use, deal with or dispose of them' as if they were a gift? The Act provides two ways.

First, if you can show 'that during the period of six months beginning with the day on which you received the goods, the sender did not take possession of them and you did not unreasonably refuse to permit the sender to do so' then you can hold on to the goods as if they were a gift to you.

Second, if you do not want to wait for the end of the six months' period you can serve written notice on the sender stating your name and address and 'if possession of the goods in question may not be taken by the sender at that address, the address at which it may be so taken'. The notice must also contain a statement that the goods are unsolicited and must be served 'not less than thirty days before the expiration of the six month period'. Provided that the sender does not take possession of the goods within thirty days from the date of the notice and you do not unreasonably refuse to permit them to do so you are entitled to keep the goods.

Now for Section 2 – which protects traders, as well as private citizens:

'A person who, not having reasonable cause to believe there is a right to payment, in the course of any trade or business makes a demand for payment, or asserts a present or prospective right to payment, for what he knows are unsolicited goods sent ... to another person with his view to acquiring them, shall be guilty of an offence and on summary conviction shall be liable to a fine not exceeding £1,000.'

So if suppliers send you unsolicited goods to your business, you will not acquire any right to them. But if they make a demand for payment without reasonably believing that you had agreed to acquire the goods, then they may be fined up to £1,000 by a Magistrates' Court.

Further, if a sender 'who not having reasonable cause to believe there is a right to payment' threatens to bring legal proceedings or places you on a list of defaulters or threatens to do so or 'invokes or causes to be invoked any other collection procedure or threatens to do so' may be fined up to £2,000.

The senders of unsolicited goods take a very considerable risk. People who send unsolicited goods 'for the purpose of a trade or business' may be guilty of a criminal offence if they demand payment or make threats, even if the recipient was a trader and could acquire no right to those goods, under the Act.

So anyone who sends goods to your business which you do not want should be warned: 'Do not try to extract payment from me, or you will fall foul of the law.'

Warning: Only after six years will the sender lose his rights to the goods sent to you for your trade or business; until then, they remain the sender's – so if you use, sell, dispose of (or, for that matter, smoke, eat or otherwise consume) those goods, you will have 'acquired a property' in them. Then you will become liable to pay.

Meanwhile, the 1971 Act gives single protection to the trader and double to the ordinary consumer.

73 Commission When the Deal Goes Off

Every business and professional person should know the rules on the payment of estate agents. Since the case of *Christie Owen and Davies v. Rapaccioli*, it has become all too easy to be forced to pay an estate agent even if he does not introduce the eventual purchaser.

There is no law which says that an estate agent is only entitled to his money if he introduces the eventual purchaser. There is nothing to prevent you from agreeing to pay your agent if he produces someone who is 'ready, able and willing' to buy. Indeed, vast numbers of estate agents' arrangements are on that basis – and their documents say so. But in the past, these arrangements have been interpreted as meaning: 'The agent is to be paid only if the deal goes through.'

Estate agents maintain that this is grossly unfair. After all, an architect may not get his whole fee if the building is neither erected nor completed but if he has prepared the plans in accordance with instructions, then he is entitled to at least a proportion of the money. His earnings are not dependent upon the erection of the structure.

The answer to that one? That estate agents may effect a sale through one phone call, a single advertisement or a sign in window. If they are lucky, with minimal effort they will get the entire fee. They are not like architects, who have to sweat over the original plans and then supervise while those plans are put into operation.

To this background, Messrs Christie Owen and Davies were instructed by a caterer called Rapaccioli to help sell his restaurant. Mr Rapaccioli wanted £20,000 plus stock and valuation.

The agents were to be entitled to commission in the event of their 'effecting an introduction either directly or indirectly of a person ... ready, able and willing to purchase at the above price ... or for any other price' which Mr Rapaccioli might be prepared to accept.

Christie's duly introduced a Mr Abbas as prospective purchaser and he telephoned to a director of the plaintiffs, offering £17,700 for the lease and goodwill, plus stock and valuation. Mr Rapaccioli agreed to accept the lower price and solicitors were instructed on both sides.

Draft contracts were approved and the deposit was paid – but Mr Rapaccioli, having apparently got a better offer, declined to go on with the transaction.

Question for the court: was Mr Abbas a person 'ready, able and willing to purchase'? The trial judge held that he was not, because no binding contract had been entered into between him and the defendant. It was conceded that Mr Abbas was 'able' to purchase at the price mentioned. But was he 'ready and willing'?

On appeal, Lord Justice Cairns set out three principles which now regulate the interpretation of 'readiness and willingness'.

1 The decision as to whether commission is payable depends on the terms of the contract and on the ordinary rules of interpretation. It follows that clients may make whatever agreement they like with estate agents, however unfavourable to themselves, and they will be bound by it. To find out whether you or your client are bound to

pay commission, look at the documents or correspondence and interpret them according to their ordinary meaning. If that is impossible, then get the help of a lawyer to establish how courts have interpreted the phrase in question.

2. When the agreement between principal and agent is for commission to be payable on the introduction of a person ready, able and willing to purchase, the commission is payable if a sale actually results. Obviously. More important: it 'may become payable when the transaction becomes abortive'. So the mere fact that the deal goes off will not necessarily deprive the agent of his remuneration.

3. Commission is payable when a person who is able to purchase is introduced and expresses readiness and willingness by 'an unqualified offer to purchase', even though such offer has not been accepted and could be withdrawn. Assuming that this offer comes within the terms that the agent has been authorized to invite and that the offer is not withdrawn by the purchaser but is refused by the vendor, the agents will be entitled to their money.

Mr Rapaccioli had turned down a good offer made by a purchaser who was ready, willing and able to buy – therefore Christie Owen won their case and were entitled to £835 commission.

So the old rule that, unless there was a contract of sale, the purchaser could not be 'willing' has gone. The principal may be forced to pay commission, even if there is never any contract.

Equally, you may find that if you are prepared to accept a certain sum and your estate agent finds you a buyer who is ready, willing and able to purchase at that price, but you accept a higher price thereafter from someone else and call off the first deal, you will have to pay two lots of estate agents. The first one earned the money by introducing the contact, the 'ready, willing and able' purchaser, in accordance with his contract with you. The second one produced the purchaser who actually bought the premises.

So where a purchaser makes an unqualified offer at a specified or minimum sum as a result of the efforts of the estate agent concerned, the seller is not bound to accept that offer – but if he rejects it, he cannot prevent the estate agent from getting his money.

So nowadays, wise business and professional people who know the rules will do their best to enter into contracts which enable the estate agents to get their money only where a sale is *actually* effected as a result of an introduction made by those agents. It is bad enough to have to pay agents once – but far worse to have to produce twice the money, when one of the agents has earned it but in a way that is useless to you.

74 Product Liability – the New Scene

At last, strict liability for defective products is to become part of UK law. Under the pressure of European requirement, the burden of proving liability where a defect in a product causes death, injury or loss will shift from plaintiff to defendant. There are limitations on the spread of the new rule – some special defences will apply, in limited cases – but overall, the scene is changing. Insurance premiums are already rocketing; and once this doorway to consumer protection has been opened, it will be pushed ever wider.

So here is your breakdown of the essentials of the new rules – set into the practical realities of the law on contract; the civil wrong (or 'tort') of negligence; and the spillover into the laws on crime.

* * *

In ordinary English 'product liability' means: liability for a defective or dangerous product. In legal jargon, it has acquired a different meaning: 'strict' or 'no fault' liability: liability, that is, on the part (broadly) of those who put defective products into circulation, without the sufferer from the defect having to prove that the defect resulted from some fault on the part of the supplier. Instead of the plaintiff (or, in Scots, the 'pursuer') having to prove fault, the defendant must disprove it.

In a civil action (in contract or in negligence, for instance) the court must decide on liability, 'on the balance of probabilities' – what probably happened. In criminal proceedings, the burden is higher. The court or jury must be satisfied 'beyond all reasonable doubt'. But whether the burden is civil or criminal, its discharge can be a serious problem, especially if the other party is wealthy and you are not.

Contract

Under the law of contract, fault is irrelevant. If people break their legally binding agreement with you, the reason for the breach is irrelevant. You will normally be entitled to your legal remedy – probably to damages.

The new rules on product liability in no way alter the basic contractual principle. Liability has always been – with diminishing exceptions – 'no fault'.

Until 1973, exceptions were often the rule.

Since 1893, the Sale of Goods Act (now consolidated into the 1979 Act) has implied terms into most contracts for the sale of goods. The most important are (broadly):

1 That goods must be 'of merchantable quality'; and
2 That they must be 'reasonably suitable for the purpose supplied'.

So if a product is defective, then it is not 'merchantable', and the supplier is in breach of contract. Equally (and generally) if it will not do the job which the supplier knows or must be taken to realize that it is intended to perform, then (once again) he is in breach and the buyer can claim damages, even if there is no express provision in the contract to that effect.

Unfortunately for buyers, this benevolent protection was habitually removed by contractual clauses, often disguised in so-called 'guarantees' or 'warranties', generally guaranteed to replace the Sale of Goods Act rights with others less extensive, and warranting trouble.

The Supply of Goods (Implied Terms) Act 1973 effectively destroyed most such exclusions. In general, where a contract is made with a 'consumer' (a non-business buyer), or is on the supplier's 'own, standard written terms', the exclusions are dead – void, unenforceable and useless.

Even in business contracts, a judge may proclaim a particular exclusion clause to be 'unfair' or 'unreasonable', in which case it dies. In practice, few business exclusions have been considered by the courts and even fewer upheld.

Under the Unfair Contract Terms Act 1977, similar rules are introduced for contracts for the provision of services. The general rule is that terms are implied into contracts for the provision of services that the job will be done in a proper and workmanlike manner and with reasonably suitable materials and to the standard of skill which should reasonably be expected from a supplier with those qualifications, standing or experience. The clause which excludes that liability will only be upheld:

1 If it is not on the supplier's own standard written terms; or
2 If it is on standard, written terms, then if it 'satisfies the test of reasonableness'. If it is reasonable in all circumstances of the case, then it will be effective – otherwise not.

In a recent Court of Appeal case, it was held that where a building society's surveyor knew that his report would be relied upon by the prospective purchaser, the society was liable for his negligence. The exclusion clause was unreasonable.

There have been few decided cases on 'reasonableness'. In general, exclusion clauses are barely enforceable.

The Unfair Contract Terms Act also provides that no exclusion will have any effect if it seeks to reduce or remove liability whether in a notice or in a contract, if it applies to causing death or personal injury by negligence.

So liability for products supplied under contracts is already powerful, extensive and no fault. The change has come in the law of negligence, which is moving swiftly in the same direction.

Negligence

To get damages for negligence, it is not enough to show that someone's behaviour – whether action or inaction – caused you to suffer damage. You must normally also prove that the person acted without due care. Negligence is carelessness – failure to apply that standard of care which a person should reasonably apply, in all the circumstances of the particular case.

Exception: Under the Employers' Liability Defective Equipment Act 1969, where an employee suffers death or personal injury due to a defect in plant or equipment supplied at work, the employer is 'deemed' to have been negligent. Negligence is presumed against the employer. In effect, strict, no fault liability is imposed on him.

Note: neither under this Act nor in the product liability rules is that liability 'absolute'. It is strict and no fault but the presumption of fault or negligence may be discharged. Defendants may prove that they were careful.

Anyway, until now, this has been the principal example of strict or no fault liability in UK law.

When the parents of the Thalidomide children sued the Distillers Company for damages, they faced grave difficulties. To win a negligence action, you have to prove: a duty of care; breach of that duty; and damage, flowing naturally as a result of that breach. The parents' problem was proving breach of duty.

In the famous case of *Donoghue* v. *Stevenson* (see also Chapter 75), a woman suffered severe injury through drinking defective ginger beer, bought for her by a friend, in a café, and poured out of a frosted glass bottle. The liquid contained a decomposing snail.

Clearly, there was no contractual duty between the café and the sufferer – there was no 'privity of contract'. The woman was not a party to the contract and could not therefore sue under it.

The only substantial exception to this rule comes where a manufacturer or other supplier induces people to buy their goods through some guarantee or advertisement, making a side (or collateral) warranty (or promise). That undertaking enables strangers to the contract to sue successfully if the goods do not come up to the standard promised.

Anyway, the woman who became ill had no contractual rights against the café ... still less against the wholesaler who supplied the drink. So she sued the manufacturers, who said: 'You are a stranger. We have no duty to you.'

The House of Lords declared that we all owe a duty to take care for the safety of our 'neighbours'. They are any people whom we ought to have in mind as being liable to be affected by a wrongful act or omission, if we apply our mind to the situation.

So, if you manufacture soft drinks, you must realize that the people who are likely to be poisoned are not those with whom you make the contract but are the 'ultimate consumers'. The 'ultimate consumer' is the manufacturer's 'neighbour' and is owed a duty of care.

It followed that the ginger beer makers should have been careful for the safety of the woman who drank the substance; they failed to take such care, and hence were negligent; and the illness obviously flowed as a direct and foreseeable result of the defective drink. The woman won the case.

Manufacturers of drugs like Thalidomide do, therefore, owe a duty to take care for the 'ultimate consumers'. Neither the parents nor the children could successfully sue the chemists or others who supplied the drug, because (presumably) they could no longer prove where they had bought them. So they went for the manufacturers, under the *Donoghue* v. *Stevenson* principle.

Unfortunately for them, though, the burden of proving negligence rested on them. Luckily for them, some got legal aid. But the defendants denied liability, claiming that they had taken all such reasonable precautions as could be expected, having regard to the current state of medical and scientific knowledge – and as they could well have won, all cases were settled, the Thalidomide parents agreeing to accept about half the sum that they would probably have received had they been successful.

Public opinion was outraged by the Thalidomide disasters. So three Commissions considered this area of law:

1 The English and Welsh Law Commission recommended that strict liability should be introduced for defective products; so did
2 The Scottish Law Commission; and, above all
3 The Royal Commission on Civil Liability, headed by Lord Pearson (known as the Pearson Commission), which echoed the recommendation, and further recommended that manufacturers should not be allowed off the hook by claiming that they had done all that was

reasonable having regard to the current state of knowledge (the 'state of the art' defence).

In addition, the EEC produced a Draft Directive on Public Liability, and a Revised Draft. Action was blocked by the UK.

The New Directive

In July 1986, the UK Government agreed to accept the EEC Directive to introduce product liability legislation, to come into force not later than August 1988. Parliament agreed. The Consumer Protection Bill was introduced into Parliament and received the Royal Assent just before the General Election in June 1987.

Now, then, for the new law. The Consumer Protection Act 1987 became law in May 1987 and is expected to come into full effect early in 1988. Where damage is wholly or partly caused by a defect in a product, the producer, importer or 'own brander' is liable for the damage. The burden of proving negligence shifts. Once the plaintiff proves that a product was defective and that the defect caused the damage, the defendants must disprove liability, if they can. This remedy is in addition to existing remedies in contract and tort.

First, the definitions: 'Agricultural produce' means any produce of the soil, stock farming or of fisheries.

'Dependant' or 'relative' (who may have a claim under the Fatal Accidents Act 1976 or the Damages (Scotland) Act 1976 has the same meaning as in those Acts.

A 'producer' in relation to a product, means:

a The person who manufactured it;
b In the case of a substance which has not been manufactured but has been 'won or abstracted' the person who won or abstracted it;
c In the case of a product which has not been manufactured or won or abstracted but essential characteristics of which are 'attributable to an industrial or other process having been carried out (for example in relation to agricultural produce), the person who carried out that process.

'Product' means any goods or electricity and generally includes a product 'which is comprised of another product, whether by virtue of being a component part or raw material or otherwise'. So: That in general means goods. It includes services like gas, water and electricity, but not immoveables, like buildings. Other utilities are not covered, nor is professional liability.

Primary agricultural products are specifically excluded. But 'product' includes components that are parts of finished products, and also raw materials. So if a final product contains a defect in a particular component, the manufacturers of the component and of the final product are both liable.

'A person who supplies a product in which products are comprised, whether by virtue of being component parts of raw materials or otherwise, shall not be treated by reason only of his supply of that product as supplying any of the products so comprised.'

So if your product includes components contained from elsewhere, you are not regarded as the 'supplier' of the components, merely because they are incorporated into your product. Conversely: component manufacturers cannot duck down behind the shelter of the main product itself.

Section 2: In general, where 'any damage is caused wholly or partly by a defect in a product' all the following people are liable:

First. Generally speaking, this means the manufacturer. In the case of raw materials, it means whoever mined or otherwise obtained them. Processors are covered, even if they would not normally be considered 'manufacturers'. But you do not become a producer merely by packaging goods, unless the packaging alters essential characteristics of the product. *Note*: Even if you are not a 'producer', you may be a 'supplier'.

Next, importers. That means: 'A person who has imported the product into a Member State of the EEC from a place outside the Member States in order, in the course of any business of his, to supply to another'.

So, importers means those who import into the EEC, and not merely into the UK. Suppose, for instance, that you buy equipment from Germany, which your suppliers have brought in from, say, Taiwan, you are not the 'importer' under the Act. The reason, of course, is that your suppliers are covered by equivalent law to our own and may, if necessary, be held liable under German product liability legislation.

So (as we have seen) questions of jurisdiction and which law applies to contracts remain extremely important.

Third, 'any person who, by putting his name on the product or using a trademark or other distinguishing mark in relation to the product, has held himself out to be the producer of the product', will be liable for the damage. That means 'own branders'. You have to put your own name or mark on the product, and hold yourself out to be its producer. One or the other will not suffice.

The only other people liable under the Act are those who do not identify their own suppliers of the product. For instance: retailers are not liable unless they refuse to identify their sources. Section 2(3) makes retailers and others liable if:

1 The sufferer requests the supplier to identify the source;
2 That request is made within a reasonable time after the damage occurs and where the sufferer cannot himself identify the source; and
3 The supplier fails within a reasonable time after receiving the request either to comply with it or to identify the person who supplied the product to him.

Now, what is a defect? Section 3 provides that, in general, there is a defect in the product if 'the safety of the product is not such as persons are generally entitled to expect; and for those purposes, 'safety' in relation to a product, shall include safety with respect to products comprised in that product and safety in the context of risk or damage to property, as well as to the context of risks of death or personal injury.'

The measure of safety, then, is that which people would generally expect from products of that sort. You apply the principles of common sense, the test of objectivity. You look at 'all the circumstances of the case', as you do when considering reasonableness in any other legal context. But you specifically take into account three matters:

a 'The manner in which, and purposes for which, the product has been marketed; its get up; the use of any mark in relation to the product and any instructions for, or warnings with respect to, doing or refraining from doing anything with or in relation to the product'. So check the particular way in which the product is marketed and the instructions given with it – and warnings, their presence, extent and adequacy.
b What might reasonably be expected to be done with or in relation to the product. Commonsense, again; and
c The time when the product was supplied by its producer to another.

Time is intended to cover the fact that because safety standards improve, goods put into circulation some years ago might not when new have been as safe as comparable goods circulated at a later date; and also the goods deteriorate and may therefore become less safe with age.

Next: Damage covered. As we have seen, the Employers' Liability (Defective Equipment) Act is only concerned with death or personal injury. The new Act extends to damage to the property of an individual, provided that:

a Property is of a sort ordinarily intended for private use, and *b* The damage done exceeds £275.

A defect, of course, must cause the damage. As with ordinary negligence cases, the damage must flow as a normal, probable and foreseeable result of the damage.

Which leaves: defences. Liability is 'strict' but not 'absolute'. So apart from your pre-existing rights to plead contributory negligence or to claim an indemnity from others who are in reality at fault, you may use any of the specific defences provided for in the Act.

There are six main defences. The most controversial is development risks. The defendant may claim 'that the state of scientific and technical knowledge at the relevant time was not such that a producer of products of the same description as the product in question might be expected to have discovered the defect if it had existed in his products, while they were under his control.'

In the light of current knowledge, the producer would claim, it was not reasonable to expect him to track down the defect – or alternatively, that it would not have been possible for him to do so.

This defence is not as powerful as the Confederation of British Industry (CBI) had wanted; consumer protection bodies, (and the Pearson Commission) do not consider that it should be included in the Act at all; but it does provide a potential route out for those whose defects are created during the course of development of new products.

Second, if the defect is 'attributable to compliance with any requirement imposed by' law, then that is a complete defence.

Third, a defendant may maintain that he 'did not at any time supply the product to another'. It was not his. They have made a mistake.

Fourth, the supplier may prove that he did not circulate the goods in the course of any business. The Act does not apply to the sale of (for instance) second-hand goods by private individuals.

Fifth, if the defect did not exist in the product at the time it was supplied, then the supplier will not be liable. The fault may be (for example) that of those who installed, maintained or erected the product, or who did not install or maintain it properly.

Finally, the defendant could maintain that the product was a component and that the defect had arisen because of the specifications given by the producer of the finished product to the component manufacturer, or to the design of the finished product itself.

The Schedule to the Act contains detailed rules on the 'limitation of actions' – periods within which actions must be brought if the Act is still to apply. In general, the period is ten years; but for causing death or personal injury, it is (broadly) three years.

There is no upper limit on the damages. And the rules do bind the Crown, so as to cover (for instance) the supply of drugs under the National Health Service.

So what will be the real effects of these potent new rules? How will they affect UK business and industry in practice?

The danger of manufacturing, importing from outside the EEC or 'own branding' defective goods will undoubtedly increase – and insurance premiums will rise accordingly. A premium will be placed on quality assurance. And an extra-ordinary variety of premiums are already being charged by an insurance market in a new field, which cannot yet assess the financial effect of the new product liability law.

When hunting for insurance, do shop around. Special points to remember include:

1 Exclusion clauses in insurance contracts still bite (see above).
2 Premiums vary according to the particular view of the risk taken by those prepared to quote for it. So check carefully before you buy.
3 Premiums also vary according to the cover required – including the answer to such questions as: Is the cover to apply to products marketed before the policy comes into effect – and for how long is it to remain effective after the products have reached buyers' hands?

As the burden of proof has shifted, so it has become easier for sufferers from defective products to bring successful legal actions. The result, though, will not be the same explosion of damages as has occurred in the United States. For this there are two main reasons.

First, it will remain more difficult to sue in the UK than it is in the US because lawyers there are permitted to take on actions on the basis that they will share in any winnings, but not otherwise make any charge. Both solicitors and barristers in the UK are forbidden to act on a contingency fee basis.

It follows that even if the burden of proof has shifted, the burden of finding money to sue has not. Unless the plaintiff (or, as in the thalidomide cases, one or some of them) can get legal aid, suing will remain a problem for all but the wealthy.

Second, the level of damages awarded by UK courts is far lower than those given in their American equivalents. Damages are rising in the UK, but remain far lower than those in the USA.

So what practical steps should you now be taking, to meet the new realities? Checking up on your insurance policies, present and potential, of course. Ensuring that your quality assurance is the best. Training someone senior to study and know product liability rules – if only so as to know when a lawyer's help should be sought – whether in the drafting of contracts, the perusal of insurance forms or the avoidance, fending off or winning of litigation.

Your financial planning should take the new scene into account, recognizing the potential hazards of your particular set-up.

By all means face reality, with insurance, assurance and knowledge. But there is no need for panic. Your colleagues in business and trade who operate in the United States, France and the Federal Republic of Germany have long lived with product liability law. And anyway, you cannot be sure that the day may not arrive when you will bless the rules which provide you with protection if you or yours are the sufferers – the thalidomide parents and children did not have this protection, and without them we would not now have it ourselves.

Part Six
Negligence, Nuisance and Other 'Torts'

75 Negligence – Gratuitous and Otherwise

The milk of human kindness can be a very expensive commodity. The law has no sympathy for those who do harm in the course of doing good. We all owe a 'duty of care' to our neighbours – whether or not we are paid for the jobs done.

Let us start with the snail that created legal history way back in 1932 (referred to in the previous chapter). It was quietly decomposing in the opaque depths of a ginger-beer bottle when it was rudely disturbed by a Miss Donoghue, who had been given the drink by a friend. She consumed the alleged beverage and as a result became ill. She sued the manufacturers. 'Ridiculous,' they retorted. 'We don't know you. We owed no duty to you. Even if we were negligent in our preparation of the ginger beer, you should have sued the person who gave you the drink.' 'Wrong', pronounced the House of Lords. Lord Atkin said this:

'You must take reasonable care to avoid acts or omissions which you can reasonably foresee would be likely to injure your neighbour. Who, then, in law is my neighbour? The answer seems to be – persons who are so closely and directly affected by my act that I ought reasonably to have them in contemplation as being so affected when I am directing my mind to the acts or omissions which are called in question.'

The most hard-hearted soft-drink maker must realize that the person likely to drink his poison is not the person who buys it from him, but 'the ultimate consumer'. Miss Donoghue was the 'neighbour' of the manufacturers. And she won a triumphant victory.

The next great leap forward came in 1963, in the House of Lords case discussed in Chapter 36.

'If a reasonable man knows that he is being trusted or that his skill and judgement are being relied on,' said the learned Law Lords, in effect, 'and he gives the information or advice sought without that reflection or enquiry which a careful answer would require, and as a result of his negligent behaviour the enquirer suffers loss or damage, he will be liable in damages.'

The defendants in question wriggled off the hook thanks to their disclaimer. But we now know that anyone who gives advice, provides information or does any sort of service for anyone else is under a legal duty to take proper care. If they are negligent and their negligence causes damage, it will be no excuse to say: 'You didn't pay me ... I only acted out of pure goodness of nature ...' Even a completely gratuitous kindness must be carefully performed.

So be sparing with your free advice. If you do not wish to deprive others of the benefit of your counsel, cover yourself by saying that the recipient of your wisdom follows it at their own risk ... that you give your reference 'without responsibility'. But remember that the Unfair Contracts Act 1977 will render void any such term in so far as it purports to exclude or restrict liability for death or personal injury caused by your negligence, and in respect of any other loss or damage caused by your negligence you can only exclude or restrict your liability if the term by which you purport to do so satisfies the requirement of reasonableness.

76 Vicarious Liability

Simon Smith was worried. 'It's not that I object to smoking in itself,' he said. 'But it's dangerous and unnecessary while working. So I forbid it. I've always realized that this meant that some of my employees would sneak off to see a man about a dog-end, so to speak. But I'd never realized the real danger – that surreptitious smoking and the furtive stubbing out of tell-tale butts might lead to fire. And last week it did.

The whole place caught alight – and the worst of it is that I'd only reduced my insurance cover a few months before. What's more, some valuable goods belonging to customers were damaged or destroyed, and I'm not covered at all for them.

Now, what I want to know is this – am I liable to compensate the owners of those goods, when I'd taken every reasonable and proper care for their safety? After all, while they were damaged because of the negligent act of my servant, that act was forbidden by me. My man was disobeying my orders, and was doing something not only which he wasn't employed to do, but which was not permitted whilst doing the work for which he was employed.'

* * *

This common problem raises the whole question of employers' liability for the wrongful acts of their servants – their 'vicarious liability', in lawyers' jargon.

The basic rule is simple. Each of us is liable to compensate people who suffer loss and injury due to our own personal negligence. And we are equally liable to pay up when damage is caused by the negligence of someone acting for us and on our behalf – that is, by our servants acting in the course of their employment. That is where the troubles begin.

What is 'in the course of a person's employment'? To take Mr Smith's case, his servant was not employed to smoke, or allowed to do so while working. So was his wrongful and negligent act done 'in the course of his employment'?

Ask yourself, 'Was the man about his master's business? Was he doing something which he was employed to do, even if he was doing so in an improper or, indeed, in a forbidden manner?' If the answer is yes, the master is liable. If it is no, he is not.

Not long ago, a judge had to decide the case of two boys who were stoking a fire on a building site. One of them pulled out a red-hot poker and waved it at the other boy's leg, to 'make him jump'. The lad jumped all right ... but the poker set light to his apron and he was seriously burned. But was his boss liable in respect of those burns? Were they caused by the other boy's negligence 'within the scope of his employment'? The judge decided that they were. The boys were employed to stoke the fire and they skylarked around while doing so. To the extent that the injured boy was hurt by the negligence of his mate (and not, that is, through his own fault) the master was just as much to blame as the lad. And that was so even though the boys had been shown how to light and tend the stove, and warned not to skylark.

The test is not whether the wrongful act was forbidden – only whether it was done in the course of the employment.

A case similar to Mr Smith's problem concerned a petrol-station attendant who, in spite of being warned against smoking, caused an explosion by flicking a cigarette-end into some inflammable material. After long argument, the court decided that he was doing his job, filling customers' tanks, and the fact that he did so negligently and dangerously and in a manner forbidden to him did not take his act outside the scope of his employment. His firm would have to compensate the third party injured in the explosion.

But Mr Smith's man had left his actual work when he caused the damage. He was, it might be argued, on 'an independent frolic of his own'. An 'independent frolic' does take the act outside the scope of employment.

Suppose your van driver is delivering goods for you and causes an accident – you will have to pay up. If he goes off his route and races a friend down a new motorway and negligently causes damage while doing so, you will not be liable. The damage was not caused 'in the course of his employment'. In another recent case an office cleaner took advantage of an opportunity created by his employment to use a client company's telephones to make expensive long distance calls. The cleaning company was held not vicariously liable for these acts outside the scope of the employee cleaner's employment.

The difficulties arise in the borderline cases — where the driver goes off in your van to get a bite to eat, and deviates from his route, or where Mr Smith's employee leaves his work for a forbidden smoke, but does the damage on his master's premises and in working hours. Here one cannot definitely say whether or not the master will be found liable. The reason, of course, that most of such cases do not reach the courts is that the employers (or their insurers) as well as the legal advisers of the injured person all realize the uncertainties ... so the cases are nearly all amicably and sensibly settled long before they get to trial.

One of the comparatively recent changes in the law of vicarious liability has been the abolition of the so-called 'doctrine of common employment'. This excluded vicarious liability on the part of the master where the damage was caused to one servant by another in the same employment. Today, the employer may be vicariously liable to anyone, be they servant or stranger, negligently injured or damaged by an employee in the course of their employment.

This does not imply that employees are not themselves liable in law for the results of their own negligence. The fact that the boss may be responsible as well does not free them from liability. The reason why the boss gets sued is that employees are often not worth powder and shot. They are 'men of straw', and as such, not worth going for. But they can be sued, and sometimes are.

Indeed, employers are entitled (in theory at least) to be indemnified by their servants in respect of any losses suffered by them as a result of that servant's negligence. In practice, this is usually a hopeless proposition. However, it is a technical possibility if the servant is not a man of straw, and was upheld by the House of Lords in a case in 1957. This case caused a good deal of consternation at the time and, following the report of an interdepartmental committee appointed by the Minister for Labour, employers' liability insurers entered into an agreement not to institute claims against employees of insured employers in respect of the death or injury of fellow employees unless the weight of evidence indicated either wilful misconduct or collusion. While this decision is entirely sensible it still leaves the law in a rather unsatisfactory state.

So if the act of negligence by your servant is not sufficiently serious to merit dismissal, you will probably decide to keep him or her on your staff and forget about the damage.

As for Simon Smith, he was advised that if his case came to court, he would probably lose – but that room for doubt would give good grounds for bargaining. In fact, he was let off lightly. The other side eventually agreed to take 50 per cent of what they might have won. It was a classic case of the bird in the hand.

77   Neighbours and Nuisances

The closer you live to your neighbours, the less likely you are to love them. But the fact that they may be a nuisance to you in fact does not mean that they are creating a nuisance in law. It is a question of degree.

We must all expect to put up with a certain amount of disturbance as 'part of the give and take of neighbourly life'. For perfect peace, you must wait for the world to come. But if the degree of disturbance from which you suffer goes beyond that which a reasonable person should be called upon to endure, the law will come to your aid.

There are many forms of 'nuisance'. Noise, vibration, smoke, dust and fumes are the most common. If any of them emanate from your neighbour's home, what are your chances of acquiring comparative peace with the aid of the law?

The first question to ask is: should you reasonably put up with the disturbance in question? The sound of your neighbour's child practising her scales may drive you to distraction, but if she practises at reasonable times, you will just have to grit your teeth and bear it. Or you could leave the district. But if she destroys the calm of the night, you may obtain an injunction – an order of the court, forbidding any continuation of her nasty behaviour.

However much you hate the smell of a bonfire, your neighbours are normally entitled to incinerate their garden refuse. But if they choose only occasions when the wind will waft the smoke into your kitchen ... if your windows must be kept permanently closed because their garden fire is the rule rather than the exception ... if a person of normal sensitivity would consider that the nature, timing or volume of the smoke went beyond the bounds of reasonableness – then if you cannot get results through courteous requests or threats of legal action, you will have to let your solicitors get on with it.

It is always the standard of the average, healthy, normal person that the law applies in cases of nuisance. For instance, noise that would be quite unobjectionable to a woman in good health or to a man who works normal hours and sleeps through the night may be torture for the woman who lies ill in bed or for the night-worker trying to snatch some sleep while the sun shines. But they have no special rights or remedies in law. If you choose to deviate from the norm – or if you have no alternative – that is your bad luck.

Then again, in assessing the degree of disturbance, the court considers the area in which it takes place. Live in the country and you may reasonably expect to be fairly free from industrial noise, but you will probably have to put up with the ordinary smells of the farmyard. Take a flat in a busy, industrial centre and while you may legitimately complain if your neighbour keeps pigs or poultry in the backyard, you may have to suffer in dignified silence whilst the machinery crashes and bangs across the street.

Occupy a home in semi-detached suburbia, and while you must expect a certain amount of family altercation through the party wall, if the do-it-yourself enthusiast engages in round-the-clock shift work, you will probably be able to prove a 'nuisance'. In other words, what is a nuisance in Bath may not be in Battersea.

Suppose that builders move in next door. They kick up a dust and din. Assuming that they have taken normal precautions to damp down the dust and to keep the noise to reasonable proportions and normal working hours, you will just have to endure, with as much fortitude as you can muster, one of the miseries of life that has existed since time immemorial. But if the dust and the din make your life unbearable, you may not only obtain an injunction but also damages. Why should you have to bear the cost of having your spotless linen and upholstery dry cleaned?

Every case, then, is considered on its own facts. 'Reasonableness' is enthroned as the sole criterion. If you survey the wreckage of Guy Fawkes' night ... look back with horror on noise that woke your children and caused the dog to howl ... console yourself with the thought that it comes but once a year. So does Hogmanay ... the Christmas dance ... the birthday binge ... after all, you probably have them yourself. And you may not always ask the neighbours to join you. But when it comes to persistent, all-night music from the café below ... banging on the wall that wakes you, night after sleepless night ... family rows that permeate your home from below ... constant jumping of well-shod children on the uncarpeted floors above ... then the time has come to take action. You too can make a nuisance of yourself. And the law will show you how.

78 Coming to a Nuisance

Dr Sturges built a consulting room next door to a factory. 'What better place for business?' he asked himself, rhetorically. The answer came in the form of bangs and hisses, squeals, rattles and clattering – all the row of particularly noisy modern machinery. The result? The doctor could not hear himself diagnose or prescribe, nor listen to the complaints of his patients. The time had come, he decided, to make his own complaints.

'Sorry,' said the factory people. 'We've been carrying on business in this industrial area for a long time. You decided to set up shop next door to us. That was your decision and not ours. We have to make a living. You will just have to put up with the noise and vibration as best you can – or move out to the foreign parts whence you came.'

But Dr Sturges was not a man to be easily moved (literally, if not metaphorically). Instead, he sued the proprietors of the factory.

Now, no one is allowed to use their land in such a way as unreasonably to disturb their neighbour's enjoyment of their property. But what is or is not 'reasonable' in any particular case is (as we have seen) a question of fact and often has to be hammered out with a great deal of (very dignified, of course) sound and fury in a court of law. And that is where the case of Dr Sturges ended up.

The doctor won his day. Lord Justice Thesiger held that the degree of disturbance caused to the good physician was more than that which an ordinary, reasonable individual would expect to have to endure as 'part of the give and take of neighbourly life'. Having regard to all the circumstances of the case, including the nature of the neighbourhood, the factory created a 'nuisance'. The doctor was entitled to an injunction, restraining the factory owners from continuing their unlawful behaviour.

Many morals may be drawn. First, the fact that you 'come to a nuisance' does not mean that you cannot complain of it. You are entitled to reasonable quiet for your work, no matter how new you are to a particular district. But the district you are in does matter.

As Lord Justice Thesiger said, 'Whether anything is a nuisance or not is a question to be determined, not merely by an abstract consideration of the thing itself, but in reference to its circumstances; what would be a nuisance in Belgrave Square would not necessarily be so in Bermondsey: and where a locality is devoted to a particular trade or manufacture carried on by the traders or manufacturers of a particular and established manner not constituting a public nuisance, judges and juries would be justified in finding, and may be trusted to find, that the trade or manufacture so carried on in that locality is not a private or actionable wrong.'

So you cannot expect the same quiet in your dockland office or surgery as you would in the hallowed precincts of Harrow or Harley Street.

79 The Value of Life and Limb

The most likely place for a businessperson to suffer injury is on the road. But there are accidents in every place of work and even the most sedate and middle-aged executive may (literally) fall down on the job.

So assume the worst. You are injured. You are entitled to damages against the other driver – or against your employers – because you can prove that your injuries were (wholly or in part) the result of their negligence or breach of statutory duty. How much will you get?

First, there are those items which can be assessed in terms of hard cash. These include loss of wages or salary (minus the tax which would have been paid on it and also less one-half any National Insurance benefits received). There are convalescent and medical expenses, the cost of repairing or replacing a damaged vehicle – in fact, all those items which can be totted up in precise figures.

But what of your physical injuries? Who can put a price on human life or limb? You would not exchange your right arm for all the gold in Threadneedle Street? But if it has to be amputated because of someone else's negligence, you will require compensation in pounds and pence. And if the case gets to court, a judge will have to decide how much you receive. Your life and those of your family and friends could not be bought at any price. But where there is a fatal accident, caused by negligence, a judge may have to assess the damages payable to dependants of the deceased. How? If you are involved in this sort of trouble, how much 'damages' will you get?

The answer depends on the sums awarded by courts in respect of similar injuries suffered by others as unfortunate as yourself. This is how insurers decide how much to offer to settle a case – and, happily, the majority of claims are haggled to a satisfactory compromise, long before they get to court. This is how lawyers base their advice on the proper amount to accept – and the nearer the case gets to court, the more likely it is that lawyers have become involved.

The experts delve into the Law Reports and their own memories for awards in similar cases. Like as not, they discuss the problems with their colleagues – the more experience you can concentrate on the problem, the more likely you are to reach a sensible result.

But no two injuries are ever identical. And even if they were, people's reactions to pain differ enormously. If two people are knocked down the same way by a car, one may walk away with a shrug whilst the other dies. Everything depends upon the person's constitution. One man has a thick skull (literally). Another's is thin and brittle. One woman can shrug off a severe shock with minimal after-effects. Another will suffer months of depression from a minor blow. In law, 'you take your victim as you find him'. Every case, like every victim, is different. And lawyers and insurers can never work out prospective damages for personal injuries with any absolute certainty.

Suppose, for instance, that a singer or a lawyer suffers damage to their vocal cords. They may lose their livelihood. But if the same person loses a leg, however mighty their misery, their loss of earnings may (if they are lucky) turn out to be minimal.

But suppose that the victim of the same accident was a labourer. His leg and his earning power go together. Even though his earnings may be a fraction of those of the limbless lawyer or artiste, his damages might be fifty times as great. But if the labourer lost his power of speech, his financial loss might be minimal. Lawyer, labourer, performer – and man of commerce – alike may obtain the same sort of award in respect of their pain and suffering. But there may be spectacular differences in their loss of actual and prospective earnings.

So reported awards cannot do much to help the layman to estimate what he would get for his injuries. There are too many variables. Newspaper summaries are too brief – or too full of the human interest angle which fascinates the reader but which may obscure the legal issue.

So if you get involved in a claim for damages for personal injuries, do not try to deal with it on your own. If you are at the receiving end of the trouble, then the odds are that your insurers will be behind you and you will have to do as they say. But if you are the claimant, it is most unwise to attempt to assess your own damages.

If your claim is to succeed, then you have nothing to fear from getting the help of a solicitor. The odds are that your case will settle and as part of the bargain your legal costs will be paid. If you are merely claiming lost cash (such as the cost of repairing your van, lorry or car), then you can probably assess the amount of that claim without too much difficulty. But when it comes to personal injuries, the chances of your being able to assess the right answer are remote. The more serious the injury, the greater the claim, the more vital it is that you should consult an experienced solicitor at the first possible moment.

Solicitors' services are often dispensable – but never for the potential litigant with a serious personal injuries claim. The lawyer will not only push for a quick settlement, where this is advisable, but (often equally important) not allow you to settle too early, when the course of the illness or injury and hence its after-effects are unclear. The lawyer will make certain that if you require Legal Aid, you will get it – and that if medical reports are necessary, they are obtained. If counsel's opinion is required, either as to your prospects of success or as to the damages you are likely to recover, your lawyer will obtain it. He or she will see that you do not lose your rights through suing too late, or your money through settling too soon.

80 Accidents and Injuries

Dangers are divisible

More than one person may be injured in an accident. If, for example, you are a consulting engineer, both you and your client may be liable for its results. Consider *Driver* v. *William Willett (Contractors) Limited and R. G. Richardson-Hill & Partners*.

Rodney Driver sued his employers (Willett's) and Richardson-Hill (consultant safety and inspecting engineers). He had been employed as a general labourer on a building site. A scaffold board fell from a hoist and he was seriously injured.

The court held that the employers were negligent and in breach of their statutory duty because they permitted the hoist to be used in an unsafe manner. 'Not our fault,' they retorted. 'We contracted with the engineers, who had agreed to advise us on safety requirements and compliance with the relevant regulations. They undertook the duties of a safety officer under the Building Regulations then in force. They had not advised us to discontinue the unsafe use of the hoist.'

'It is plain from the evidence,' said Mr Justice Rees, 'that the consultants knew and could reasonably foresee that the employers' employees would be working on the site and that their safety would be endangered if the safety regulations were not observed or the work not safely conducted. In my judgment, the consultants also knew that the employers relied on them for advice as to the steps to be taken in relation to the safety precautions on the site generally and, in particular, as to the safety of the hoistway. ...

The Plaintiff fell clearly within the class of persons whom the consultants must have reasonably foreseen would be injured if they failed to give advice to the employers as to the safety precautions to be taken, and they therefore owed a duty to the Plaintiff. ...'

'We were not in breach of that duty,' argued the consultants. The judge disagreed. They had 'clearly failed in their duty to advise the employers to have the hoistway enclosed by wire mesh as soon as their site inspectors observed that the hoist was adapted for carrying scaffold boards and long timbers. They must have observed the state of affairs several months at least before the accident.'

'But even if we had complied with our duty and given the proper advice, that advice would not have been accepted and the precautions advised taken and the accident prevented,' said the engineers.

'I am satisfied on the balance of probabilities,' said the judge, 'that the employers would have implemented that advice.' The result? Responsibility was apportioned in the ratio of 40 per cent to the employers and 60 per cent to the consultants. But the employers were entitled to recover from the consultants as damages for breach of contract such sum as the Plaintiff was awarded against the employers. Although the injured man could have recovered from either Defendants for the 'tort' of negligence, the engineers were in breach of their contract and were liable to indemnify the employers in full. This was no joke. The trial judge assessed the damages at £21,646.

Moral: Damages and responsibilities may be divisible – but are not necessarily payable in the same proportions. Watch out for the wording of contracts. Make sure that you are insured.

The range of awards of damages for death or personal injury is enormous; the claims are common; and the amounts are constantly climbing. So check your insurance policy and make certain that you are properly covered, for all eventualities. And remember that awards of damages also carry interest.

Protect your staff

Of course, it is much better not to have to claim under your policy. If you become too bad a risk, your insurers will decline to renew your cover when your present policy expires. Anyway, your premium is unlikely to remain where it is. So you must take care for the safety of those whom you employ – and not just when they are in your premises, either.

A Mr Bradford was sent by his employers on a 500-mile journey in a vehicle which was not only unheated but which 'had a defect necessitating frequent halts for "topping up" the radiator'. It was cold and (believe it or not) the man suffered frostbite. He sued his employers – and the judge decided that they had 'failed to take steps to protect him against the reasonably foreseeable hazards of weather conditions'. They were liable in damages.

Accidents to others

Finally, note that you are responsible not only for your own personal due care. You get the benefit of the good deeds of your staff, in the course of their employment? Conversely, you are 'vicariously liable' for their sins, provided only that these are committed within the scope of the duties for which they are employed.

Messrs ITW Limited employed a Mr Kay, who got into the cab of a lorry and started the engine so as to move it out of the premises; it ran backwards down a slope and injured the chief storekeeper. Kay should have confined himself to driving forklift trucks. His employers maintained that when he entered the cab of the lorry he left the scope of his employment.

The Court of Appeal decided unanimously that once it was conceded that he was doing something in his working hours, on his employers' premises, and was seeking to act in his employers' interests, that 'his act had a close connection with the work which he was employed to do'. The burden of shifting responsibility was therefore on the employers to show that the act was one for which they were not responsible. This burden they could not discharge. So they lost their case.

81   An Occupier's Liability

How far are you liable when someone is injured on your premises? Does it make any difference if it is a child or an adult? What about the window cleaner, the plumber, the insulating engineer – do they come at their own risk or at yours? And what about the traveller, the postman, the uninvited guest ... are they in the same position as other visitors? The Occupiers Liability Acts 1957 and 1984 tell you all the answers.*

* * *

---

* In Scotland the equivalent of the Occupiers' Liability Act 1957 is the Occupiers' Liability (Scotland) Act 1960. Under that Act, however, the question of reasonableness in the duty of care is left entirely to the courts.

An Occupier's Liability

In the old days, there were varying 'duties of care' depending on the capacity in which the visitors came on to the premises. There were 'licensees' and 'invitees' – and a forest of case law had been allowed to block the view of the basic essentials. But today there is a 'common duty of care' which an occupier owes 'to all his visitors, except in so far as he is free to and does extend, restrict, modify or exclude his duty to any visitor or visitors by agreement or otherwise'.

What is this 'common duty'? It is 'a duty to take such care as in all the circumstances of the case is reasonable, to see that the visitor will be reasonably safe in using the premises for the purposes for which he is invited or permitted by the occupier to be there'. So 'reasonableness' is once again made the criterion. The view and actions of 'the reasonable man' become the test.

But the Act helps a little more in telling us the sort of circumstances which a court must take into account when seeing whether or not 'reasonable care' has been taken. 'Circumstances relevant for the present purpose,' it tells us, 'include the degree of care, and of want of care, which would ordinarily be looked for in such a visitor, so that (for example) in proper cases: (*a*) an occupier must be prepared for children to be less careful than adults; and (*b*) an occupier may expect that a person, in the exercise of his calling, will appreciate and guard against any special risks ordinarily incident to it, so far as the occupier leaves him free to do so.'

So there is a difference between children and adults. You may expect your visitors to take care of their own safety – but you must not expect children to have such a high standard as adults. You must take more care for their safety than you would for that of grown-ups.

Equally, you don't have to wet-nurse the window cleaner or pamper the plumber. In so far as their professions entail special risks, they will have to watch out for them – unless you make it impossible for them to do so.

'In determining whether the occupier of premises has discharged the common duty of care to a visitor,' the Act goes on, 'regard is to be had to all the circumstances, so that (for example):

a where damage is caused to a visitor by a danger of which he had been warned by the occupier, the warning is not to be treated without more (i.e. on its own) as absolving the occupier from liability, unless in all the circumstances it was enough to enable the visitor to be reasonably safe.'

On its own, then, a warning of danger will not free you from liability if it was not enough to amount to 'reasonable care' for your visitor's safety. And, we are told:

b where damage is caused to a visitor by a danger due to the faulty execution of any work of construction, maintenance or repair by an independent contractor employed by the occupier, the occupier is not to be treated without more as answerable for the danger if in all the circumstances he had acted reasonably in entrusting the work to an independent contractor and had taken such steps (if any) as he reasonably ought, in order to satisfy himself that the contractor was competent and the work had been properly done.

'The common duty of care does not impose on an occupier any obligation to a visitor in respect of risks willingly accepted as his by the visitor,' says the Act. And 'the question whether a risk was so accepted is to be decided on the same principles as in other cases in which one person owes a duty of care to another.'

Suppose, then, that you occupy a rickety building and a prospective buyer wants to look it over. If you warn him of the danger, that warning may or may not be sufficient to free you from liability. It will depend on all the circumstances. But if you have made it clear to him that he came in entirely at his own risk, and he willingly agreed to do so, then *volenti non fit injuria* – a volunteer has no remedy – and if the visitor tumbles down the stairs due to some defective treads, that will be, in all respects, his own downfall and not yours.

Now we come to the policeman, the man who inspects your meters, a person who enters premises 'for any purpose in the exercise of a right conferred by law'. These people 'are to be treated as permitted by the occupier to be there for that purpose,' says the Act, 'whether they in fact have his permission or not'.

What about the trespasser, the person who has come onto your land unlawfully? The duty owed to trespassers is now laid down by the Occupiers Liability Act 1984. Section I of the Act provides that:

'3 An occupier of premises owes a duty to another (not being his visitor) in respect of [any danger due to the state of the premises or to things done or omitted to be done on them] if –
  a he is aware of the danger or has reasonable grounds to believe that it exists;
  b he knows or has reasonable grounds to believe that the other is in the vicinity of the danger concerned or that he may come into the vicinity of the danger (in either case, whether the other has lawful authority for being in that vicinity or not); and
  c the risk is one which, in all circumstances of the case, he may reasonably be expected to offer the other some protection.
4 Where, by virtue of this section, an occupier of premises owes a

duty to another in respect of such a risk, the duty is to take such care as is reasonable in all the circumstances of the case to see that he does not suffer injury on the premises by reason of the danger concerned.

5 Any duty owed by virtue of this section in respect of a risk may, in an appropriate case, be discharged by taking such steps as are reasonable in all the circumstances of the case to give warning of the danger concerned or to discourage persons from incurring risk.

6 No duty is owed by virtue of this section to any person in respect of risks willingly accepted as his by that person (the question whether a risk was so accepted to be decided on the same principles as in other cases in which one person owes a duty of care to another).'

So if there is a possible danger to persons on your land and you think that there is some risk of a person coming into the vicinity of it, then you should take positive steps to give warning of the danger.

Finally, remember: the above is *civil* law. Failure to comply may lead to a civil action for damages by the sufferer. The Health and Safety at Work Act is a criminal statute. The same careless act or omission may lead to a prosecution as well as to a civil action.

82 Guard Dogs

Business and professional people frequently use guard dogs to protect their premises or property. It is therefore important to be aware of the decision of the Court Appeal in the case of *Cummings* v. *Granger* and the provisions of The Guard Dogs Act 1975.

Mr Granger acquired an Alsatian dog from the Battersea Dogs' Home. He kept the dog in a scrapyard which he ran, to guard the premises. Everyone seemed agreed that Alsatians are normally quite docile but that this animal was one of the odd exceptions – both vicious and nervous. A Mr Hobson was allowed to keep his stock cars in the yard and often came in, with helpers, in the evenings or at weekends. Miss Cummings, his friend, was savaged by the dog. The judge found that she had entered the yard as a trespasser.

Section 2 of the Animals Act 1971 provides that where damage is caused by an animal which does not belong to a dangerous species (which a dog does not) a keeper of the animal is liable for the damage (subject to certain provisions of the Act) if:

a the damage is of a kind which the animal, unless restrained, was likely to cause or which, if caused by the animal, was likely to be severe; and

b the likelihood of the damage or of its being severe was due to characteristics of the animal which are not normally found in animals of the same species or are not normally so found except at particular times or in particular circumstances; and

c those characteristics were known to that keeper.

One of the provisions of the Act which prevents liability under Section 2 is that contained in Section 5. This Section provides that there is no liability for any damage where:

a it was caused wholly by the person who suffered it; or

b the person who suffered it had voluntarily accepted the risk of the damage; or

c the person who suffered it was a trespasser and the animal was not kept there for the protection of persons or property; or

d the person who suffered it was a trespasser and the animal was kept there for the protection of persons or property, but the keeping of it there was not unreasonable.

The Court of Appeal held in *Cummings* v. *Granger* that if the dog were to bite anyone the damage was likely to be severe; that the likelihood of such damage was due to characteristics not normally found in Alsatians except in the 'particular circumstances', namely, an untrained dog roaming a yard which it regarded as its territory; that it could be assumed that those characteristics were known to Mr Granger; and accordingly, that the requirements of Section 2 were satisfied. However, they held that in all the circumstances, it was not unreasonable for Mr Granger to keep the dog in his yard to protect his property and that since Miss Cummings was a trespasser he was therefore not liable to her. The court also decided that since she had entered the yard knowing all about the dog she must be taken to have voluntarily accepted the risk of the damage.

At the time that *Cummings* v. *Granger* was decided the Guard Dogs Act 1975 had been passed but could not affect the decision because the events with which that case were concerned occured in 1971. The Master of the Rolls, Lord Denning, did, however, comment that the effect of the Guard Dogs Act might be that in civil proceedings the keeping of a dog free in a yard at night would be regarded as unreasonable, and thus remove the defence under Section 5 of the Animals Act 1971.

The Guard Dogs Act 1975 makes it a criminal offence to use or permit the use of a guard dog at any premises unless a person who is capable of controlling the dog is present on the premises and the dog is under his control at all times while it is being so used, except while it is secured so that it is not at liberty to go freely about the premises. It is also made an offence to use or permit the use of a guard dog at any premises unless a notice containing a warning that a guard dog is present is clearly exhibited at each entrance to the premises. These offences are punishable with a fine of up to £2,000. Therefore, if you have a guard dog guarding your premises, make sure that you comply with the provisions of this Act.

83 A Question of Contributory Negligence

I am a highly skilled and well paid executive – or, to be precise, I was. Unfortunately, I suffered a severe accident at work. I maintain that the company was entirely at fault and that I am entitled to heavy damages. They answer that the responsibility was mine.

Please explain how far an employee can be held responsible for his own accident.

* * *

To recover damages for negligence, you must prove that your mishap was caused through the failure of someone else to take due care for your safety. Before 1945, even if you could prove that the defendant had been negligent, they could avoid having to pay you any damages whatsoever by showing that your own lack of due care contributed to some extent at least to the accident. But since the Law Reform (Contributory Negligence) Act 1945, this rule has been returned to the limbo where it belongs. The full extent of that return was shown by the House of Lords, in the very important case of *Smith* v. *National Coal Board*.

Section 1 says: 'where any person suffers damage as a result partly of his own fault and partly of the fault of any other person or persons, a claim in respect of that damage shall not be defeated by reason of the fault of the person suffering the damage, but the damages recoverable in respect thereof shall be reduced to such extent as the court thinks just and equitable having regard to the claimant's share in the responsibility for the damage.' In general, you can reckon that the damages recovered by the plaintiff will be reduced proportionately to their own share in the blame.

Suppose, for instance, that you are involved in a crossroads collision. Neither of you was taking proper care and you are each 50 per cent responsible. Before 1945, neither could obtain any damages from the other. But today the damage of each would be totted up and divided by two. Suppose, for instance, that the proper recompense for your pain and suffering, loss of salary whilst off work and repair costs for your vehicle amount to £1,000. Those of the other driver come to £500. You are entitled to 50 per cent of your £1,000 as against him and he to half of his £500 against you. Result? You are £250 in pocket.

In practice, you may not have to worry about this. Insurers on each side may settle on a knock-for-knock basis, leaving you without your no-claims bonus (if you had one) and with a real risk of an increased premium. But if the case comes to court, then if the liability was divided in that way, this is how the figures would work out.

Suppose, now, that you are injured at work. If the entire fault was that of your employer, you recover damages in full. If you were wholly to blame and your employers in no way negligent, then the fact that you suffered your injuries during the course of your employment would not make them liable in damages. And if they were partly at fault, then they (or their insurers) would doubtless do their best to attribute as much contributory negligence to you as reasonably possible.

The case of *Smith* v. *National Coal Board* arose from the tragic death of a shunter, run over by a train of three wagons being moved from one siding to another. The employers maintained that if the deceased had paid proper attention to his own safety, he would not have been killed. His widow contended that if the NCB had conducted their business with proper care, the accident would never have occurred and that they were entirely to blame. By a majority of three to two, the House of Lords found the deceased one quarter to blame and reduced his widow's damages by 25 per cent.

'An employer', we are told, 'or those for whom he is responsible, must always have in mind not only the careful man but also the man who is inattentive to such a degree as can normally be expected.' You cannot expect your employees to be on the alert all the time. You are entitled to expect them to take proper care of themselves, but you must make allowances for normal, human failings. You are not responsible for the safety of others only in their brighter moments. Allowances must be made for their times of inattention. Once again, the law accepts that it is made for the protection of the fallible. And while a failing on the part of the sufferer may reduce the amount of damages awarded, it in no way absolves the other party from his duty of care.

So even if the injured party was asleep on the job, the law was not. In spite of the finding by a majority of their Lordships that the deceased was guilty of contributory negligence, the shunter's widow got £3,792. It would only have taken one more of their Lordships to have absolved him altogether of liability and the majority would have gone the other way. Do you wonder that lawyers are cagey when asked to assess the odds in litigation?

In practice, whenever there is an industrial accident, the employer's insurers ask themselves the question: 'Who caused the mishap?' If the answer is clear, then the only question that remains is: How much? If the answer is in doubt, then the haggling begins – and the injured parties are certainly wise to put their own solicitors on the trail. If there is any sort of settlement, the chances are that their legal costs will be paid by the employer's insurers.

If no agreement can be reached, then legal proceedings are likely to be issued. Happily, the vast majority of cases settle long before they reach trial. But if there is no settlement, then a judge will eventually have to answer precisely the same question: who was negligent?

To the extent that employees are careless and their carelessness contributed towards their accidents, their damages will be reduced. Employers must not expose their staff to unnecessary risk. They must provide and maintain proper equipment. The workplace must be reasonably safe. And so must the system of work.

On the other hand, employees must take care what they do. Employees who cause their own injuries entirely through their own stupidity will get no compensation from the company.

It should also be remembered that if you are liable to any person, whether in tort, contract, breach of trust or otherwise you are entitled to recover a contribution to any damages which you have to pay from any other person who is responsible for the same damage, whatever the basis for his liability. This is so by virtue of the Civil Liability (Contribution) Act 1978.

The practical effect of this Act is that, for instance, a retailer who sells goods which are not of merchantable quality, so that he or she is liable for breach of the implied term in the contract of sale, can recover contribution from the manufacturer of the goods whose negligence caused the goods to be unmerchantable.

The amount which is recoverable from a person in contribution proceedings is such sum as 'may be found by the court to be just and equitable having regard to the extent of that person's responsibility for the damage in question'.

84   Trespass – and Assault

Unoccupied properties are creating new law. Squatters move in one day, the law the next. Whatever your connection with the world of commerce, you need to know the rules on trespass – and assault. How far are you entitled to determine who may or may not be in your office or on your premises? To what extent are occupiers entitled to regulate their own visitors? If you are invaded by trespassers (singly or in numbers) are you entitled to use force to eject them?

* * *

In theory, your home is your castle. So is your shop, office, factory or farm. But the law lays down strict rules as to when and how unwanted guests may be evicted. And the laws on trespass and assault not only creep into the lives of us all, but are curiously interwoven.

We are all entitled to decide who may and who may not be on our property. With the exception of privileged persons (such as police officers with search warrants and people who arrive by statutory authority to read our gas and electricity meters) anyone on your land without your consent is a trespasser.

Consent may be either express or implied. You may invite representatives to try to sell, or clients to visit you for business discussions. But the postman does not require a gilt-edged invitation. Nor do your neighbours whom you have long allowed to cross your yard or forecourt. The representative who arrives on the doorstep of your office, factory or home is normally a lawful visitor.

If you put up a sign saying: 'No hawkers or canvassers', the position might be different – just as it is when Americans erect their quaint signs: 'No solicitors'. No invitation (express or implied) equals no right to be on your property.

Even if visitors are entitled to come in, you are still free to turf them out. Ask them to go and if they refuse they become trespassers. So it is with the customer or client who declines to leave your shop or office … the representative who declines to remove his foot from your door … the employees whose sit-down strike is on your factory floor .. 'It's a free country,' they say, refusing to budge. Not so.

You are entitled to demand that trespassers leave your property. If they fail or refuse to do so you may use reasonable force to eject them. How much force will be reasonable would depend upon all the circumstances of the case. First, you must ask them to go. Then a firm frogmarch would normally be justified. But to cripple them with your paperweight, scalp them with a letter opener or pepper them with buckshot will seldom be appropriate.

Only if the trespassers offer real violence to you will the law smile upon your use of fierce force against them. As Baron Parke put it, in 1841: 'If a man finds another breaking into his house, he has a right to push him out and to use as much force as is necessary for that purpose.'

So it may often be a defence to a civil or a criminal charge of assault to show that you were acting reasonably in the defence of your rights as an occupier of property. And it is always a good defence to an assault charge to prove that you struck only in self-defence. But the force you use must bear reasonable relation to that offered against you. In a case where 'the prosecutor lifted up his staff and offered to strike the prisoner', that was sufficient justification for the prisoner to take avoiding action. 'He need not in such a case wait until the other has actually struck.'

But if you are provoked by words alone – however stinging, obscene or accurate – you commit an assault if you respond with sticks or stones. If you happen to kill your victim and can show that you were so provoked by their remarks as to lose your self-control, the jury before whom you appear when charged with murder may reduce the offence to manslaughter. If the provocation was enough to make a 'reasonable man' behave as you did, then you may avoid life imprisonment. 'But no provocation whatever can render homicide justifiable, or even excusable,' saith the law. Thou shalt not kill.

Again, the law insists that, rather than strike, you must if possible retreat. Only when the trespasser on your property refuses to budge are you normally entitled to initiate the attack. The law is a cowardly creature.

In one case a man who was charged with assault proved that he was gravely provoked, but the prosecution satisfied the court that, had he wished to run away, he could have done so. He was convicted. The provocation, of course, was a very powerful portion of his counsel's 'plea in mitigation'. But it provided no defence to the charge.

In practice, if faced with a trespasser who declines to move, the sensible step to take is a swift one in the direction of the nearest policeman. Or dial '999'. If there is liable to be a breach of the peace, it is rare that the police will not intervene. If you suffer from a major invasion of squatters, then the police may require an order of the court before they take steps to assist you. But as hordes of hippies have learned to their cost, such an order will be readily available. And in more minor incursions, the formalities are generally dispensed with. The law abhors assaults, deplores trespassers and does its best to allow businesspeople to make their own rules on who may and who may not visit their premises.

85 Remoteness of Damage

Just as you are not liable to pay damages merely because there is an accident in your office, shop, factory, works or other premises, so damages are not payable in respect of every injury for which you are responsible. Anyone who wants damages from you must prove that you were negligent or in breach of statutory duty and that the damages claimed are not 'too remote'.

So there is an accident. Question number one: Can the employee establish that the employer was negligent or in breach of statutory duty? If so, then the action proceeds. If not, then it must be dismissed.

Next questions: What damage can the employee prove that he or she suffered as a result of the employer's wrongful act or omission? And how much of that damage is sufficiently 'foreseeable' to give rise to a claim?

Suppose that you yourself are injured. Perhaps you tripped over an obstruction which someone had carelessly left in a passageway, or into a pool of oil negligently allowed to accumulate alongside a machine. You break your leg; you are carted off to hospital; you are off work for a month, and return grinning bravely, supported by crutches.

Your company is insured against employer's liability and you claim. What would you get?

First, there is your actual provable financial loss. If you were paid while off work, your 'special damage' would probably be quite small. Maybe there were medical or convalescent expenses. Next, there are damages for pain and suffering. Their amount would depend upon the nature and seriousness of the injury and whether or not you will suffer after-effects (quite minor injuries, for instance, may trigger off painful osteo-arthritic conditions).

Now suppose that the day following the accident you were due to attend an interview for another post. Had you been successful in your application, you would have improved your salary and working conditions. Instead of sitting in the interview room, you are lying on your hospital bed. You lose the job.

Immediately you can get to a telephone, you speak to your proposed interviewer. 'I am terribly sorry,' he says, 'but the matter was urgent. We have appointed someone else. I'm sure that you would have had an excellent chance of obtaining the position ... but ...'.

'The company was negligent,' you tell your lawyer. 'I am therefore entitled to damages to compensate me in so far as possible for my financial loss.' Correct?

'Agreed.'

'I did not lose a mere few weeks' pay, but an immensely important opportunity to improve my financial position on a permanent basis.'

The lawyer shakes his head. 'The damage is too remote,' he says.

Unfortunately, unless you can show that the loss actually flowed from the accident as a reasonably foreseeable result, you get no damages.

In the Court of Appeal decision in the case of *Hinz* v. *Berry*, the judges unanimously decided that, in certain circumstances, damages for 'nervous shock' arising out of an accident which occurred to someone are not 'too remote' to be recoverable.

The unfortunate Mrs Hinz had been married for ten years. She had four children and was again two months pregnant. In addition, she was looking after four foster children. She and her husband drove in their Dormobile van down to Canvey Island. On their way back, they pulled into a lay-by and Mr Hinz was making the tea. His wife and one child walked across the road to pick blue-bells.

At this moment, a Jaguar car went out of control – a tyre had burst. The car crashed into the Dormobile. Mr Hinz was injured and a few hours later he died. The other children who had been in the Dormobile were injured.

Mrs Hinz heard the crash. She turned around and saw the disaster. She ran across the road and did her best to comfort her husband and care for her children.

In due course, Mrs Hinz claimed damages. She was awarded £15,000 in respect of the pecuniary loss which she suffered as a result of her husband's death. But what of damages for the shock she suffered 'by turning round and seeing her husband injured and the children strewn about'?

Damages, said the court, could be given 'for nervous shock caused by the sight of the accident'. This is not too remote.

On the other hand, 'By English law no damages are awarded for grief or sorrow caused by another's death, or for worry about children, or for the difficulty of adjusting to a new life.' There are many wrongs for which the law provides no remedy.*

---

* In similar circumstances in Scotland a widow would be entitled to claim damages in respect of the grief and suffering caused to her by her husband's death.

'Damages,' said the Master of the Rolls, 'are recoverable for medical effects, the nervous shock, and any recognised psychiatric injury. In some way the line has to be drawn so as not to give damages for grief and sorrow but for the medical consequences of the injury to health.'

There was 'telling evidence' that poor Mrs Hinz suffered 'far more than a widow would have done had her husband been killed in an accident 50 miles away'. A 'sound, level-headed, robust, hardworking capable woman', she might in the course of time have got over it. But in fact she was suffering from 'a morbid depression', two years later. She was 'physically ill'. And she was 'entitled to be compensated effectively for the extreme mental anguish that she had suffered during the past five years as a result of being present at the scene of the disaster.'

In the case of *McLoughlin* v. *O'Brian*, the House of Lords extended the recovery of damages for nervous shock to a person who did not witness the actual infliction of the injuries but witnessed the 'immediate aftermath'. In that case, the plaintiff, a mother, was at home when she was told that her family had been involved in a car accident. She went to the hospital and learned that her youngest child was dead, she saw her elder daughter and son in a pitiable condition and her husband dazed. She recovered damages for nervous shock which she sustained as a result of this from the person who had caused the accident.

86 No Loss, No Damage

In the case of *Sykes* v. *Midland Bank Executor and Trustee Company Limited*, a firm of architects and surveyors won a Pyrrhic victory, and in the process made new law. The Court of Appeal unanimously agreed that they had been negligently advised by their former solicitors, but the judges were equally unanimous in their reduction of the £9,000 damages awarded by the trial judge to a nominal, miserable, two pounds.

'A solicitor acting for a client in negotiations for a lease of premises,' said the court, 'is under a duty to draw the attention of his client to any unusual clause that may affect the client's interest, even if the client himself is a professional man experienced in property transactions.' Architects, surveyors, builders, estate agents, property people or directors in charge of their company's property may themselves be well acquainted with property transactions. They still have a right to receive the correct advice from their solicitors.

In Sykes' case, there was an underlease with some complicated and unusual clauses. The solicitor, said the court, should have drawn his client's attention to the complications and, in particular, to have pointed out that the superior lessors were entitled 'arbitrarily to withhold consent to a change of use'. The trial judge described the clause as a 'trap' even for the 'careful lay reader'.

'When a solicitor is asked to advise on leasehold title,' said Lord Justice Harman, 'it is his duty to draw his client's attention to any clauses in a lease in an unusual form which might affect the client's interest.'

The solicitor had failed to warn the architects of the powers of their proposed superior landlords. He was therefore 'in breach of duty under his contract'.

Before anyone can obtain damages for breach of contract, he must show that 'loss flowed as a foreseeable result of that breach'. In one famous case, for instance, a man fell off a high scaffold and was killed. His employers had been negligent in failing to provide proper safety-belts. But the court was satisfied that even if the man had been provided with a belt he would not have used it. There was therefore no 'causal connection' between the negligence and the loss.*

In Sykes' case, the solicitor had in fact died before the matter got on for trial. But counsel for his executors argued that 'there was no evidence that the failure to give proper advice to the plaintiffs made any difference to them'. At the trial, the judge had 'pressed the sole witness for the plaintiffs on that point, very hard, but he answered that he really did not know whether warning of the trap... would have prevented the plaintiffs from taking the underlease at the same rent'.

In other words, even if the solicitor had given the correct advice, the architects might well have declined to act upon it.

'The probability was', said Lord Justice Harman, 'that the warning which should have been given would have made no impact on the plaintiffs' minds and that they would have disregarded it.' So there was negligence – but no provable financial loss flowing from it. So the 'nominal award of £2' was substituted for the £9,000 awarded by the trial judge.

On the question of the solicitor's negligence, Lord Justice Salmon added this: 'Although there are no degrees of negligence, the negligence committed by the solicitor was slight and was such that many a professional man might commit on an isolated occasion in his career.' To err is human, and kindly judges recognize the fallibility of lawyers.

---

* There is, of course, no need for damage – nor even for an accident to occur – for there to be a successful prosecution under the Health and Safety at Work etc. Act.

Finally, the judges said that 'there is no duty on a solicitor acting for a firm to communicate his advice to all the partners; it is sufficient if he tenders his advice to the partner dealing with the matter'.

So you are fully entitled to expect the correct advice – and all necessary warnings – from your solicitors. But if it is given to one member of your firm, that is sufficient. There is no duty on your solicitor to send a memorandum to every member of your firm – or, for that matter, to all those who sit on the board of your company.

You must keep the appropriate lines of communication open within your own outfit.

Finally, let us look at the 'trap' in rather more detail. Clause 2 of the underlease provided that the tenants would 'not use the demised premises otherwise than as offices in connection with their business of architects and surveyors or as office and showrooms in connection with any other business for which the permission in writing of the lessor and the superior lessors had first been obtained such permission by the lessor not to be unreasonably withheld.'

A further clause provided that the tenants would 'not assign or part with possession' without first obtaining the written consent of the lessor and the superior lessors, such consent not to be unreasonably withheld in the case of a respectable and responsible person.

'To a lawyer,' said Lord Justice Harman, the first of the two clauses 'was perfectly clear – it distinguished between the lessor, who could withhold his consent to a change of user only if he had reasonable grounds, and the superior lessor, who had an absolute and arbitrary right to hold consent.' The second clause provided that both the lessors and the superior lessors could withhold consent to an underletting – but only if they had reasonable grounds. The architects 'were under the mistaken impression that in both clauses consent could not be unreasonably withheld and they executed the lease in that belief.'

The solicitor should have disabused them of that belief. He was negligent in failing to do so. Even though the negligence was 'only slight', it gave rise to a good claim for damages.

As we have seen, it was at the next stage that the plaintiffs' case fell down. The architects might well have taken the lease at exactly the same rent, even if proper advice had been given by the solicitors. So the plaintiffs emerged from the battle theoretically the victors but in practice with nominal damages only. They applied for leave to appeal to the House of Lords. Leave was refused.

Part Seven
Crimes

87 The Theft Acts

The Theft Act 1968 revolutionized the laws on stealing and other offences of dishonesty. As a frequent prey to thieves and 'con men' every business and professional person should be aware of the provisions of the Theft Acts.

The offence of larceny was abolished. In its place is the offence of theft which is committed by a person who 'dishonestly appropriates property belonging to another with the intention of permanently depriving the other of it'. Any assumption of the rights of an owner amounts to an appropriation, and this includes, where the taker has come by the property (innocently or not) without stealing it, any later assumption of a right to it by keeping or dealing with it as owner. If a person appropriates property in the belief that if the owner knew of the appropriation and the circumstances of it he or she would consent to it, the taker has a good defence. A taker who believes that the owner could not be found by taking reasonable steps also has a defence. However, if you find property and fail to take reasonable steps to find the owner, and merely dispose of it or use it for your own purposes, you are guilty of theft.

In general, borrowing is still no crime. But a borrowing is illegal if the taker's intention is to treat the thing as their own to dispose of regardless of the owner's rights. Nor are people who walk out of a shop without paying for something in a moment of genuine absentmindedness guilty of theft. They lack the element of dishonesty.

The maximum penalty for theft is ten years. For robbery (using force or the fear of force in the course of stealing) the maximum is life imprisonment.

A person who enters a building and steals or intends to steal is guilty of burglary. Burglary also covers entering a building to rape or inflict grievous bodily harm. The maximum sentence is fourteen years, but burglars who have with them any firearm, imitation firearm, any weapon of offence, or any explosive may be sentenced to life imprisonment.

A person who by any deception dishonestly obtains property belonging to another with the intention of permanently depriving the other of it commits an offence punishable with ten years' imprisonment. This offence covers the situation where you are duped into parting with possession of your property and where a theft is probably not committed.

The 1978 Theft Act was introduced to block a number of loopholes in the law by creating a series of new offences of deception. It is an offence to obtain services by deception – where another person is induced to confer a benefit by doing some act, or causing or permitting some act to be done, on the understanding that the benefit has been or will be paid for. The maximum imprisonment for this offence is five years.

Anyone who dishonestly secures the remission of a liability by deception, or by deception dishonestly and with an intention to make permanent default induces a creditor to wait for or forgo payment, or by deception dishonestly obtains an exemption from or abatement of liability to make payment, commits the offence of evasion of liability by deception which is also punishable by up to five years' imprisonment.

Another important offence introduced by the Theft Act 1978 is that of making off without payment. It is intended for those who leave restaurants, self-service petrol stations and suchlike without paying. The offence is committed by a person who 'knowing that payment on the spot for any goods supplied or service done is required or expected from him, dishonestly makes off without having paid as required or expected and with intent to avoid payment of the amount due'. It is punishable by up to two years' imprisonment.

If your business is running into trouble and you unwisely decide to 'cook the books' or your finance director decides that the only way he is going to be entitled to a bonus this year is if he falsifies the profits, you should bear in mind the specific offences created by the Theft Acts in respect of false accounting and false statements by company directors. It is an offence to destroy, deface, conceal or falsify any account or any record or document made or required for any accounting purpose. It is also an offence for an officer of a company to publish or concur in the publishing of a written statement or account which to his or her knowledge is or may be misleading, false or deceptive in a material particular with intent to deceive members or creditors about its affairs. Both of these offences carry a maximum of seven years' imprisonment.

You should also not forget that the making of unwarranted demands may be a criminal offence. People who, with a view to gain for themselves or another or with intent to cause loss to another, make any unwarranted demand with menaces are guilty of an offence unless they do so in the belief that they have reasonable grounds for making the demand and that the use of menaces is a proper means of enforcing the demand. The punishment for blackmail is a maximum of fourteen years' imprisonment.

This is only the broadest outline of some of the principal offences under the Theft Act (for handling stolen goods, see Chapter 89). If you get entangled with it, the sooner you see a solicitor the better.

88 A Criminal Mistake

A customer given too much change who knowingly keeps the extra is probably guilty of theft. The Court of Appeal's much criticized decision in the case of *Regina* v. *Gilks* is of great assistance to business or professional people who carelessly overpay, and a warning to anyone who sees fit to hold on to money overpaid in obvious error.

Donald Gilks went to a Ladbroke's betting shop in North Cheam. There he placed money on the noses of horses including a creature called Fighting Scot. The race was won by a Welsh relative named Fighting Taffy.

By mistake, the relief manager paid Mr Gilks £106 over the odds on the day's betting. 'At the moment of payment', said Lord Justice Cairns, 'Mr Gilks knew that he was not entitled to the money. But he kept it, contending that it was hard lines on Ladbroke's.'

In due course, Mr Gilks was convicted of theft. He appealed, arguing that the bookmakers had, in effect, 'made him a gift'.

Section 1 (1) of the Theft Act 1968 says (as we saw in the previous chapter) this:

'A person is guilty of theft if he dishonestly appropriates property belonging to another with the intention of permanently depriving the other of it, and "thief" and "steal" shall be construed accordingly.'

Where there is a 'dishonest appropriation' with the intention that the owner will never get his property back, that is stealing.

Section 2 (1):

'A person's appropriation of property belonging to another is not to be regarded as dishonest ... if he appropriates property in the belief that he has the right in law to deprive the other of it ... '.

If the person who has your property and keeps it honestly believes that he or she is entitled to it, then he or she is not a thief. Even if their belief is entirely unwarranted, provided that it is genuine they are entitled to be acquitted.

Suppose, for instance, that one of your employees believes that he is entitled to use your stationery and stamps as a 'perk' of his job. Even if he is totally misguided and incorrect, he is not a thief – because of Section 2 (1).

'On the face of it', said the judge, 'Mr Gilks' conduct was dishonest. The only possible basis on which the jury could find that the prosecution had not established dishonesty was if they thought it possible that the appellant did have the belief that he claimed to have.'

Mr Gilks had alleged that he thought that there was 'nothing dishonest about keeping the money'. But he did not say: 'I think that I am entitled in law to keep it.'

Under Section 2 (1), Mr Gilks would have been entitled to keep the money if he had a genuine belief that he had 'in law the right to deprive the other of it'. He had not even argued that he held such a belief. So he was 'dishonest', he was properly convicted; his appeal was dismissed.

The morals of this cautionary tale are abundantly clear. If you make an overpayment, you are entitled to the return of your money. Only when six years have passed will your claim in civil law have become 'statute barred'. In criminal law, the beneficiary of your mistakes is a thief.

Better still, thanks to Section 40 of the Magistrates Courts Act 1980, you do not even have to sue the offender in a civil court. If you apply to the criminal court which convicts the offender and if you do so at the time of the trial, the judge may order that the thief pay compensation to you. In a Magistrate's Court, this may not exceed £2,000.

'Upon the application of any person aggrieved and immediately after the conviction ...' the court may '... by way of satisfaction or compensation for any loss of property suffered by the applicant through or by means of' the crime order the criminal to make payment. 'The amount awarded for such satisfaction or compensation shall be deemed a judgment debt due to the person entitled to receive the same from the person so convicted.'

You will have what amounts to a judgement of the court, without having to spend time or resources on taking the criminal before a civil court.

So the victory of Fighting Taffy over Fighting Scot has led to new rights for business people – and new risks for the person who dishonestly takes advantage of their mistakes.

The reason for the considerable criticism of this case is that it leads to a conflict between the civil law and criminal law in relation to the passing of ownership. This is undesirable. As a matter of civil law, since the relief manager made no mistake as to the identity of Mr Gilks or as to the property delivered, the whole ownership of the money would have passed to Mr Gilks upon delivery. Be that as it may, until the law is changed a person should be very careful in taking advantage of another's mistake.

89 Handling Stolen Goods

It takes a tough person to turn down a big bargain. But when it comes to buying goods from strangers, the bigger the bargain, the greater the risk that the goods are stolen. As the Theft Act 1968 provides a penalty of up to fourteen years' imprisonment for 'handling stolen goods', here are some suggestions on how not to get wrongfully charged with that particular, nasty, offence.

* * *

'A person handles stolen goods,' says Section 22 of the Theft Act, 'if (otherwise than in the course of the stealing), knowing or believing them to be stolen goods, he dishonestly receives the goods, or dishonestly undertakes or assists in their removal or retention, disposal or realisation, by or for the benefit of another person, or if he arranges to do so.'

In the old days, to convict of 'receiving' the prosecution had to show that the accused actually physically handled the goods. Nowadays, a person may be convicted of 'handling' who has never set eyes on the property. Anyone who dishonestly deals, directly or indirectly, with stolen property may find themselves charged with 'handling' even if they never clapped a dishonest eye (still less, a thieving hand) on the 'hot' goods.

As the law seeks to knock down the dishonest fences (and so to see that robbery does not pay), it is inevitable that some foolhardy (and usually greedy) business and professional people get wrongly caught up in the web. And while it is a joy to be acquitted, it is much better not to get charged. So how do you achieve this careful result?

First, know from whom you buy. Even if goods turn out to be stolen, if you can both identify the seller and show that you have cause to trust them, you will be let off the legal hook. What then happens to them is their concern.

Next, look at the circumstances of the sale and see whether they are even apparently honest. If a fellow appears in the dead of night, for instance, send him on his way.

Then do make sure that you obtain a full receipt, setting out the name and address of the seller; identifying the seller, if possible (perhaps by the number of their car, van or driving licence); describing the goods; bearing the seller's signature – and also saying that the goods belong to the seller and (in appropriate cases) are not the subject of any charge or outstanding hire purchase agreement.

Naturally, all purchases should go through the books. But even if some escape the formal accounting net, you must make absolutely certain that any casual purchase, the origin of which is potentially in doubt, is entered into your ledgers – and can be traced going out of them. The greater the bargain ... the less you know the seller ... the more suspicious the deal could look to the trained police mind ... the more vital it is that you can show that you dealt with the matter in an entirely normal way.

In fact, the police should be consulted before you buy, if there is ever any real doubt. Say to the seller: 'Look, I don't know you. I have an arrangement with the local police that when I buy in this way, I have them check their books on the goods beforehand. Have you any objection?'

If there is the least flinching on the part of the seller, do not buy. If they agree, then you may still check with the authorities. By the time you come back from the telephone, the dishonest person will probably have disappeared.

Above all, remember that if the circumstances are sufficiently suspicious a jury might well take the view that you must have known that the goods were 'hot' ... that you were dishonest ... that you either 'knew' or 'believed' that they were stolen. It is sometimes very difficult to believe that honest people who fall for a dishonest bargain are as simple as they would like to seem. And when it comes to buying, it is up to you to see that you do not buy stolen goods. If in doubt, say no.

Naturally, it is up to the prosecution to prove beyond reasonable doubt that the accused 'handler' knew or believed that the goods concerned were stolen. A dishonest intent is not presumed against the purchaser. But where a purchase is made in suspicious circumstances; where the price is low and the buyer has taken insufficient precautions; where the books are inadequate and the buyer's excuses likewise – then it may take good fortune to be acquitted. To be tried and found innocent is excellent; it is much better never to be tried at all.

So when you are offered a bargain by a stranger, take care. You may find it much more expensive than it seems.

90 The Trade Descriptions Act – and the Employer's Liability

In the good, safe old days, provided that employers guarded their machinery, deducted PAYE and let their staff get on with their own criminal activities without encouragement or support, they would keep out of the dock. And the chances of anyone making them criminally liable for the sins of their servants were remote. No more. Today the law requires the boss to exercise external vigilance – or take the consequences.

The Trade Descriptions Act, as everyone knows by now, is a criminal statute, imposing maximum penalties of two years' imprisonment and fines of unlimited amount in suitably serious cases. But employers do not sufficiently realize that they may not be protected from prison because they happen to enjoy a cosy seat in the boardroom or a proud, executive position in the company. They may be 'vicariously liable' (see also Chapter 76), in a sense, for their employees' misdeeds – that is, liable personally to pay if their staff apply false trade descriptions to goods or services supplied by the company (or, for that matter, by the firm or individual employer).

Section 20: 'Where an offence under this Act which has been committed by a body corporate is proved to have been committed with the consent and connivance of, or to be attributable to any neglect on the part of, any director, manager, secretary or other similar officer of a body corporate, or any person who was purporting to act in any such capacity, he as well as the body corporate shall be guilty of that offence and shall be liable to be proceeded against and punished accordingly.'

So the company itself will be liable for the offence, but so will any guilty 'officer' (and in nationalized industries members of boards of management are defined as 'officers'). What really matters is that, in order to obtain a conviction, the Crown (via the Weights and Measures authorities, whose duty it is to enforce the Act) do not have to show 'consent' or 'connivance'. If there has been 'any neglect' on the part of the individual, the crime of the company may be laid at their door.

In general, then, the law imposes a 'duty of care' on employers for the safety of their staff and of the public. The boss who wishes to avoid paying damages must avoid negligence. But due care must also be taken to ensure that the Trade Descriptions Act is complied with. Failure to do so may lead to jail.

On the other hand, if care is taken, the employer will be let off this particular legal hook. Section 24:

'In any proceedings for an offence under this Act, it shall ... be a defence for the person charged to prove:

a that the commission of the offence was due to a mistake or to reliance on information supplied to him or to the act or default of another person, an accident or some other cause beyond his control;

b that he took all reasonable precautions and exercised all due diligence to avoid the commission of such an offence by himself *or any person under his control.*'

It is, of course, those last six words (italicized by me, not by the legislators) which employers must note. Assuming they can prove that the false trade description was applied by someone under their control, but despite 'all reasonable precautions' and 'all due diligence' on their part directed towards the avoidance of the offence, they will be acquitted. They must also give (in general) seven clear days' notice to the prosecution that they intend to rely upon this defence – but, subject to that, a good defence it will be.

So the Trade Descriptions Act does not establish 'absolute offences'. If a prosecution is thrust at you, you may shield yourself with proof of your 'reasonable precautions' and 'due diligence'. But you will have to prove them. All the prosecution must do is to show that your employee applied a false trade description and the two of you are likely to find yourself side by side in the dock – a thoroughly unhealthy and unpleasant experience. Only if you can prove no default on your part will you be acquitted.

Naturally, we may expect the authorities to wield their considerable power with a great deal of circumspection. While the livelihood of a Weights and Measures Inspector does not depend upon all their prosecutions being made to 'stick', too many acquittals of too many important executives might well result in a well-merited rebuke. And, anyway, you will not be persecuted for your position. If you take 'reasonable precautions' and exercise 'due diligence', your chances of being prosecuted are remote. But connive at or assist in misleading the public through misdescribing the goods your company sells, or allow misdescriptions to occur through your lack of due care in directing your staff – and you are asking for trouble.

So if you have not yet applied your mind to the application of true and accurate trade descriptions, now is the time to do so – with new warnings to your staff of the perils that beset them, and of the dire consequences to them if they lead you into trouble with the criminal law. Help them to comply with the Act and you will do both yourself and them a good turn.

Finally, what of the civil law? In a recent case, it was held that while an employer cannot normally be held liable for the criminal acts of his servants, provided that he did not authorize or co-operate in their commission, yet if someone else suffers damage as a result of those acts, the employer will be 'vicariously liable'. If, for instance, one of your staff steals goods belonging to your customer, the chances are that you can be made to pay up. The answer, of course, lies in careful personnel selection and supervision – and adequate insurance. These are hard days for the soft employer.

* * *

Finally, note that the law on trade descriptions is being tightened up. Here's how:

a It is now possible for a court not only to fine and/or imprison a defendant for breaches of this Act, but also to require the defendant to make a compensation payment to the innocent party deceived by the false trade description of up to £2,000.

b Judges have warned that the Act will be enforced more rigorously – possibly by using the powers of imprisonment. Meanwhile, enormous fines have been levied, notably on tour operators;

c The Act may be amended further, so as to bring providers of services (car repair outfits and sellers of travel, for instance) within similar rules to those which apply to sellers of goods. At present, a seller of services is only liable under the Act if the prosecution can prove positively that they either knew that the statement they made was false or that they made it 'recklessly'. But to sell goods under a false trade description is an 'absolute' offence, and neither 'knowledge' nor 'recklessness' need be shown.

So watch out for new fireworks – and for firm enforcement of the old law.

91 Bribery and Corruption

The borderline between bribery and legitimate business greasing-of-the-palm is a narrow one. Ordinary business kindnesses are lawful and proper, but bribery and corruption are highly criminal.

Suppose, first, that you induce someone to work harder by offering an increased wage. That is not bribery. Equally, if you try to get people to join your firm by offering them better pay or conditions than they at present enjoy, that is not corruption. But if someone gives a gift to one of your staff in return for some special favour, then, unless the transaction is done with your knowledge and consent, this is both bribery and corruption. Moreover, although few employers or personnel managers seem to realize it, both the giver and the receiver are criminals in the eyes of the law.

'If any agent corruptly accepts or obtains, or agrees to accept or attempts to obtain, from any person, for himself or for any other person, any gift or consideration as an inducement or reward for doing or forbearing to do, or for having ... done or forborne to do, any act in relation to his principal's affairs or business, or for showing or forbearing to show favour or disfavour to any person in relation to his principal's affairs or business', then he is an offender against the criminal law and is liable to a term of up to two years' imprisonment or to an unlimited fine or both imprisonment and a fine. These are the penalties which can be imposed 'on indictment' – that is where the offender elects to be tried by jury. Offenders who stand trial in a magistrates' court are liable 'on summary conviction' to up to four months' imprisonment or a £2,000 fine or both.

That covers the 'agent'. Any person who acts on behalf of their employer is an agent. Any effort on an employee's part, successful or otherwise, to obtain some special benefit for themselves in return for some act done in relation to their employer's business is a criminal offence, provided that it is done corruptly. So says Section 1 of the Prevention of Corruption Act 1906.

But for a successful bribing operation, there must be two parties. And the Act goes on to deal with the corrupting giver.

'If any person corruptly gives or agrees to give or offers any gift or consideration to any agent as an inducement or reward for doing or forbearing to do, or for having done ... or forborne to do, any act in relation to his principal's affairs or business, or for showing or forbearing to show favour or disfavour to any person in relation to his principal's affairs or business', then he is liable to the same penalties as the person bribed.

What is more: 'If any person knowingly gives to any agent or if any agent knowingly uses with intent to deceive his principal, any receipt, account, or other document in respect of which the principal is interested, and which contains any statement which is false or erroneous, or defective in any material particular, and which to his knowledge is intended to mislead the principal', then he, too, may find himself suffering the same penalties from the law.

Take an all too common example. Joe is a buyer. In order to induce him to purchase a certain line of goods, Mr X quietly offers him a commission of *y* per cent on all business accepted by his company. At once Mr X is a criminal. As soon as Joe accepts the offer (even though he has not yet got the money), he too is an offender, just as much as he would have been if he had sought the bribe. And if, to cover the deal, Mr X supplies Joe with false receipts, then the giving of the false document is a further offence against the law.

But what does 'consideration' mean? The Act says that it 'includes valuable consideration of any kind'. Money, a right to buy goods at a discount, gifts in kind – all these are covered.

As for the word 'agent', this is very broadly defined. It includes 'any person employed by or acting for another'. And the expression 'principal', we are told, 'includes an employer'.

'But what about public servants?' you ask.

'A person serving under the Crown or under any corporation or any municipal borough, county or district council, is an agent within the meaning of this Act.'

Mind you, public employees are even more stringently restrained from bribery. Under the Public Bodies Corrupt Practices Act 1889, the penalties for bribing, attempting to bribe, receiving a bribe or trying to get one when a public official is concerned are considerably higher than those where the public is not concerned. And under the Prevention of Corruption Act 1916, where 'the matter or transaction in relation to which the offence was committed was a contract or proposal for a contract with Her Majesty or any government department or any public body or a sub-contract to execute any work comprised in such a contract', the offender is liable to a minimum of three years' and a maximum of seven years' imprisonment – in addition to any punishment which could otherwise have been imposed. Moreover: 'Where it is proved that any money, gift, or other consideration has been paid or given to or received by a person in the employment of Her Majesty or any government department or a public body, by or from a person, or agent of a person, holding or seeking to obtain a contract from Her Majesty or any government department or public body, the money, gift, or consideration shall be deemed to have been paid or given and received corruptly as an inducement or reward ... unless the contrary is proved.'

The general rule in criminal law is that a person is presumed innocent until found guilty. But where there is any question of the bribery of a public servant, corruption is generally presumed, once a gift is shown to have been given or received, offered or requested.

True, there have been some court battles over the meaning of 'public body'. If you are in doubt whether your own outfit comes within that definition, you should ask a lawyer. Nevertheless, the general rules are clear. Bribers and the bribed – givers and receivers of the 'dropsy' – those whose palms are greased and those who do the greasing – are often far more open to legal penalties than they realize.

This is not to say, of course, that the mere offering or receiving of a tip makes the offerer or recipient a criminal. If everything is done openly and with the knowledge of the employer, all is usually well. But if someone 'slips' one of your employees 25p or a £5 note, so as to jump the queue for the service you offer ... if one of your staff takes a secret cut out of the proceeds of some operation in which the company is involved ... if Christmas presents are kept hidden and unannounced ... then the law has probably been broken, and if the offender replies that he 'did not know he was doing anything wrong', that will not save him from a possible heavy fine and/or prison sentence. Ignorance of the law, as usual, is no excuse.

92 Race Relations

Whether race relations is a field in which Parliament can effectively interfere is a question of argument and philosophy. However, employers have to cope with the legislation which is enacted as best they can. The Race Relations Act 1976, which amended and strengthened the provisions of the Acts of 1965 and 1968, establishes machinery for the enforcement of race relations legislation which runs along very similar lines to that of the Sex Discrimination Act 1975.

'Discrimination' under the Act occurs in three ways:

- *a* if a person on racial grounds treats another less favourably than he treats or would treat other persons; or
- *b* if a person applies to another a requirement or condition which he applies or would apply equally to persons not of the same racial group as that other but:
    - (i) the proportion of persons of the same racial group as that other who can comply with it is considerably smaller than the proportion of persons not of that racial group who can comply with it; and
    - (ii) which he cannot show to be justifiable irrespective of the

colour, race, nationality or ethnic or national origins of the person to whom it is applied; and

(iii) which is to the detriment of that other because he cannot comply with it; or

c by victimization, for instance if a person treats another less favourably than he would treat other persons because the person has brought proceedings or has given evidence in proceedings under this legislation.

Part 2 of the Act deals with discrimination in the employment field. By Section 4 it is unlawful for a person 'in relation to employment by him at an establishment in Great Britain, to discriminate against another –

a in the arrangements he makes for the purpose of determining who should be offered that employment; or

b in the terms in which he offers him that employment; or

c by refusing or deliberately omitting to offer him that employment.'

Access to opportunities for promotion, transfer or training 'or to any other benefits, facilities or services' must not be afforded or withheld on grounds of racial discrimination. Nor must an employee be 'dismissed or subjected to any other detriment' on such grounds.

'Racial grounds' means: 'colour, race, nationality or ethnic or national origins'. The word 'nationality' is new. Under the old rule, you could discriminate against people because of their current nationality although not because of their national origin. The words 'ethnic origins' were scrutinized by the House of Lords in the case of *Mandla* v. *Lee*. In that case a Sikh boy had been refused entry to a school because of his insistence upon wearing his turban. The headmaster, against whom the claim was brought, sought to argue that the Sikhs are not a racial group. However, the House of Lords held that 'ethnic origins' meant a group which was a segment of the population distinguished from others by a sufficient combination of shared customs, beliefs, traditions and characteristics derived from a common or presumed common past, even if not drawn from what in biological terms was a common racial stock, in that it was that combination which gave them a historically determined social identity in their own eyes and in those outside the group. Accordingly, the Sikhs were held to be a racial group within the Act by reason of their ethnic origins. Likewise, although it is noteworthy that religion is not covered by the Act, Jewish employees, for instance, are probably protected by reason of their 'race ... or ethnic ... origin'.

Employment agencies, vocational training bodies, the Manpower Services Commission, the Employment Services Agency and the Training

Services Agency are specifically covered. So is discrimination against contract workers, as opposed to people who are actually on your payroll.

It is unlawful for a partnership of six or more partners in relation to a position as partner in the firm to discriminate on racial grounds – although partnerships of one to five people may still select on whatever grounds they wish. Trade unions and employers' associations are also covered by the Act. And it is unlawful for those who confer authorization or qualification to discriminate in this way.

Matching the Equal Opportunities Commission, which seeks to help women to get their rights, the 'Commission for Racial Equality' has power to establish Codes of Practice; conduct investigations; seek information; and assist those who are discriminated against.

Enforcement of the Act against defaulting employers is (as in Sex Discrimination and Equal Pay cases) via complaints to Industrial Tribunals.

If a complaint of discrimination is established, the tribunal may make a declaration; it may order the payment of compensation; and it may make a 'recommendation' that the employer take within a specified period such action as the tribunal considers 'practicable for the purpose of obviating or reducing the adverse affect on the complainant of any act of discrimination to which the complaint relates'. Failure to comply with the recommendation may lead to further compensation.

There is much more in the Act than a book of this scope can deal with. However, it is important to note that there are certain exceptions to the provisions in the Act in particular in relation to genuine occupational qualifications, so that, for instance, if you own a Chinese restaurant you can insist upon employing only Chinese waiters.

The Act also outlaws discriminatory advertisements and creates an offence of inciting racial hatred. A useful guide to this tricky area of law can be found in the Code of Practice issued by the Commission for Racial Equality.

Note: Racial discrimination can be very expensive. There is no minimum period of employment before an employee acquires a right not to be discriminated against.

93 Prosecution Laws

To prosecute or not to prosecute – that is the question which the business or professional person must frequently ask. Do you hand a suspected thief or pilferer – whether or not you employ them – over to the police? The decision is yours and the days are gone when keeping silent was itself a crime.

If the prosecuting authority decides to prosecute, then you are powerless to prevent the march of the law. But if it is left to you to decide whether or not to sign the charge sheet, you have a tactical question of great importance on your hands. Before you make up your mind, check the following list. It sets out the main considerations to be borne most carefully in mind.

* * *

1. It is pointless to prosecute if the accused is likely to be acquitted. So have you obtained a written confession? If so, did you remember to caution the suspect, warning them that anything they said would be taken down in writing and might be used in evidence? No caution would probably mean that no mention could be made of the confession in court.
2. Could you prove beyond all reasonable doubt that the employee had acted dishonestly and that they intended 'permanently to deprive' you of the property taken? If they genuinely believed that they were entitled to the goods – perhaps as a 'perk' – or that if you had been asked for your permission to take it, you would have agreed, then prosecution would fail.
3. Assuming that you have a reasonable prospect of making the prosecution 'stick', but the accused is acquitted, could the accused show that you brought the prosecution out of 'malice'? If so, they would have a good civil action for damages for 'malicious prosecution'. They would have to prove that you put them at risk out of desire to harm them or from some other unlawful motive, and not because of your wish to see justice done. The mere fact that the prosecution fails will not of itself give any rights to the accused.
4. Is the accused a member of a minority group, extra sensitive to any unfairness? If so then be especially careful and tactful.
5. Have you enough evidence – oral or documentary – to prove your case? If it is your word against that of the accused, and the burden of proving the case rests upon you, then you would probably be wise not to proceed.
6. Are you sure that you wish to prosecute? A civil action may be withdrawn at any time on payment of the costs of both sides. A criminal prosecution may only be withdrawn with leave of the court – which will only be given for excellent reason and not (for instance) because you now feel sorry for the accused or because you realize that the prosecution will bring bad publicity to your business.

7 Will a prosecution lead to trouble with others in your workforce? Examples:

   a Are any trade unions concerned on your side? Sometimes workers' organizations apply pressure to prosecute – perhaps because continuing pilfering or 'shrinkage' causes ill will among the workforce; perhaps because property has been stolen from members. Sometimes the pressure is in the opposite direction. It is totally proper to bear this in mind.
   b Is it in the best interests of your business to prosecute – to discourage thefts by others or because you have a specific policy that all those caught thieving are handed over to the law?
   c Will the prosecution add to the temptation for other employees by (for instance) revealing a shrewd mode of dishonesty which they have probably not thought of?
   d Will a prosecution lead to bad publicity because it will show how poorly the person concerned was paid in comparison to their responsibilities; the extent of the temptation open to them; or the inadequate system which you have operated for the protection of your property?

8 Are there special mitigating circumstances in the case of the individual concerned which would encourage you not to prosecute?

   a Is the theft a minor one and the employee a person whom you wish to keep on your books, in spite of this slip from grace?
   b Is the employee a person who has given long service; someone from a decent background; a person with heavy family responsibilities; a normally decent person who acted in an uncharacteristic way under particular stress – of ill health or debt?
   c Is the employee willing to resign – or will you wish to dismiss them – and do you feel that the loss of the job is sufficient punishment, both from the employee's point of view and from that of others who will hear of your decision?

9 What are the views of the police as to the prosecution? How far are they prepared to help? Do they consider that the prosecution is likely to succeed? And what is their estimate of the length of the trial?

10 What are the costs likely to be involved? Assuming that the prosecution is brought properly, your legal expenses should be

recoverable from the Crown, even if the prosecution fails. But consult your solicitor to find out what risk there may be to your pocket.

11 How much time would have to be devoted by how many (and which) of your staff, if the appropriate evidence is to be placed before the court? If the accused pleads guilty, both the costs and the time will be minimal; but a plea of not guilty will inevitably involve time – and possibly anxiety.

12 Finally: If the offender is convicted, are they likely to receive such a leniency that other potential offenders will actually be encouraged? If the case is likely to be heard by your local bench, how do they generally treat pilferers, petty thieves or other villains of the category concerned?

* * *

Having checked the list, if you are still in doubt then consult your solicitor. If you prosecute privately you will in any event need legal help. So get it before you make your decision, if you are in any doubt as to what the decision should be.

94 The Rehabilitation of Offenders

The Rehabilitation of Offenders Act 1974 was introduced to rehabilitate offenders who have not been reconvicted of any serious offence for a specified number of years and to penalize the unauthorized disclosure of their previous convictions. Among exceptions to the provisions of this Act are those who deal with the sections of society regarded as being particularly vulnerable. Thus, doctors, nurses, pharmacists, opticians, dentists, vets and teachers all retain their bad names for life. But the Act does not merely cover professional people in such positions, it also makes exception for persons employed by local authorities in their social services departments, youth workers, probation officers, prison officers and even persons employed within a cadet force concerned with naval, military or air force training for persons under the age of eighteen.

These people all join the more predictable exceptions to the Act, such as judges, barristers, solicitors, justices' clerks and policemen. Most other people are allowed to wipe the slate clean.

The Act raises important questions for the employer, particularly when asked to provide references not merely for staff but also for customers or clients. So consider: What can and should you reveal about a disreputable past when you give a reference? How far can you expect an applicant for a job to go back in the past if they have served time, when considering appointing them to a post of trust? And are you free to ignore a person's past improprieties when giving them a reference which will affect not only their future, but also that of others – including especially those who are intending to employ them?

* * *

Anyone who applied for a job with you before 1974 could have been required to reveal their criminal past. If you did not see fit to enquire, then that was your misfortune and the applicant's good luck. Assuming that the applicant told no lies, you were (and are) not entitled to dismiss them merely because you discover some unpleasant truth about their past. The Rehabilitation of Offenders Act goes much further. It allows everyone who has ever been convicted of a criminal offence and has been given a sentence not exceeding *two and a half years* in prison to become a so-called 'rehabilitated person' at the end of a specified period. The 'rehabilitation period' will generally restart if the person is again convicted of anything other than a minor offence during that period. Once the period has passed, the conviction is 'spent'. They have what amounts to a clean licence to show prospective employers.

In general, 'a person who has become a rehabilitated person ... in respect of a conviction, shall be treated for all purposes in law as a person who has not committed or been charged with or prosecuted for or convicted of or sentenced for the offence or offences which were the subject of that conviction'. Evidence of the conviction will not be admissible in any Civil Court. The Act does not apply, though, to criminal prosecutions or to proceedings involving the care or custody of children. However, in 1975, Lord Widgery CJ recommended in a Practice Direction that courts and counsel should give effect to the Act's general intention and should not refer to spent convictions when that can be reasonably avoided.

Next: 'Any person who, in the course of his official duties, has or at any time has had custody of or access to any official record or the information contained therein, shall be guilty of an offence if – knowing or having reasonable cause to suspect that any specified information he has obtained in the course of those duties is specified information – he discloses it, otherwise than in the course of those duties, to another person.'

So there is a maximum fine of £1,000 for anyone who makes improper disclosure from their records – and that includes doctors or nurses giving away secrets. When you or your colleagues or subordinates give references, be careful not to reveal any conviction which is 'spent'.

Again: 'Any person who obtains any specified information from any official record by means of any fraud, dishonesty or bribe' may be fined up to £2,000 and/or imprisoned for up to six months. Those behind-the-scenes, private investigations of other people's files have become legally perilous operations.

How long, then, is the 'rehabilitation period' which must pass before a person's conviction is 'spent'? That depends upon the length of the sentence; for example:

Absolute discharge – six months.
Fine or community service order – five years.
Imprisonment for six months or less – seven years.
Imprisonment for between six months and $2\frac{1}{2}$ years – ten years.

The rehabilitation period for people under 17 is halved, except in the case of an absolute discharge. And where a sentence may only be imposed on the young person, the periods of rehabilitation are fixed. On the other hand, where the person has been sentenced to more than 30 months in prison – or to life or to preventative detention or their equivalents for young offenders – the period can never be suspended.

Note: what matters is the period imposed by the court, and not the actual time served. So even if a sentence is suspended, the above periods apply. Where someone is imprisoned while serving in the armed forces, the rehabilitation periods are the same as in civilian life. And where a serviceman is discharged with ignominy or disgrace, the period is ten years.

Here, then, are the main consequences, in the law of employment:

1 It is normally unlawful to refuse to employ or to dismiss an employee on the ground that he or she has a criminal record, once that record is 'spent'.
2 You may give a reference about the rehabilitated person, without mentioning any spent conviction.
3 If the spent conviction comes to light, the employee must not be prejudiced for having failed to disclose it.

Over a million people are said to have stale convictions for indictable offences. In general, they now no longer live under the fear of the threat of their past being brought to light. And yet another opportunity for blackmail has been removed. But (as I said) certain professional people will have no such legal luck. And it will be small consolation for them to know that their long term misery is shared by lawyers who have strayed from the required paths of righteousness.

Finally: note that when a person has become rehabilitated, this applies for all purposes – including the making of insurance contracts. In general, insurers are entitled to avoid liability if there has been any 'material non-disclosure'. The assured is bound to reveal any facts which would be likely to affect the mind of the prudent insurer when considering whether or not to grant protection and if so, then at what premium.

Today, though, you are not usually bound to reveal the criminal past of people engaged in your business. Indeed, to do so may itself constitute an offence against the law.

Part Eight
Courts, Cases and Lawyers

95 To Sue or Not to Sue?

The average business person tends to regard the courts as places of last resort. To an extent, they are right. Civil litigation is a luxury and criminal prosecutions (as we saw in Chapter 93) should only be brought after careful thought and consideration. But if you know your courts and how best to use them, you can save a great deal of time and worry. And they are designed to bring justice not only to criminals and their kind, but also to business and professional people ... to the world of commerce. ...

So we now consider the question: To sue or not to sue?

* * *

Leaving matters of arbitration on one side, the alternative to justice meted out by an impartial judge is war. In the old days, the tribal chief or king used to sit on his throne (or under the leafy tree in his courtyard) and do justice to his loyal subjects. As the tribe grew, so the royal powers had to be delegated. Judges were appointed. The squire was created a 'justice', empowered to keep the king's peace by acting as a mediator between his subjects, or by imposing discipline upon them. Princes of power, temporal and spiritual, acquired the power to judge, each in his own sphere.

'Hear ye, hear ye, hear ye ... all those who have business before Her Majesty's Justices of Oyer and Terminer of the City of London, draw nigh and give your attendance. God save the Queen!' The court usher's cry rings down through the centuries. No longer claiming to represent divine infallibility on earth, the Crown is still the symbol of justice. And Her Majesty's judges and justices and the members of all juries do their best to fail as rarely as possible.

Naturally, the courts cost money. If you appoint an arbitrator, you would expect them to be paid for their time and trouble. The courts are provided as part of the facilities of every civilized State. But the litigant must pay the lawyer. If they manage to win their case, then they should get an indemnity from the other side.

Normally, 'costs go with the event'. The loser in a civil suit is ordered to pay the costs of the winner. All those costs regarded by the law as essential for the doing of justice must normally be paid by the party whose intransigence, unreasonableness or error has resulted in those costs being incurred. Still, there is usually a balance of legal costs, properly incurred but not regarded as essential, which have to be paid by the winner out of his own pocket. These costs sometimes dig deep into the winnings.

Nor can litigants expect to be paid for their own time. The loser will usually have to pay the expenses of witnesses, lay and professional. There is no recompense, though, for the litigant's loss of his own time – still less for the worry and aggravation involved in the legal proceedings.

Naturally, if the potential winnings are sufficiently high it is well worth investing your own time and money in legal process. So when deciding whether or not to sue, the first question is: Is there sufficient cash involved? If not, then write off the debt or the row and put it down to experience ... deduct the losses from your taxed income or profits ... and keep away from the law. Battles over principles are all very well – but in business and professional life, it is seldom worth fighting over trifles.* The most principled of litigants tend to settle, when they see the costs mounting up and the time bearing down on their already heavy days.

Next, time must be considered. A sensible settlement today is usually better than a potential victory the day after tomorrow – or the year after next. Maybe yours is a claim so clear and unanswerable that you could get 'summary judgment'. Where the defendant cannot raise a 'triable' or 'arguable' issue, then you may be given swift, cheap judgment in the High Court. For a smaller sum, a default summons in the County Court may do the trick.

On the other hand, has the other party a good defence to your claim? If they were to argue that the goods you supplied were delivered defective or late or that the services rendered were inadequate or unworkmanlike, might they be believed? The greater the opposition, the less you should be inclined to do battle.

Then consider the documentation involved. How intricate are the issues, of fact or of law? The greater the stakes and the more involved the problems, the more time the lawyers will have to spend and the longer the case is likely to last if it reaches trial. In addition, the weightier the matter, the more experienced (and expensive) the lawyer whom you will want to instruct.

So before you launch litigation, by all means ask your solicitors to

---

* Indeed, it is said that a good businessman will sell the shirt off his back to become a millionaire.

attempt to estimate the likely costs involved. They will doubtless hedge vigorously and explain how impossible it is to give any precise assessment. They will be right. On the other hand, they will at least be able to tell you the sort of sums involved if you take the case through its various stages.

Maybe it is worth while to hazard a certain sum at the start, to see whether proceedings bring results. You will have sent out the usual letters of demand. Your solicitor will have tried a 'letter before action', threatening proceedings if monies due are not paid. Those two steps usually bring results. If they fail, though, and a writ or summons is issued, the debtor generally pays up. Only a tiny minority of cases ever reach trial.

Even if the start of the proceedings does not spell the end of the opposition, you should get some sort of compromise settlement before the day of trial arrives. But this cannot be guaranteed. Once you start a case, you should be prepared if necessary to fight it or else to throw in a certain figure as costs, in return for withdrawing the action. Alternatively, you could probably 'let it go to sleep' (as lawyers put it), hoping that the other party will not seek to 'wake it up', or to have it 'dismissed for lack of prosecution' merely for the sake of costs which he himself has incurred to date.

Unfortunately, though, there are other worries to be put into the balance. Do you know where to find the debtor? Will you have to throw good money after bad in setting up a search for them? If you obtain your judgement, is it likely to be satisfied? Suing a man of straw or a shell company is a profitless pastime.

So before you waste powder and shot in court proceedings, look at the issues; tot up the likely or potential legal costs; examine the defences and the defendants – and then decide on your legal action in a cool, commercial way, and with due regard to the advice you receive from your experts.

96 Representing Yourself

Most businesses are blessed with limited liability. They operate through companies. A company is a brilliant invention of the law, which has no existence apart from those who run it. It is defined as a 'person', by certain statutes. But its personality is distinctly inhuman.

Still, a company may sue and be sued – and it may also be convicted of criminal offences. It may be fined, banned or otherwise punished. It may not, of course, be imprisoned. For that, you need flesh, blood and bones.

The same applies to appearing in court. There is nothing whatsoever to prevent a company from employing its own lawyer to act as company secretary, accounts administrator, property supervisor or any other sort of general factotum. If they are a qualified solicitor, holding a current practising certificate, then they may appear in court and represent the company. True, they are limited to those courts at which solicitors may appear – they have no right of audience in the High Court, for instance, but County Courts, Magistrates' Courts, tribunals and certain Crown Courts are open to them.

What of any other company employees? They have no right of audience. In practice, companies do sometimes obtain a cheaper representation through putting their staff into a court in the guise of witnesses. This is particularly common when it comes to debt collecting. But in general, corporations must appear through solicitor or counsel.

Individuals (including professional men and women), on the other hand, may fight their way up to the House of Lords, if they wish, entirely in person. Take, for instance, the case of a Mr Robin Samuel Buckland, shopkeeper, who conducted a successful action in person against a chartered surveyor, against whom he alleged professional negligence.

In general, 'costs go with the event'. If you win your case, you are entitled to your costs. There will often be a balance left over which clients must pay to their own solicitor, even though the case is won. Be warned – this may be as much as one-third of the total costs billed by a solicitor. The only costs which will be allowed against the other side are normally those which are regarded as absolutely essential for the doing of justice. Apart from the 'solicitor and client' costs, the winner is usually entitled to force the loser to pay.

'I won my case,' said Mr Buckland, in effect. 'I had to study my law books in an attempt to "do it myself". I have had to draft Particulars of Claim, to prepare the case for trial, to consider the law and so on. I estimate that I had to spend a vast amount of my time – which is also my money. I have been awarded costs, but nothing for my time. This is wrong.'

'Sorry,' said the Court of Appeal. Lord Justice Danckwerts put it like this:

'Although solicitors who act in person for themselves and claim to be remunerated for necessary professional services may recover these costs, a layman not skilled in the law may recover only out-of-pocket expenses. ... A layman cannot charge for his time...' So Mr Buckland got nothing for his 'time and labour expended'.

Sir Gordon Willmer: 'When a solicitor successfully conducts his own case, there has been an exercise of professional skill and he is treated differently from any other litigant in person. The court is not concerned with the exercise of other skills. Other professional people who become involved in litigation might recover something in so far as they are qualified witnesses and are called as such. But nobody except a solicitor is entitled to make charges in respect of the exercise of professional legal skill, which is what Mr Buckland seeks to do in this case.'

The learned judge expressed 'much sympathy for Mr Buckland'. But he could find 'no ground either in principle or in authority for allowing him anything by way of remuneration for the exercise of professional skill which he had not got'.

That's the essence of it, then. No professional skill exercised? Then you get no costs from the other side. You may recover your out-of-pocket expenses ... your disbursements ... what you have to lay out in order to win your judgement. But you provide your time and labour, at your own expense, win or lose.

This, of course, is a mighty argument for obtaining legal representation. An even better one? That the lawyer is likely to do a far better job for you. You are dealing with parking summonses and the like? Then by all means represent yourself. But if (for instance) you are likely to lose your licence, then it is the height of folly to attempt to handle the court without the assistance of the best lawyer whom you can afford to instruct.

You have a lawyer for your business? They are no good? Then find another. They are splendid? Then do not keep a dog and do your own barking. Even if you are allowed to appear and you win your case, you may still find yourself out of pocket on costs ... as the unfortunate Mr Buckland discovered.

97 When You Need Your Lawyer – a Checklist

To know when your lawyer's services are vital may be worth a fortune to you or your business. Here is a checklist of occasions when the wise business person will not attempt to go it alone.

1 Drafting and vetting standard terms of service. The Employment Protection (Consolidation) Act 1978 requires written particulars of

all main terms to be supplied within 13 weeks of the start of the employment or any variation within four weeks of the change. At least once in a business lifetime it is worth getting the terms drafted by experts. If you are offered a document containing your own proposed terms of service and you do not fully understand it, then take it to your lawyer.

2 Restraint clauses – new or old, yours or those of your employees – need professional drafting and interpretation. In the absence of a reasonable (and hence binding) restraint clause, an employee may compete against the company immediately on leaving its service. Definition of 'reasonableness' depends upon all the circumstances of the case – and upon knowledge of all recent decided cases. Do not attempt to draft restraints upon your own employees – you are likely to fail, disastrously. Conversely, if there is no restraint clause in your own contract of service, you may leave and compete as you see fit; but if you find a restraint clause, it may not be binding on you. Obtain and follow your solicitor's advice.

3 Standard documents require legal drafting. In the light of the large amount of legislation which now exists to protect consumers in particular (see Part Five) this drafting or re-drafting should be done by lawyers.

4 Disputes over complicated contracts need expert sorting out. To find out, for instance, whether you can cancel, bring all the documents (order forms, 'acceptances', acknowledgements, correspondence and the like) to your lawyers. They may find loopholes for you – or advise you whether there are any available to your suppliers or customers.

5 Court actions can seldom be fought without legal help. Individuals may represent themselves; a company must (except in comparatively rare and unimportant cases) have solicitor or counsel. If you are sued, ask your solicitors the following questions:

a What are the plaintiff's prospects of success?

b When is the case likely to come on for trial?

c Can you give any estimate of the legal costs likely to be involved – if not in the entire proceedings, then at least within the foreseeable future?

d Do you advise attempting a settlement – and if so, then should we wait for the approach to come from the other side; should it be made between solicitors; or should we wave the olive branch personally?

e What additional documents, statements or information do you require from us?

6 If you wish to sue, then ask your solicitor the questions posed in (*a*) to (*e*) above (in reverse, where necessary), plus the following:
   a If we obtain judgement, what are our prospects of getting it enforced?
   b Have we – or could we obtain – information about the liquidity or means of the defendant? It is useless to sue a man or a company 'of straw', however successfully.
   c Would the defendant (if an individual) be likely to obtain legal aid? If so, then they may not be worth suing because even if you win, it is most unlikely that they would be ordered to pay any substantial part of your costs;
   d Should we place a limit on the costs which we are prepared to incur, without re-assessing the situation? After all, very few cases reach trial; a writ or a summons usually brings the desired result; but litigation is a gamble and it is often wise to assess and limit that gamble in advance.
7 If you are prosecuted for anything other than a parking summons (which you might as well deal with on your own), then you need your lawyer – as soon as possible and preferably before you have made any incriminating statements. In civil and in criminal cases alike, clients habitually go to lawyers when their cases are already ruined – through incautious oral statements or careless correspondence. Do not ruin your own case beyond repair – particularly when that ruin could cost you a fine, your driving licence – or your freedom.

Typical prosecution cases which may require swift legal help include the following:

Trade Descriptions Act.
Factories Act.
Offices, Shops and Railway Premises Act.
Health and Safety at Work Act.
Serious driving offences – including those involving allegations of drink or danger or situations where the number of points already endorsed upon the licence lead to a significant risk of disqualification.
Also (and more serious) theft; taking or driving away a motor vehicle or other conveyance; handling (or receiving) stolen property.

8 Before prosecuting a suspected thief, if in doubt then take advice. While a civil action may be withdrawn on payment of the costs of the other side, the prosecutor may only discontinue a prosecution with the leave of the Court.

9. Do not draft your own will. There are too many snags. Samples: A witness cannot get a legacy; if both parents are dead, the executors may automatically become guardians of the children; and there are complicated formalities, the absence of any one of which can make the will invalid. Anyway: You are unlikely to achieve your wishes if you draft your will yourself.
10. The acquisition or sale of premises needs an expert in conveyancing. Traps include: problems of title; plans for compulsory purchase for development or road widening; complicated clauses in leases – particularly concerned with repairs; and technical terms which the layman cannot hope to understand.
11. When dealing with tenancies or tenants, let solicitors vet or prepare and serve (as the case may be) all necessary notices – including notices to quit; notices required for increases of rent following a break or rent revision clauses; counter-notices or applications to the court in connection with business tenancies (under the Landlord and Tenant Act 1954).
12. When approaching liquidation or bankruptcy (personal or corporate, your own or other people's), there are too many intricacies for the business or professional person to cope with on their own.
13. Where an accident causes personal injuries either to you or to another person for whom you are responsible, a solicitor's help is vital. While special damage (items like loss of earnings or cost of repairing a vehicle) is easily assessed, 'general damage' (compensation for pain and suffering, loss of expectation of life and loss of future earnings, for instance) is extremely difficult; based upon decisions of courts in similar cases; and leaves the layperson totally out of his or her legal depth.
14. Unless you have an employment law specialist on your staff, then consider consulting a lawyer before dismissing an employee. Unfair dismissal claims can be extremely expensive. Your lawyer may help you to avoid the claim and to behave 'fairly'.

If in doubt in any case, the sooner you consult your lawyer, the less their services are likely to cost you in the long run.

98 Problems of Legal Aid

One of the greatest joys of winning your case is collecting the costs from the loser. 'Costs go with the event', says the law. He who emerges triumphant from court is entitled to have at least the bulk of his costs paid by the other side. But what happens if the loser has legal aid?

Conversely, what are your chances (as a business concern or as a private individual) of having your litigation financed as part of the wonders of the Welfare State? If you need solicitor and counsel, it is best to be rich or poor. The middle-grade executive or professional person is out of luck.

So let us look at legal aid from every commercial angle.

* * *

If operatives are injured and wish to sue you, the chances are that they will get legal aid. This will not necessarily be free. Their income will be assessed; various items of expenditure will be deducted; and if the balance is sufficiently high, they will have to make a contribution towards their costs. Still, the chances are that the legal battle will cost them far less than it would if they had to finance it on their own.

Perhaps the greatest advantage of legal aid comes to the losers. The chances are that they will have to contribute exactly the same towards the cost of the winner as they do to the Legal Aid Fund for their certificate. If this contribution was nil, then the winner will probably have to bear all his or her own costs, even if he or she emerged from court unruffled and triumphant in every respect.

Winners cannot be sure of getting all their costs. Generally, these will be 'taxed' (or assessed by an official of the court) and the loser will have to pay those which are regarded as essential for the doing of justice ('party and party' costs, so called). There is usually a balance ('solicitor and client costs') which the winner will have to pay in any event. Litigation is always a luxury, to be avoided where possible.

Still, it is possible in most cases to rescue a great deal from the wreckage if you can only convince the court of the justice of your cause. But when you fight a legally assisted person, whatever happens you are almost always bound to lose. If you cave in at the start and pay up, the chances are that you will not only save time, worry and aggravation but that you will have to pay out less than if you had taken the case to court and fought it to a conclusion. In other words, if you are advised by your solicitors that if you win against a legally assisted person your own costs will exceed the amount of his claim, the sooner you come to a sensible compromise, the better. This is a form of blackmail, if you like. But it is legitimate and it works.

'What about my litigation, then?' you say. 'If I want my doctor on the National Health, I can have him. Can I force the State to pay for my lawyer as well?'

The chances are that – as a reader of this book – your income will exceed the prescribed limit for legal aid. If you operate through a company, then even if it is on the rocks ... about to go up the spout ... operating at a loss ... legal aid will certainly not be available to that ompany. If you are an individual and your income exceeds the limit, the fact that you cannot afford to litigate without legal aid does not mean that the State will help you by paying one single penny towards your costs – or by saving you from the grim necessity of finding the costs of the other party, if you lose.

The departmental manager of a substantial factory recently settled a High Court case. He dropped his claim and even agreed to pay his own costs. His counsel pointed out to the judge that if the hearing were to last, as expected, for the best part of a week, to lose would have meant complete financial ruin. The stakes were too high. He had to throw in his hand and lose every penny that he had spent on the litigation.

'I sometimes feel,' said the judge, 'that our courts are like the restaurant in the Ritz. In theory, they are open to all. ...'

American lawyers avoid this problem by agreeing to work on a contingency basis. A client who loses may pay nothing. When one wins, as much as 50 per cent of the proceeds may go to the lawyers. This system is forbidden to counsel and solicitors in Britain. There are many who feel that while both the rich and the poor are better off without it, at least it would enable the industrial and commercial executive, professional person, and even the better paid modern operative or engineer to fight cases which they ought to win but which today they do not even dare to fight. It is a brave person who risks ruin, even when their cause is just.

99 Arbitrations

King Solomon used to sit under a palm tree dispensing justice. In the main, his loyal subjects willingly submitted their disputes for his wise decision. The modern equivalent of this procedure is arbitration. Its success or failure depends almost entirely upon how much of the wisdom and experience of Solomon has passed to the arbitrator.

Every commercial community (alas) has its disputes. It is essential to understand how these may best be settled. And you need that understanding not merely before trouble breaks out but preferably even before a contract is made.

So consider the vices and virtues of arbitration, as opposed to the efforts of courts of law. When can you be forced to arbitrate – and when is it to your advantage? If you do not like the arbitrator's decision, what can be done? When will a court set aside an arbitration award?

* * *

There can seldom be arbitration without the consent of the parties. That consent may have been given when they agreed on their terms of business. It may come later. But whereas you can drag your opponents unwillingly to the courts of the land, you cannot lay them (or your case) at the feet of an arbitrator without their consent.

It follows that the form of arbitration is also a matter for agreement. Just as the variety of disputes and disputants is almost endless, so arbitrators may be individual business people, Presidents of Chambers of Commerce, former Official Referees or other court officials, or the Chief Rabbi's court (known as the 'Beth Din', or 'House of Judgment'). Just as you may choose the persons with whom you do business, so you may pick your arbitrator.

Most arbitrations are held because the original agreement contained a clause under which the parties agreed to settle their disputes through arbitration. Most such clauses provide that either party may give notice, requiring arbitration; that an arbitrator shall be chosen by consent; and that if the parties cannot agree upon an appropriate arbitrator, then the arbitrator shall be chosen by person holding a particular office – maybe the President of the Royal Institute of British Architects or the President for the time being of the local Chamber of Commerce.

On the other hand, there is nothing whatsoever to prevent people from saying: 'We cannot agree. Let us submit our dispute to an independent engineer, surveyor, or suitably qualified person whom we both trust.'

Once a case gets before an arbitrator, the arbitrator has the power to settle it and both parties are bound by the decision. The rules are laid down by various Arbitration Acts – but the procedure is generally informal. In most cases, the parties will set out their contentions in 'points of claim' and 'points of defence'; the arbitrator will give directions as to the trial; documents will be disclosed – and, with good fortune and a first-class arbitrator, the result may be obtained more quickly and cheaply than if the parties had gone through the courts.

In practice, though, arbitrations have a number of snags. First, the party being kept out of their money and who could get 'summary judgement' in the High Court will have their patience sorely tried. In that case, arbitration takes much longer to produce results than do the courts of law.

Next, whereas judges at every level are skilled in deciding disputes – that is, in hearing and sifting evidence and coming to a just conclusion – most arbitrators have little or no judicial experience. Unless they happen to be retired judges, or perhaps practising lawyers, they will lack judicial experience and training. However great their knowledge of the particular trade or industry, their acquaintance with the law will probably be minimal.

Again, rights of appeal from courts of law are far greater than from arbitrators – which is a double pity when you consider the judicial inexperience of many of those who arbitrate. In general, the courts will only upset an arbitrator's decision if it is made in bad faith, contrary to the rules of natural justice or in disregard of the law of the land.

There have been cases where arbitrators have heard one side while the other was out of the room or where the documents themselves show some clear error. But however many dissatisfied litigants there undoubtedly may be (and are) in courts of law, most lawyers consider that dissatisfaction is far more common with arbitrations.

Still, arbitrations do have their advantages. For instance, there may be no formal hearing. An arbitration is, in any event, generally held in private – and one or both parties may welcome a total absence of publicity. Only if the arbitrator's award is appealed is the press likely to be involved. Again, although the parties may be represented by solicitor or counsel before an arbitrator, the costs are generally lower than they would be in a legal proceeding of equivalent complexity and length. But it would be interesting to know (although impossible to find out) whether there is truth in the general belief that a far higher percentage of arbitrations in fact reach hearing than commercial cases in which writs or summonses are issued.

Finally, consider one arbitration case in which Mr Justice Willis dismissed a motion in which builders sought to set aside an arbitrator's decision that they make payments to a Mr Pywell.

'Only within a very limited sphere,' said the judge, 'will the courts interfere with arbitration awards. An error in law or in fact on the faith of an award means that there can be found in the award – or in a document actually incorporated thereto – some legal or factual proposition which was the basis of the award and which could be said to be erroneous.' In other words, only where the arbitrator is in obvious and patent error will the courts interfere. Whether or not that is a happy thought depends entirely upon your view of the decision of the arbitrator.

So before you decide to incorporate an arbitration clause in your commercial contract – or to appoint an arbitrator to sort out your dispute – consider the pros and cons with care. There are many of each.

100 When You Owe the World a Living

If we lived in China, no doubt the present time would be dubbed 'The Era of the Great Debt'. As each New Year arrives, the prospect of anyone emerging into it in universal credit is remote. Both for business, professional and personal reasons, the debtor needs to know some basic law. So here are some thoughts on staving off your creditors.

If you owe money, then (assuming that the time for payment has arrived) your creditor is entitled to sue. Unless you have some special credit arrangement, the moment that a debt falls due, your creditor may use the law as a stick to beat your money out of you. And – in spite of an almost universal belief to the contrary – there is some point to the Sword of Justice, which may somehow be wielded to swift effect.

Where the defendant can raise no 'triable issue' ... where there is not even an arguable answer to the claim ... then a plaintiff can get 'summary judgment' – short-circuit the usual, lengthy legal procedures and obtain judgment in a matter of weeks and at a fairly low cost.

So if you are sued, look for a 'triable issue'. Maybe the goods delivered turned out to be defective or the contractors' workmanship was shoddy. Do you suspect errors in accounting? The old gambit, 'I ordered the goods for my company not for myself', is treated with merited suspicion. The company in question is, no doubt, teetering on the brink of liquidation. But if that is the best you can do then at least put it on paper as soon as you can.

In fact, the time to prepare your issues is before they arise. If you have no correspondence to corroborate your alleged complaints, then your purported defence will probably be regarded as a sham and you will be refused 'leave to defend'. If you do have genuine grounds for refusing to pay any account which is at present on your 'Damn'd Bills' clip, the sooner you write off to the alleged creditor setting out those complaints in clear and unequivocal terms the better.

This procedure is, at the worst, likely to deter or at least to postpone the issue of the writ. With luck, your creditor will have as sound a realization as you do that litigation (at least for the non-legally-aided) is a luxury, to be avoided wherever possible. You both know that while an order is normally made that the loser pay the winner's costs, there may well be some part of the winner's legal expenses that will have to be met out of their own pocket. Then there's the time and energy expended, the loss of goodwill, the general aggravation and the risk (however remote) of failure.

However much the creditor may despise litigation, it is worse for the debtor. So if you do receive a 'letter before action' from a solicitor, you should either put your own lawyer into action – or else see whether you cannot come to some reasonable arrangement for payment by instalments.

This sort of gambit is particularly apt for your bank manager. A bank loan is like any other. And an overdraft is a form of loan. In the absence of some special agreement to the contrary, it is repayable on demand. So if the Bank of England squeezes those honoured with your custom and they react by requiring you to liquidate your debt to them, the odds are that they are within their rights. If you refuse to comply, then they may be able to dispose of the securities you have lodged with them, to repay themselves from the proceeds and to and over any balance.

If you would like to keep your shares or other securities, then off you go to the manager's office. The stars foretell that the most fashionable future position in such circumstances will be prostrate. But if you can manage to convince them that you are only waiting to be paid what you are owed, you may find them a good deal more patient than the law could require.

Many of us (especially those who are self-employed – or whose incomes depend upon receipts of family companies) could pay off all our debts with ease, if only others would do the same courtesy to us. If your creditors become nasty, you will have to pass the misery along the line to those who owe you a living. Demand your money. If it is not received, let your solicitor send a 'letter before action'. If this fails and you are advised to issue a writ, go ahead – remembering that you may get summary judgement. Console yourself, too, with the thought that most people pay up when they get a solicitor's letter and that those who do not will seldom allow a case to get to trial. Even where a writ is issued, the odds are heavily against eventual legal battle.

My advice, then, in a hard-up future? Treat thy debtor as thyself. If your creditors are cruel to you, the least you can do is to return the compliment — to those in your debt. When solvency is at stake, the forthcoming years are unlikely to be known as 'The Era of the Gentlemen'.

101 Legal Aspects of Billing*

The larger and more modern the aircraft, the greater the tragedy when the crash occurs. The finer the computer, the greater the hazard if it hiccups — or is fed the wrong material — and the wrong bills emerge.

So consider: If you send out the wrong account, can you later correct it? If you undercharge, are you bound by your mistakes? If you overcharge and your client or customer has a heart attack as a result, can you be held liable in law?

* * *

A bill is born of a contract. When the contract contemplates that payment is due, the debtor is bound to pay.

The bill merely takes account of existing circumstances. An error in that account in no way affects the obligations of the parties, one towards the other — at least for the first few years.

If you charge too much, your customer is still only bound to pay the proper contractual price. A customer who overpays is entitled to the return of any balance overpaid.

Conversely, if you undercharge, you are entitled to demand the difference between the sum on your account and the amount which should have been billed.

The creditor is not bound by the mistakes that he or she makes in accounts, which are 'post-contractual documents'. They do not contain the deal between the parties. The bargain remains the same and either may still enforce their rights.

The situation is, of course, entirely different where the supplier agrees to provide goods or services at a mistakenly low cost. Suppose, for instance, that you receive a firm quotation for repairs to your premises. The contractor has underquoted. This is their own misfortune. The law will not let them say: 'I made a mistake — so I must charge more.'

Equally, you may accept a quotation and then find someone

---

* See also Chapter 63 for the Rights of the Unpaid.

else prepared to do the job (or, for that matter, to provide the goods) at a much lower cost. You are bound by your error.

There are some possible legal loopholes. For instance, if goods are advertised or shown in a shop window, marked with a price, and you write (or say) that you will have them, you are making the offer. The supplier is merely (in law) issuing an 'invitation to treat' – inviting you to offer to pay the sum which they have indicated that they will accept. They are not bound by their indication (see Part Five).

Anyway, the bill has nothing to do with the bargain. It comes afterwards. Mistakes will cause ill will – but they have no legally binding effect.

What if an overcharge causes ill health?

The law is very unlikely to provide any balm for the customer's wounds. The damage is 'too remote', from the wrongful act or omission. I know of no case in which an overcharge – even a deliberate one made by a public utility to jolt the customer into action – has led to successful legal proceedings. Not every wrong leads to a legal remedy.

As for undercharging, the creditor runs one risk only – that time may run out. The law says that all good things – and all bad ones – must come to an end. It applies a 'period of limitation' even on claims for debts when there is and can be no valid answer to the original claim, and even where the account is both accurate and entirely justified.

A claim for a debt becomes 'statute barred' when six years have passed from the date when the debt was originally incurred or (in appropriate cases) the date when the debtor last gave a written acknowledgement of his debt. If someone owes you money and asks for time to pay and you grant the request, then 'time begins to run' all over again, from the date of the request. But if the debtor simply sits tight and says nothing, you must start your proceedings within six years from the date when the money originally fell due for payment.

Conversely, if you do not receive an account for a while, do not rejoice too soon. Only when six years have passed can you relax and regard the transaction as closed.

102 The 'Harassment' of Debtors

A debt collecting firm attempted to obtain money from a housewife in payment for goods. It sent a letter threatening that a van marked 'debt collection company' would arrive at her home. Charged and convicted of an offence under the Administration of Justice Act 1970, the proprietor made legal history – and emphasized that traders who are owed money are going to find it even harder to collect in the future than they have done in the past.

So before you put a list of debtors in your window or threaten to humiliate your debtors in some other way, consider the rules.

Section 40 of the Act says this: 'A person commits an offence if, with the object of coercing another person to pay money claimed from the other as a debt due under a contract, he –

a harasses the other with demands for payment which, in respect of their frequency or the manner or occasion of making any such demand, or of any threat or publicity by which any demand is accompanied, are calculated to subject him or members of his family or household to alarm, distress or humiliation.'

The object of telling a customer that a van will arrive at her home marked 'debt collection company' is obviously to subject her and her household to 'distress or humiliation'. To put the name and address of the debtor in the window would produce the same result. Either way, the odds are that the trader commits an offence.

Equally, it is unlawful 'falsely to represent, in relation to the money claimed, that criminal proceedings lie for failure to pay it.' By all means threaten to put the matter in the hands of your solicitors or of a debt collecting agency. But do not say that you will call in the police when you know perfectly well that no prosecution lies for failure to comply with your contract.

Further, it is unlawful to represent that you are 'authorised in some official capacity to claim or enforce payment'. So do not tell the debtor that you are a court official or the like. Also, if you send out a document which you have falsely represented to have some official character, you will commit an offence.

A trader who 'concerts with others' in the taking of such action under (*a*) above may be guilty of an offence 'notwithstanding that his own course of conduct does not by itself amount to harassment'. If you plan harassment with some debt collecting agency, you may find yourself in the dock, even though you have taken no specific action on your own behalf.

Penalties? The maximum fine for this offence is now £2,000. You cannot be imprisoned for your pains, but it may cost you a great deal more to break the law than it would to write off the debt.

The Section does provide one defence: The above rules do not apply 'to anything done by a person which is reasonable (and otherwise permissible in law) for the purpose –

- *a* of securing the discharge of an obligation due, or believed by him to be due, to himself or to persons for whom he acts, or protecting himself or them from future loss; or
- *b* of the enforcement of any liability by legal process.'

Lawyers may still harass debtors by serving writs or summonses – and the wise course now is quite clearly to let your lawyers get on with the job for you. On the other hand, if you are owed money – or honestly believe that a particular person is in your debt – then you may take such steps as are 'reasonable and otherwise permissible in law' in order to get payment. What is 'reasonable', as always, will depend on all the circumstances of the case.

103 Time Passes

If a train or a plane arrives late, its occupants may be irritated but the effects of the delay will not be fatal. In law, though, delay may spell death.

When suing for damages for personal injuries, for instance, the claim must normally be brought within three years of the accident. But 'time' may run from the date when the patient first could or should have known of the existence of the ailment or of its cause. Claims against the estate of the deceased person must generally be brought within 12 months from the grant of probate or, in the case of an intestacy, of letters of administration, of the start of the winding up of their affairs. Actions for debt must (as we saw in the previous chapter) be brought within six years of the date when the debt was incurred or the date when it was last acknowledged to be due, in writing. Most other actions for breach of contract have a six-year limit.

If you are to be sued for professional negligence, the time limit is also six years (unless, of course, you caused personal injuries, in which case the three-year limit applies). Negligence is a 'tort' – a civil wrong – as are nuisance, defamation and assault. Six years with no writ or summons means that the potential action disappears.

There are other and much shorter limits imposed by individual statutes. The most important for the business or professional person? Those laid down by the Landlord and Tenant Act 1954 – which protects business and professional tenants whose leases or tenancies are coming to an end (see Chapter 23).

Suppose that you are tenant of your shop or office. Unless and until your landlords serve a notice on you, in the prescribed form, stating whether or not they are prepared to grant a new tenancy, you may remain – on the old terms.

Once you have received a notice, though, you must take appropriate action. You must serve a counter-notice, saying whether or not you are prepared to give up possession of the property. You must give your notice within two months – and you must do so in writing.

Now suppose that you give your notice and the haggling procedure begins. Your landlord asks for a rent that you regard as too high. You offer terms which are unacceptably low. Still, there is no doubt that you are entitled to a new tenancy. Your landlord cannot show (for instance) that he needs the place for the purposes of his own business or home, or that he intends to redevelop the premises.

Unfortunately for you, the haggling goes on too long. You are suddenly faced with Section 29 (3) of the Act: 'No application ...' to the court for a new tenancy 'shall be entertained unless it is made not less than two nor more than four months after the giving of the landlord's notice ...' The four-month period has passed. You are out of luck. No court, however mighty, can restore your rights. You are at your landlord's mercy.

If you decide to handle your own legal affairs, you do so at your own risk – if you make a mistake ... if you forget to take action within the appropriate time ... then you have only yourself to blame. In that case, you will have to bear any loss on your own shoulders.

If, on the other hand, you have seen fit to put your problems into the hands of solicitors, it is up to them to watch out for the time limits. Whether you are seeking a new tenancy of your old office or shop – or whether the local planning authority is challenging your use of the premises – it is highly dangerous to go it alone.

In Conclusion

Whether you handle your legal anxieties yourself or through lawyers, please use the information and guidance in this book well and with discretion. Watch for changes in the law; know when to take legal advice and how to follow it; and stay as far away from courts and lawyers as you can.

Good luck, then ...

Index

ACAS, 115, 118, 119, 133
Accidents, 141, 244–8, 253, 258, 294
    notification of, 160
Accounts, 4, 41
Administration of Justice Act 1920, 201
Administration of Justice Act 1970, 303
Agents, 187–9
AGM, 34–5
Air pollution, 171
Animals Act 1971, 251–3
Annual report, 119
Arbitration, 287, 296–9
Arbitration Acts, 297
Assault, 256–8
Assignment of lease, 4, 40
Atmospheric pollution, 171
Attachment of earnings, 81–2

Banking, 46–8
Bankruptcy, 65, 294
Billing, legal aspects of, 301
Bills of Exchange Act 1882, 209
Binding agreement, 190
Bomb warnings, 160
Bonfires, 241
Bonus, 88–90
Borrowing, 265
Breach of contract, 93, 214, 224, 304
Breach of warranty of authority, 189
Bribery and corruption, 273–6
Builders, 242
Business closure, checklist, 39–41
Business name, 4
    unlawful use, 48–50

Business Names Act 1985, 4
Business premises, 4, 5, 39, 60–4, 69–70
    acquisition or sale of, 294
    deposits on, 5
    see also Leases
Business start-up, 3–7
Business termination, 27–9, 64–8
Buyers, 163

Cammell Laird Shipbuilders Ltd, 126–31
Cash flow, checklist, 194–7
Caveat emptor, 178, 183
Central Arbitration Committee (CAC), 119
Charles Rickards Limited v. *Oppenheim*, 198
Cheques, dishonouring, 48
Christie Owen and Davies v. *Rapaccioli*, 221
City Code, 19
Civil Jurisdiction and Judgments Act 1982, 201, 204
Civil Liability (Contribution) Act 1978, 255
Codes of Practice, 126, 133, 144, 278
Collective bargaining, 116–19, 136
Commission, 88–90, 221–2
Commission for Racial Equality, 126, 278
Commission on Industrial Relations, 118
Common Market law, 204–7
Companies Act 1947, 32
Companies Act 1948, 32

Companies Act 1985, 7, 15, 26, 29, 31, 34, 67, 80, 118, 119
Companies Consolidation (Consequential Provisions) Act 1985, 67
Companies (Tables A–F) Regulations 1985, 31
Company formation, 3
Company meetings, 34–6
Compensation, 83–4, 106, 107, 111, 113–15, 238, 244–6, 259
Competition, unfair, 86–8
Computer programs, 53
Conciliation, 119
Confidential information, 41–6
Confidentiality clause, 76
Conspiracy action, 23–5
Consumer Credit Act 1974, 184–5
Consumer Protection Act 1987, 150, 204, 228
Consumer Protection Advisory Committee, 180
Contract of service, 77–8, 80, 85, 87, 88, 94, 95
Contract variation, 78–82
Contractors
    cost of, 209–11
    definition, 209
    rights of the unpaid, 213–18
    see also Repairers
Contracts
    binding, 209–11
    breach of, 93, 214, 224, 304
    checklist, 175–7
    disputes, 211, 292
    employment, 75–8, 158
    fixed-term, 114
    import/export, 200–4
    insurance, 232
    litigation, 211
    terms of, 209–11, 213
    time factor in, 197–200
    see also Billing
Contractual documents, 40
Control of Pollution Act 1974, 168
Copydex Limited, 43–4
Copyright Act 1956, 50
Copyright (Computer Software) Act 1985, 53
Copyright laws, 50–3

Corporation tax, 71
County Courts Act 1984, 208–9
Creditors, 39, 65, 67, 81
    fending off, 299
    checklist, 194–7
    winding up, 66
Cummings v. Granger, 251–2
Customs and Excise Act 1952, 16

Damage
    general, 294
    remoteness of, 258–60, 302
    to property, 230–1
Damages, 72, 232, 247–8
    claiming, 93, 189
    for breach of contract, 224
    for negligence, 226, 253, 260
    for personal injury, 244–6, 304
    for wrongful dismissal, 113
    in defamation action, 97
    suppliers, 40–1
Damages (Scotland) Act 1976, 228
Data Protection Act 1984, 55–6, 206
Debt recovery
    checklist, 191–4
    litigation, 192–4
Debtors, 81, 299
    harassment of, 303–4
Debts, 65, 81
    payment of, 81
    preferential, 138
    priorities, 65
    statute barred, 302
Deception, 266
Defamation, 97, 99
Defective products, liability for, 224
Department of Trade and Industry (DTI), 34
Depositors, protection of, 31–4
Deposits on premises, 5
Depression, 68
Director
    dismissal, 23–7
    duties of, 16–18
    fiduciary relationship, 13
    personal liabilities, 11–13
    removal of, 29–31
    title implications, 14–16
Disclaimers, 100

Index

Dismissal
  definition, 113
  director, 23–7
  problems of, 94–6, 104
  summary, 114
  unfair, 106, 107, 111, 113–15,
    122, 123, 294
  wrongful, 111, 113
Disputes, 211, 292, 297
Dissolution of company, 66
Disturbance, assessing degree of, 242
Doble v. *Firestone Tyre and Rubber Co. Ltd.*, 102
Documentation, 161
Donoghue v. *Stevenson*, 226
Driver v. *William Willett (Contractors) Limited and R.G. Richardson-Hill & Partners*, 246
Duty of care, 248

Earnings, attachment of, 81–2
Earnings Act 1971, 81
EEC, 204–7, 228
Employees
  housing for, 5–6
  in business closure, 39
Employees' rights, 134
Employers' liability, 238, 258, 271–3
Employers' Liability (Defective Equipment) Act 1969, 226, 230–1
Employment Act 1982, 111
Employment Appeal Tribunal, 102
Employment contracts, 158
  requirements of, 75–8
Employment Protection Act 1975, 40, 65, 111, 116, 123, 127, 134, 135
Employment Protection (Consolidation) Act 1978, 5, 78, 94, 96, 100–1, 106, 107, 111, 113, 120, 122, 131, 291
English Law Commission, 227
Equal Opportunities Commission, 126
Equal Pay Act 1970, 111, 126, 127
Equal Pay Act 1975, 121, 122
Equal Pay (Amendment) Regulations 1983, 126
Equal Pay Regulations, 205
Estate agents, payment of, 221–3
European Economic Community, 204–7, 228

Exclusion clauses, 160

Factories Act, 145, 158
Failure of businesses, 3
Fair Trading Act 1973, 178, 180, 186
Fair Wages Resolution, 127
Fatal Accidents Act 1976, 228
Financial planning, 233
Financial Services Act 1986, 32, 34
First aid regulations, 159
Fletcher v. *Budgen*, 181–2
Flixborough disaster, 163
Foreign contractors, 200–4
Foreign Judgments (Reciprocal Enforcement) Act 1933, 201
Franchise, 71–2
Fraser v. *Evans and Others*, 44
Fraud, 24
Freelance help, 107
Fund-raising, 3

Gaming licence, 16
Guarantee payments, 120
Guard dogs, 251–3
Guard Dogs Act 1975, 251–3

Hall v. *Wickens Motors (Gloucester) Limited*, 182
Handling stolen goods, 269–70
Hayward, Julie, 126–31
Health and Safety at Work etc. Act 1974, 141–8, 150–53, 156, 158–64, 166, 251, 261
Health and Safety Codes, 144
Health and Safety Commission, 133, 144, 165
Health and Safety (Emissions into the Atmosphere) Regulations 1983, 166
Health and Safety Executive, 144
Hire purchase, 184
Hiring, 184–5
Hourly paid workers, 120
Housing for employees, 5–6
Hubbard v. *Vosper*, 45
Huckerby v. *Elliot*, 16, 18

Import/export contracts, 200–4
Individual trading, 3, 71
Industrial accidents, 141
Industrial Relations Act, 111, 116, 118

Industrial Tribunals, 114, 121, 123, 126, 137, 278
Information, 116–19
  confidential, 119
  duty of employers to provide, 116
  on safety and health, 162
Injunction, 241
Injury, 244–6, 246–8, 258, 294, 304
Insolvency, 64, 134
Insurance, 6, 160, 247, 254, 258
Insurance contracts, 232
Insurance policies, 160, 232, 247
Interest charges, 207–9
Inventions, ownership of, 83–4
Investors, protection of, 31–4
ITW Limited, 248

Landlord and Tenant Act 1927, 63
Landlord and Tenant Act 1954, 4, 60, 305
Larcency, *see* Theft Act
Law of Property Act 1969, 4, 60
Law Reform (Contributory Negligence) Act 1945, 253
Law Reform (Miscellaneous Provisions) Act 1934, 208
Lawyer, need for services of, 291–4
Leases, 4, 70, 305
  expiry, 60–4
Leasing, 184–5
Legal Aid, 246, 293–4
Liability
  personal, 152–3
  vicarious, 238–41, 271
Limited liability company, 3, 29, 289
Lindgren and Others v. *L. & P. Estates Limited*, 22
Line of business, 36–9
Liquidation, 294
Litigation, 287
  contracts, 211
  costs involved, 287–9, 300
  debt recovery, 192–4
  documentation involved, 288
  need for lawyer's services, 292–3
  representing yourself, 289–91
  time aspects, 288
  time limits on, 304–5
  see also Legal Aid
Loans, 300

Lonrho Ltd v. *Shell Petroleum Co. Ltd.*, 24

McCulloch Limited, R.H., 101
McLoughlin v. *O'Brian*, 260
Magistrates Courts Act 1980, 268
Mandla v. *Lee*, 277
Medical examinations, 159
Memorandum of Association, 37, 206
Mergers, 18–23
Misconduct, 115
Misrepresentation Act 1967, 5, 178
Mistakes, 301
  criminal, 267–9
  in pricing, 189–91, 302
Mobility clause, 76
Moonlighting, 77, 84–6

National Health Service, 232
National Insurance, 5, 82, 91
Negligence, 226–8, 237–8, 244–6, 258, 260–2
  contributory, 253–5
  damages for, 226, 253, 260
  suing for, 304
Neighbours, 241–4
Newson v. *Robertson*, 59
Noise nuisance, 170–1
Notice, preparation and serving, 93, 94, 105, 294, 395
Nuisance, 241–4
  coming to a, 243–4
  forms of, 241
  in law, 241

Objects clause, 206
Occupier's liability, 248
Occupiers' Liability Act 1957, 148, 149, 248–51
Occupiers' Liability Act 1984, 149, 248–51
Occupiers' Liability (Scotland) Act 1960, 248–50
Offices, Shops and Railway Premises Act, 145, 158
Official Receiver, 65
Overcharging, 302
Overdrafts, 300
Owen v. *Book*, 57

Part time employment, 106–7

Partnership, 3, 71
  dissolution of, 9
  duration of, 9
  fixed term, 9–10
  problems of, 7–11
Partnership Act 1890, 7–11
Patents, 83–4
Patents Act 1977, 83
PAYE, 82, 125
Pearson Commission, 227, 231
Pensions, 96
  qualifying ages for, 122
Perks, 77
Personal guarantees, 40
Personal injuries, damages for, 244–6, 304
Personal liabilities, 152–3
Poaching of staff, 92–4
Pollution control, 166–71
Preferential debts, 138
Preferred debts, 65
Pregnancy, 123, 124, 134
Prevention of Fraud (Investments) Act 1934, 32
Prevention of Fraud (Investments) Act 1958, 32
Pricing, mistakes in, 189–91, 302
Private business, 3
Privileges, 77
Product liability, 224–33
  definition, 224
  EEC Directive, 228–33
Profit sharing schemes, 88–90
Prohibition Notice, 144–5, 147
Property, damage to, 230–1
Prosecution, 287
  legal help for, 293
Prosecution laws, 278–81
Protective awards, 137, 138
Public duties, 131–4

Quality assurance, 232
Quantum meruit, 210

Race Relations Act 1976, 276–8
Racial discrimination, 276–8
Reasonableness, 242
Recession, 68
Redundancy
  payments, 100–7, 113, 120
  problems of, 94–6
  rights, 135–8
  rules concerning, 40
Redundancy Payment Act 1965, 135
References, 96–100
Regina v. *Gilks*, 267
Regina v. *Swan Hunter Shipbuilders Ltd*, 146
Registrar of Companies, 38, 39, 66
Rehabilitation of Offenders Act 1974, 281–4
Reinstatement orders, 95
Repairers, charges by, 212
Reporting of Injuries, Diseases and Dangerous Occurrences Regulations 1985, 160
Restraint clauses, 76, 86–8, 95, 292
Restrictive Practices Court, 180
Retirement, 68–72
Right to search, 76
Robbery, 265
Rolled Steel Products Limited v. *BSC*, 37
Royal Commission on Civil Liability, 227
Rules, 76

Safety committees, 162
Safety consultations, 162
Safety measures, 159–60
Safety rules, 156–8
Salaries, attached, 81
Sale of Goods Act 1970, 199
Sale of Goods Act 1979, 178, 195, 208, 214, 215, 225
Scotland, common law of, 5
Scottish Law Commission, 227
Secondhand goods, 181
Security and Investments Board (SIB), 32
Selangor United Rubber Estates Limited v. *Cradock*, 22
Self-employed, 300
Self-protection, 18–23
Servants, 187–9, 238–40
Severance pay, 69
Sex Discrimination Act 1975, 122, 127
Sex Discrimination Act 1986, 122, 123, 126
Sex Discrimination Act, 111, 125
Sick pay, 90–2, 125

Smith v. *National Coal Board*, 253, 254
Social Security and Housing Benefits Act 1982, 90
Solvency and insolvency, 64, 134
Squatters, 256
Staff
    problems concerning, 5
    stealing of, 92–4
Statutory maternity pay, 124, 125
Statutory sick pay (SSP), 90–2, 125
Stealing, *see* Theft Act
Stealing of staff, 92–4
Stock valuation, 6
Stolen goods, 269–70
Summary judgment, 288
Suppliers, 39–41
Supply of Goods and Services Act 1982, 178, 180–1, 185–6, 210, 213
Supply of Goods (Implied Terms) Act 1973, 225
Supreme Court Act 1981, 208–9
Surveys, 5
Sykes v. *Midland Bank Executor and Trustee Company Limited*, 260

Take-overs, 18–23, 69, 105
Taxation, travel costs, 57–60
Tenancies, 305
Terms of service, 291
Tesco Supermarkets Limited v. *Nattrass*, 152–6
Tesco v. *Nattrass*, 145
Theft Act 1968, 68, 265–7, 269
Theft Act 1978, 266
Time aspects, litigation, 288
Time factor in contracts, 197–200
Time off, 131–4
Torts (Interference with Goods) Act 1977, 219
Trade Descriptions Act 1968, 178, 180, 271–3
Trade Descriptions Act 1972, 180, 181
Trade-ins, 181–3
Trade marks, 53–5

Trade Marks Act 1938, 53
Trade Marks (Amendment) Act 1984, 55
Trade Marks Registry, 55
Trade union duties, 131–4
Trade unions, 105, 116–19, 135–7
Training in safety and health, 162
Transfer of Undertakings (Protection of Employment) Regulations 1981, 22
Transfer of Undertakings Regulations, 105, 205
Transport, 6–7
Travel costs, 57–60
Trespass, 149, 256–8

Uncollected goods, 218–21
Undercharging, 302
Unemployment, 68
Unfair Contract Terms Act 1977, 178, 186, 225–6
Unfair Contracts Act 1977, 238
Unoccupied properties, 256
Unsolicited goods, 218–21
Unsolicited Goods and Services Act 1971, 218–19

VAT, 5
Vicarious liability, 238–41, 271

Wages, attached, 81
Wages Act 1986, 40, 105, 138
Waste disposal on land, 168–9
Water pollution, 169–70
Weights and Measures Authorities, 154
Welsh Law Commission, 227
Wills, drafting, 294
Winding up a business, 27–9, 64–8
Windmill Clubs Limited, 16
Wright, Layman and Umney Limited, 49
Written statements, 161
Written undertakings, 163